6
Knots

Joan—
Thank you for
putting us together
spiritually as well as
in the eyes of the State
of New York. Your
friendship is invaluable
Love, Chris + Rick

Chris Flanders

AuthorHouse™
1663 Liberty Drive
Bloomington, IN 47403
www.authorhouse.com
Phone: 1-800-839-8640

First published by AuthorHouse   03/31/2011

ISBN: 978-1-4567-2348-4 (sc)

Library of Congress Control Number: 2011900476

Printed in the United States of America

Any people depicted in stock imagery provided by Thinkstock are models,
and such images are being used for illustrative purposes only.
Certain stock imagery © Thinkstock.

This book is printed on acid-free paper.

authorHOUSE®

Acknowledgements

It's a long way from an idle comment to a book. My Dad always told me that I could do anything in my life, no limits. I am doing my best to fit it all in. My friends have supported me while I work my way from observation to text, often, unwittingly, being the objects of my storytelling.

I want to thank Connie Fenney, first for her help in editing, but most of all for any of the cruising lore I used in this book. She and Ken (of OZ) gave Peaches and I a crash course in the nuts and bolts of cruising life. They compressed their years of experience into many happy hour conversations, feeding all of it to us in little bites.

My sons are the best examples for me of living life to the fullest. I want Lee to know he is my muse. There can't be enough thanks to Peaches Wagner for being as open to a new challenge as I am. We are at an age when some people just sit down to watch the world go by. It took two of us to sail this adventure I hope we have many more years of exploring the world at 6 Knots.

COVER INFORMATION: Bahamas courtesy flag, Seven Seas Cruising Association burgee, Buffalo Yacht Club burgee, Buffalo Harbor and Sailing Club burgee.
Photo: Chris Flanders Location: Nassau Harbor Club, Nassau, Bahamas

"There is nothing, absolutely nothing –
half so much worth doing
as simply messing about in boats."

Rally said to Mole in the *Wind and the Willows* by Kenneth Gibson, 1908

Table of Contents

**Our maiden voyage in Star of the Sea
(the cruising edition, not the 36.7),
with Buffalo in the background.
Where is the fast button on this thing?**

Chapter 1

Just the Facts

June 30, 2009, Buffalo NY

Like the personal columns say, I am a mature, white, long divorced, recently retired female. I am the mother of two sons, the grandmother of two red-haired girls and a tow-headed grandson. I am very active, love to sail, to cook and read. I am a closet writer. I can't dance well but I have a great personality (read that rounder than I would like for my height!) My name is Chris Flanders, a nurse practitioner with all the accompanying Type-A characteristics and the touch of OCD (obsessive-compulsive disorder) that lets medical people multitask effectively. I am throwing in the towel and simplifying my life by going sailing with a friend on a 44 foot sailing vessel, Star of the Sea. More later about the word simplifying. The destination is tentatively Trinidad and the time frame is wide open.

My friend in crime/adventure is Margaret Mary Wagner, universally known as Peaches. She is single, white, a nursing home administrator, an ex-nun, also a longtime sailor who will retire just days before we leave on the boat in September. She was a Fulbright Scholar to India. She has a PADI Master Diver ranking and a couple of fine arts degrees along the way. She has more than the required amount of Type A personality along with administrative traits. Peaches also has a touch of OCD for good measure and very deep love for sailing. Upon leaving the convent years ago, she wanted to work with the elderly, sail, scuba dive, build a fine art collection and now join the ranks of the live-aboard sailors. Place a checkmark by all but the last, she has aced them all.

In conversation a couple of years ago Peaches asked if I was interested in cruising after I retired. I've sailed since I was 6 years old and recently started racing with her and her crew on Star of the Sea, a 36.7 Beneteau First out of the Buffalo Yacht Club on Lake Erie. We smiled and talked as our minds raced with possibilities, then she said "if you want to take off and cruise for a couple of years, put your money where your mouth is." I did, we bought the boat and we are frantically getting ready for our departure on September 4, 2009.

Retiring early seemed like such a risk, but now that I have retired it seems just barely in time. I used the word simplifying a little earlier. How do you simplify and unclutter 62 years of living in a few weeks? We sold the cars, prepared a home for sale, and entrusted the other home for family to use and care for while we were gone. Household items were packed in boxes, clothes were given away, food was shrink-wrapped, artwork was loaned out and bills were switched to auto-pay. Lists were made of all our important numbers for credit cards, insurance carriers, furnace repair men and plowing services. For fathers, sisters and brothers, contact information was compiled. Peaches' sister, Susanne, was given all the information that connected us to the world. She was to care for and represent us while we are gone. Simplify was so way the wrong word for all of this.

We have 6 weeks to get ready to go down the Erie Canal. Everything electric has been installed and checked out, the six man life raft is due for delivery soon and we just need to pack the boat (I know, just is another inadequate word). We have a few trips we want to take on Lake Erie before our departure. We have lots of friends and relatives to take out on the boat for fun. They all want to picture us on this boat when we are gone. Our plans are so very open, we could be gone a year or maybe 5. There are lots of loose non-marine ends to tie up. Peaches and I can't wait.

I've read stacks of books by cruisers, historical accounts of sea voyages and blogs talking of horrible seas, insurmountable difficulties with equipment and finally the raw power of Mother Nature. We still want to go where the winds take us, changing our sails as needed and enjoying our lives untouched by work, traffic or time schedules. The world is ours at 6 knots.

Return to Buffalo on a stormy afternoon, Lake Erie

Chapter 2

Two Weeks to Cast-Off!

08/21/2-009 RCR Yachts, Buffalo, New York

We are scrambling to get everything perfect for our departure from the Buffalo Yacht Club on Friday, September 4th. I awoke a couple of nights ago to the realization that we can do a lot of this final preparation underway as long as all the necessary items are on board. Suddenly, perfect is not the absolute go-to word for everything.

Peaches and I spent a great week with friends and family at the Dunkirk Yacht Club. We celebrated birthdays, hugged grandchildren and signed up my 86 year old father, Bill, for the Baltimore to Annapolis part of the journey down the coast. We invited both sailors and non-sailors on board to see what they thought of our preparations, hoping that their comments would be encouraging. We should have been more tuned into their thoughts. "I wish I could take time out of my life to go do what you two are going to do but I can't right now."

Another said "You must be crazy to take off like this in the middle of a full recession."

My favorite was "You are going to live your dream and I am going to live mine through your stories." Alone with our thoughts again, we needed to listen to ourselves, cast off the lines to the dock and live our dream. I'll blog our stories. Maybe it'll help someone else to set themselves free.

We checked our Sirius Weather program before returning to Buffalo from Dunkirk for the chance of thunderstorms and with our newly found weather skills decided the storms were going well north of our Buffalo destination, five hours or so up the lake. I can sense your misgivings, even as I write this!

We left under sail, surfing the large waves back to Buffalo, the wind at our backs. We saw the dark band of storms looming closer and closer so we added the engine to get home sooner. We pulled in the sails, revved up the engine, cleared the decks of all loose clutter and prayed that the brand new Bimini would stay attached in the accelerating winds. It went from 18-20 knot winds and 6-8 foot waves with chop to a lightning festival complete with a strong downpour. Suddenly the waves flattened and the wind accelerated to 48 knots. We were in a downdraft of strong wind. Peaches turned the bow of the boat into the wind and we held our breath. What a sturdy and well-handling vessel Star of the Sea turns out to be.

After about half an hour of wondering how we could ever handle this for days at a time in the open ocean, the wind diminished and the waves returned. No waterspouts were in sight. We did a 180° turn toward Buffalo and started breathing again. I failed to mention that we had a good friend with us who is not a sailor. From about half a mile out of Dunkirk, she was suffering from mal de mere into a bucket from all the wallowing the boat did between waves. She had the good sense to be too frightened to throw up during the worst of the downdraft. She said her entire life was flashing by her eyes in full living color. She quickly rethought her dream of joining us later in our journey!

I am so glad this stupidity happened to us before leaving on the trip. The boat is almost fully loaded and as close to her traveling weight as she could be. So, if she could handle this little Lake Erie blow, she could handle anything. So could we. We are not invincible, but are so much better prepared for our new life because of this sudden storm.

Buffalo Yacht Club, Buffalo, New York

Chapter 3

Four Days and Counting

08/31/2009 Buffalo Yacht Club

It is hard to sleep when your head is working like a computer that seriously needs defragmenting. We are both making progress toward our goal of leaving on Friday. Peaches is retired and has fully shifted into panic mode. There are sliding piles of papers in all corners of the house, piles of unsorted clothing covering the floor and the furniture. Poor Peaches is wandering from pile to pile picking up things, shaking her head and throwing them into opened boxes or back onto the piles. I didn't think until now what a huge burden she has on her shoulders, sorting and packing for herself in just four days. I've been squirreling away things and making lists for months. I am in complete pack-it mode. The boat looks like a bomb has hit it and all her guts are exposed. We'll never get it packed before the Bon Voyage party in two days. Help!

Peaches' sister, Susanne Tocke, says she visualizes us leaving the Buffalo Yacht Club with several dinghies tied in a line behind us, loaded with all our earthly goods. It may come true. We just bought 2 car carrier bags, the kind you strap to your car roof, to tie in front of the mast on the deck. All the stuff we need, absolutely need will be packed in these hopefully waterproof bags until we get time to go through them. Now we are going to look like the families escaping the dust bowl with our rocking chair hanging off the port side and the cow trailing behind, surfing the wake behind the swim platform! These bags will allow our crew of two able-bodied men to have a place to sleep and move about the boat. There is so much stuff, so little room, poor cow.

About our crew: Burt Smith is Peaches' cousin and loves the water. He and his wife, Sue, crewed with us last summer as we tried to race our Beneteau 423 in the open class for the Buffalo Harbor Sailing Club races. We always came in last, but we got the hang of all the winches, the in-mast furling sail and even the new asymmetric spinnaker sail. Did I mention we always came in last? There were times when the race committee boat had already headed back to the warm and comfortable bar at the yacht club before we rounded the last mark! Our steep learning curve had started. Burt and Sue stuck it out for the whole season and Sue encouraged Burt to go on the Erie Canal/Hudson River part of our adventure. Two women couldn't set off without some testosterone on board. It seemed to make our families less fearful and our friends more comfortable with our crazy scheme.

John Pettis, from the Buffalo Yacht Club, is our other volunteer crew member. He is the proverbial old salt. He has been on boats, under boats, in their engines and up their masts all of his life. He knows diesel engines like he knows good food and beautiful women. Between the two of them, we can have a fear-free start to our trip. John can trouble shoot the mechanics, tell great stories and helm the boat until he drops. Burt knows the Erie Canal and boats in general. He also has stories to tell and by the end of this adventure, so will we. My job is to keep the coffee and the food coming.

We've had our immunizations and our passports and other documentation are in order. As of today we have the new and spare alternators, fuel pumps, water pumps, spare bulbs and fuses, hardware, clips and widgets. Filters of every shape and color, belts for the Volvo engine and spare bilge and shower pumps adorn the piles of stuff in the boat.

Like carrying an umbrella to keep away the rain, these spare things will keep us warm, safe, dry and well hydrated.

All that is left is to divest ourselves of the houses and cars, pack the reference books on board, have a couple of wonderful good-bye parties and shove off. Thanks to all of you who have listened to us over the past years plan our trip out loud over and over until we got it right. So, think about coming to join us for a short while in the location of your choice along our route. We hope to have the excess baggage tamed before we turn right at the Hudson River and head south from the Erie Canal to Hop-O-Nose Marina on the Hudson.

Up the Black Rock Canal, Buffalo, New York
John Pettis presiding at the start of our adventure!

Chapter 4

Turn Right at the Erie Canal

09/06/2009 Niagara River, Tonawanda, New York

We left our slip at the Buffalo Yacht Club on September 4 after a quick lunch. We headed up the Black Rock Canal, under the Peace Bridge to Canada. What an attitude adjustment it is to go right toward Niagara Falls instead of left out past the breakwater to race. The Star of the Sea is no longer a sailing vessel because the mast was wrapped up and taken by truck to Hop-O-Nose Marina on the Hudson several weeks ago. All the bridges on the Erie Canal have less than 15 feet clearance so a 58' stick is out of the question. Our mast is waiting for us.

The boat is loaded from the keel to the deck with all of our earthly goods. Burt and John's two duffle bags hardly made a difference. The boat has fenders, boat hooks and 3 car carrier bags on the front deck (yes, yes, I know it was only two but now Peaches' stuff is all here to be sorted through). We don't want to miss a minute of our journey. The camera is never out of our hands. It still seems like an afternoon boat ride, not the biggest thing Peaches and I have ever done.

The Black Rock Lock and the swing bridge were the first of many such interruptions along our way this first day. I was at the helm for this first part and the strong currents were a surprise. My learning curve angle just got way more acute! We continued on to Tonawanda and turned right, tucking into the Erie Canal. As we went through Lockport, the sides of the canal were full of friends and family waving and calling to us from the shore and bridges along our way. I had trouble steering because I wanted to wave with both hands at the same time. Thanks guys!

So, we are motoring along at about 5.5 knots in the sunny warm weather. There isn't much boat traffic even though it is a holiday weekend. We left at noon so John could finish up some business at his shop and we could arrive at a good place along the canal to spend the night. No anchoring allowed. We slipped along through the shortening daylight and pulled into the wall at Medina, NY. The town has a stone face wall with cleats spaced so we can tie up. It's almost dark but the yellow street lamps make it easier. We secure the boat, tidy up and walk into town. In most of the towns we pass, the canal runs close to the main street. Burt knows the towns, the restaurants and even the locations of the West Marine and hardware stores from other trips through the canal in his motor boats. A quiet dinner at an Italian restaurant, some wine and talk make us all realize how very tired we are. As we walk through the deserted streets back to the boat it strikes us, this boat is our new home.

At dinner, Burt and John made us a deal. They will get up early in the morning, shower on shore and when the sun comes up, motor down the canal to the next lock. Our part is to set up the coffee maker the night before and get up for the next lock. A perfect deal. I can hear them bumping around in the salon, then the boat bobbing as they get off and on the wall, the coffee maker grinding the beans and then the engine starting. Remember going on car trips with your parents, the engine humming and the movement of the car putting you into dreamland? That's how our mornings were in the canal.

We both slept fitfully in the V-berth because it was all new and also because there was not much shoulder room for two ladies with great personalities but rather Rubenesque bodies. Boxes of papers, for Peaches to go through and eventually send home, fill the floor and the sides of the room. John sleeps in the salon where the table converts the couches into a bed. Burt sleeps in the back berth. The engine starts, the water flows past the hull and we both fall sound asleep, no responsibilities for a bit.

Everyone takes their turn at the helm until we come to a lock. I take over as the rookie helmsman and bring the vessel up against the starboard wall of the locks. That part is easy. Boats coming the other way might be in the lock so waiting for the lock lights to turn green is a little harder. Watching ahead helps so you can slow your forward progress, check the other boats around you for position and check the current and the winds. Sometimes you get too close and need to turn and circle if there is room and sometimes you just go into reverse. John made a game of having me practice figure eights in slow reverse while we waited for the green light. I can't imagine where I'll use this skill, but John is always right.

The Erie Canal is beautiful, clean and practically empty of traffic. There are birds flying everywhere, swooping through the dense trees at the sides of the canal. Occasionally the shore opens up to fields of corn or pastures. Small towns are scattered here and there and sometimes a main highway runs parallel to us. We feel like we are moving along at a good clip until the cars blow by at 70mph. It takes us all day to go the same distance a car goes in one hour!

Our well-oiled team snaps to attention when a lock appears. I take the wheel, Burt and Peaches pull on their work gloves and move to the front deck. John pulls out his boat hook, dons his gloves, and mans the stern. All the locks are taken on our starboard (right) side. Hint: port is left, port and left both have 4 letters and port wine is red and the red bow light is on the left side. My heart is the only one speeding up in anticipation. We come along-side after the green light goes on. The lockkeepers are out on the wall and our fenders are down to protect the fiberglass sides of the boat. Lines are passed and the doors to the lock close. When going down, the water whooshes out with some turbulence against the hull. The walls get taller and taller. Burt, Peaches and John fend the boat off of the wall with the boat hooks and pay out the lines. When we level out, the front gates open and off we go again. There isn't much yelling or drama, just good work. It would be very trying and tiring to be just two people going through the canal. We saw several single-hander boats going through. Burt and John grew smarter, more handsome and more valuable every day.

We stopped after what I thought was a slow meandering day down the canal in a town called Lyons, Lock 27 (halfway through!). We had a lazy lunch along the way and several unnamed crew members caught short naps. We chased blue heron, trying to get a good picture of them in flight. They hid in the trees, looking just like branches. We'll see a lot more birds in the Montezuma Swamp Reserve tomorrow. Tied up at the far lock wall, we grilled steaks with mashed potatoes and peas on the side for the Irish contingent. Burt's daughter sent a pound cake for desert (and breakfast and lunches for days). We have to not be so kind to ourselves in the galley. Do you know how many times around the deck it will take just to walk off the calories from that pound cake? We've already gone through two pounds of coffee beans from Premiere in Buffalo, running on high test!

I can't believe we are really on our adventure. My mind is whirring, trying to gauge the amount of food stored on the boat. I hope our supplies make it to Hop-O-Nose Marina where we stop to have the Sean step the mast. All the fresh air blowing up your nose holes all day sure makes you hungry!

Going through a lock, the Erie Canal

Chapter 5

The Erie Canal Saga Continues

09/08/2009 Troy, NY

Should I start with the ship as big as the Fisher Price Factory coming around the bend without leaving us any room to slip by or should I talk about the amazing length of time and miles we managed to go on one tank of diesel fuel? No, I will start by saying we made it to the Hudson River today, Tuesday at six PM.

Let me get back to the stories. There's been lots of good food eaten on the way and a huge amount of coffee consumed and spilled during this trip and to run on this sentence a bit, there have been great friendships made. Our well-oiled lock passage machine reached new all-time excellence today, doing 14 locks (and actually all the locks on the canal) without an incident unless you count the number of boat hooks lost.

Let's talk about diesel fuel and how far one can go on 55 gallons. We took off with a full tank and a spare 5 gallon jerry can on deck. Off we went Friday mid-day and traveled 6 hours, 12 the next day and about 10 the day after. We watched the level go down on the dial as we motored along but there were only gas pumps at the marinas, no diesel. John said "Aw, don't worry, most boats can go half a day after the dial says empty." Okay, on we went. Peaches got more and more concerned. I was skeptical but thought maybe his vast knowledge and life experience would pull us through. Burt got more and more vocal and then got stone quiet. John even lost a little of his reassuring ways and was quiet. We all got quiet and the trusty Volvo chugged on. Eventually it was decided to pull into the wall at the next lock, if we made it.

We called Winter's Harbor in Brewerton, NY, the next place with diesel, and Elena answered, "Yes, they had diesel. Yes they were just on the other side of the lock. Yes we could spend the night." When we asked if they could bring us 5 gallons of diesel, she said she would call us back. The line went silent and I thought we were abandoned. The only good thing is we made it to the wall before the engine quit. The phone rang and she said they would be right over, and they were. They walked the can to the boat, waited for us to put it in and get the engine started again and took no money.

"Hurry up and get through the lock before the sun drops any more. We'll be waiting for you." and off they went into the trees.

It was almost dark when we pulled into their dock. We took on 50 gallons of fuel, 5 in our jerry can and they'd given us 5 so John stayed pretty quiet until the lady said, oh, it was only 4 gallons in that can we brought to you. John then continued his crowing about how far one can go in a boat after it says empty.........

Winter's Harbor, just west of Lake Oneida, had hot showers, a safe place for the boat with electrical hook-up and even offered a courtesy car to do shopping errands. We had just enough energy to cook, clean up sort of and go to bed. We are a lot like chickens, up with the sun and falling into a non-moving heap when the sun goes down. The next day we traveled the length of Oneida Lake between the buoys without going aground in the shallows. We heard stories about how horribly rough it could be on Oneida when the wind comes up. We are, after all, from Lake Erie racing stock and would have done admirably, but it was like a mill pond. There were some fishermen but not a lot of boaters considering it was Labor Day.

Our stop last night was a little more unplanned as we were aiming for the other side of Lock 14 but we could only make it to 15 when the sun disappeared behind us. We tied to the wall, safe and in the company of two other sailboats without masts. It was so dark we could only see their lights. There was only one mercury vapor light and it was at the other end of the wall. No electricity or water available but we are chickens and need very little to make us comfortable. We were traveling through the canal with several other boats and none of us went the same speed between locks. Of course the lock tenders leveled the playing field and waited for the last boat to come in before letting us through. No problem, just frustrating. We traveled alongside several people in sailboats, masts on the deck, going to the islands or to the southeast coast for the winter. When we were asked where we were headed, Peaches or I would say Trinidad to get below the hurricane belt before June 1st. John and Burt always shook their heads and said they were getting off down on the Hudson. Most boaters and the lock crews all smiled back at us, but I can read lips and they were saying "Holy shit, two women on this big boat all the way to Trinidad. No way!"

One Burt story: He takes his turn at the helm, like we all do. It is afternoon and the canal is twisting and turning like a big river. We are talking and bantering back and forth. Our conversations are not always highly intellectual, but they are comfortable and often very funny. I am down making another pot of coffee to fuel the afternoon and I hear a huge commotion from above. "Chris, you've got to see this" Peaches shouts. I go up and an enormous white cruise ship has filled the entire canal from side to side and is towering over us. It came around the bend in the canal without warning. What appeared to be a large white factory on the river bank was actually coming at us. The AIS system went off just as we saw the bow smoothly curve around the bend. The AIS is an alarm system we have to alert us to ships bigger than 100 feet who are within the one mile radius we set. Burt stood up, threw his arms up in the air like he was being held up at gun point and said "John, here, now, right now." The alarm was blaring, Burt was getting as far away from the helm as he could, John calmly got one hand on the wheel. When Peaches and I saw there was going to be room for us to pass the monster ship, we doubled over in laughter. John was laughing so hard I was surprised he could see. Our adrenaline levels dropped quickly but for some reason, Burt's adrenaline never allowed him to think this story was funny. In Burt's defense, my brother Bob sends his lame nautical sayings daily and today's hits home. "For right of way, gross tonnage rules."

The final step-locks # 6 to 2 are like going down a long tunnel of steps that falls off the side of a mountain five times. Pictures can't give you the feeling of imminent falling. The locks are just football fields apart and when you are done, you don't want to see another lock for years. We reluctantly went through the big Federal Lock #1 where the rules on how to tie up and position the boat are all reversed. We exited the Erie Canal in four and a half days way smarter than when we turned right at Tonawanda.

We stopped at the town dock in Troy, just a few miles down the Hudson. Both Burt and John couldn't wait to tie up and get to the pub next door where the burgers and the mussels in wine and garlic are to die for. Post dinner, I am uploading pictures to the blog site with everyone snoring around me. The boat is safe, we are full of good food and beer and we are so happy. I wish you could experience this too.

Tomorrow we go to Hop-O-Nose Marina to get our mast stepped by Sean and his crew (I have got to find out where that name came from). We hope we can do some rearranging of the equipment in the car carriers, the boxes in the salon and the V-berth. Looking at what is here, I can't imagine what we were thinking when we put it on the boat. We really did pack for every eventuality. Peaches' niece Kristen and Mark are coming to see us, driving across the state to make sure we are okay. They will load their car to the roof and beyond if necessary to help us debunk the boat. I would be so happy if just one of the car carriers disappeared.

**One of the many beautiful lighthouses on the
Hudson River, New York
(This one was worth running aground for!)**

Chapter 6

The Hudson River

09/10/2009 Haverstraw Marina, New York

We've finally taken off the cheesy costume from Wal-Mart that allowed Star of the Sea to run through the Erie Canal disguised as a motor boat. Whew! That was ugly! As I write we are motoring down the Hudson, having left Hop-O-Nose Marina at 10:30. We put up the sails, the radar dome, took on water and left behind two roof carrier bags of unneeded marine stuff (two, yes two, you read it right. Yippee!). I, for the first time, used all my backing up experience to back out of the slip at the marina and just about complete a figure of eight to get to a fuel dock on the other side of the inlet. Thanks John! We feel lighter and freer and can actually move about the boat without shifting piles to make a place for your foot to land. Thanks Peaches. I donated some clunky items too.

The boat looks great, is running very well and we are following the red and green buoys to the very best of our ability. Since we are heading south to the sea, the channel is marked with buoys, the green on our starboard side and the red on our port. As my brother reminds us Red, Right, Returning; red buoys on the right as you come in from the sea. The tricky thing is that the shipping lane willy-nilly switches from one side of the river to the other without much warning. Only if you are following the chart plotter, the paper charts or are following a barge do you get some inkling of where to go. There are shoals and sand bars all over the place, more on that later.

The Hudson is wide and beautiful after being in a small canal/river for several days. I feel like we are using some of the things we learned from our captain's course at last. Big barges loaded with gravel go by us. I always thought a tug is a tug is a tug, but there are so many different shapes and sizes. There are beautiful blue hills surrounding the banks and lush green trees. Some of the homes are breathtaking. There are many lighthouses, usually out on islands or long points of land.

I helmed the first couple of hours this morning and managed to make all the markers with help from the others. I went below to make lunch and heard them all calling me to come up and take a picture of a great island lighthouse. I got up the steps from the salon and was just stepping into the cockpit when the boat went from 6 knots to 0 knots. We ran aground hard, with a big oomph from us all. The beauty of it was that we were in mud, not rock. But, stuck is stuck and a certain unnamed co-owner of the boat was driving at the time.

John took over the helm and ordered us to all stand on the bow. He wiggled and twisted the boat from side to side, creating a channel in the mud for the keel to slip through. Soon we were back on track, after we got some good pictures of the red-roofed lighthouse and all was well. We call John "Saint John" now for his depth of wisdom, but also for continuing on with us down the Hudson. Another crewmember who was going to join us had to back out and I guess John thought after the grounding earlier today we weren't really ready to fly solo yet. He could have been up to his armpits in work back in Buffalo but when I look at him in the cockpit, he doesn't look one bit stressed or uncomfortable. Good decision, John.

We are passing Newburgh NY, calling every marina we can that could take a boat as large as ours and with a six foot draft. Our plans changed somewhat last night when we found that a gale was coming up the coast and we had only today to get as close to NYC as we could. We will hunker down for Friday while it blows its way north and east. Peaches is using all her toys for this; iPhone, GPS, Navionics and her full powers of persuasion including but not limited to her Nun-Card. This is something that ex-nuns utilize when the going gets tough. It is a very powerful tool.

If all works out as we plan, we'll find a safe place to be for tomorrow and then go through New York Harbor during the daylight on Saturday and on down the New Jersey coast. The weather service we use said it would be calm sailing for three days at that point. We like it when they talk like that. Going out the inlet at Sandy Hook, NJ will be our first outing into the salty ocean.

Every day is different but wonderful. We are gone a week at this point and have traveled six days that equal a quick seven to eight hour car ride from Buffalo to NYC. From a car window at 70mph you would never have seen the people, the scenery, the animals and birds we have enjoyed. You would never have had so many different conversations or felt so strongly the trust one can have for your friends and your crew. Please try going slowly some time in your lives. It is the fastest way to happiness.

We pass by the Statue of Liberty on a rainy 9/12/09

Chapter 7

New York Harbor and Sandy Hook

09/12/2009 Sandy Hook, New Jersey

On 9/11 we were safely in a marina just above the Tappan Zee Bridge. Finally, someone who could accommodate us for two nights. We came into Haverstraw Marina on the Hudson with the sun setting in front of us. John was at the helm and having a terrible time finding the entrance in the shadows of the shoreline. Even the fancy E-80 navigation system didn't help us. Peaches kept trying to get me to pass her iPhone to John and I wouldn't. When I did, he pushed it away. She pushed me again and I said "here it is, plain as day!" He took one look and stuck the bow into the opening. After some hassling we found our slip, quite narrow for our beam, but by then we weren't very fussy. Haverstraw was huge and the walk to the main buildings was the longest yet. The array of big fiberglass boats was impressive.

Clouds were starting to cover the sunset and the wind was picking up. We slept soundly and in the morning awoke to steady hard rain and shifting winds. What a great day to get some laundry done and tonight have dinner with Kristen and Mark at the restaurant. They stopped at Hop-O-Nose and picked up the two car carrier bags, probably having to rent the big crane to lift them into their SUV! They were on the way to NYC and we were happily on the way in the morning. After dinner and saying goodbye, Peaches realized she was so home sick.

We took off this morning in a misty rain. Soon under the Tappan Zee Bridge, we clicked pictures nonstop. The sights we were seeing were more and more familiar, University Heights then the west side of Manhattan. The George Washington Bridge passed over us while super-fast car ferries made our sailing vessel rock side to side dangerously. There were some large tugs and barges, police boats, more fast ferries and then all the cruise ships parked one pier after the other. Our camera never had a chance to breathe all the way. Finally we got the first view of the Statue of Liberty and Ellis Island.

I lived in Manhattan for two three year periods during the late 60s and early 70s, so I appreciated this new view of my old stomping grounds. We all alternately chattered and were silent, watching it all go by. It was my own first view of the missing twin towers. It was done way too soon. We finally made the Verrazano Bridge after ducking the Staten Island Ferry, watching a yacht race off the Brooklyn Ship Yard, waving at the tour ships and counting the ships at anchor just at the base of the bridge.

The swell of the ocean became more and more noticeable, left over from the 60 knot winds of the unnamed storm yesterday. We headed toward Sandy Hook for diesel. It was about 3PM when we arrived at the fuel pumps and our giant adrenaline rush from going through NY Harbor ran right out of our sandals. We decided to spend the night at Twin Lights Marina. All the windows are open to the warm dry breezes. After a late lunch of soup, cheese and crackers, Burt is napping. Peaches and John are going over the charts for tomorrow's trip to Cape May. I am posting all of the pictures we took today and blogging to you. Perfection.

You've all asked how we do the simple things on Star of the Sea. It has taken less than two weeks for cooking, cleaning and sleeping to be like second nature. I say second nature because I can locate the pan I need and the box of rice mix I want in under half an hour. This is not your mother's big eat-in kitchen. This is a packing puzzle requiring a manifest in a spiral book to allow me to cook, wash dishes and find a paper clip Peaches is asking for.

Let me start at the beginning. In the galley there is a refrigerator and a deep 3x1x3 foot deep freezer. They run all the time and the freezer does the cooling for the refrigerator. There are small battery-operated fans inside both to move the cold air around. Both units are full of food. Drinks are up in the cockpit in a cooler filled with ice.

There is a small double stainless steel sink. There is pressurized water that comes out of the tap and Burt installed a small faucet and charcoal filter for water used for drinking and for coffee. All our water is stored in two large water tanks totaling 150 gallons; one under each stateroom bed, fore and aft. For now water comes from hoses at the marinas.

A three burner gas stove with a small gas oven doesn't take up much space. It's on gimbals so that it swings and stays level in rough seas. Clamps hold the pots on when needed and you always use a bigger, deeper pot than you would at home. There is a wall, where the stairs come down, that I can lean on if the boat is hobby-horsing while I cook. Two propane tanks are nestled in a compartment up in the cockpit.

My first use of the oven was a total disaster. I took out some frozen rolls from the freezer to thaw. They rose all day on the small counter in the galley. Everyone who went downstairs for something checked them out. Much anticipation was evident. They were in two loaf pans made of that red plastic/silicone material from Williams Sonoma. I'd never used them before but brought them because they squish into a small space for storage. Dinner was ready so I took out the pans with a flourish and they were both on fire. A glowing hole was on the starboard side of both pans from the open gas flames. The untouched rolls were eaten only to make me feel better but were flatter than tortillas and gummy to boot. Ugh!

There is a microwave for popcorn and quick reheating. We brought a toaster that might make live-aboard sailors cringe because of the extreme amount of electricity used per second! I've cooked bacon, eggs, Bartoli chicken parm, soups, vegetables, Cajun rice and of course mashed potatoes for the Irish. We also have a grill that attaches to the back rail up on deck for chicken, hot dogs, steaks and burgers. We would have done a lot more grilling but the guys (high testosterone chefs) left the gas valve on the last time!

All dishes are done by hand in the sink and stowed in special cupboards to keep them from banging around. The ceramic coffee cups are nestled in the plastic net sleeves placed around liquor bottles when you carry them home. None of us really likes coffee from plastic mugs.

The most important piece of equipment on the boat is the coffee maker. More veteran sailors just cringed. It takes lots and lots of amps as it grinds the beans and brews the wonderful coffee!

This brings up where our electricity for lights, instruments, water pumps, radios and the flat screen TV comes from. While the engine is on and we are motoring along the alternator generates electricity and powers our things and charges the battery banks. One bank is in front of the engine under the stairs for 400 amp hours. The other larger bank is deep in the stern of the boat for 900 amp hours. If we are anchored or at a dock without an electrical outlet, we run on the D/C power direct from the batteries using and inverter to convert it to A/C power for things plugged into outlets. We try not to use this inverter a lot as it takes power to run itself as well. If needed, we could use the Honda Generator to recharge the battery banks or to run A/C stuff in the boat.

At larger marinas there are always the large 30 amp electrical outlets on the dock. This is like living in your home. Life is good! The easiest way to think of electricity is like a bank. I have all these amps to use. I choose what I really want to do like run the coffee maker for five minutes or watch a movie for a couple of hours and watch the battery bank monitor to see how the battery banks are. You can't take it below 50% of the total before recharging. I am the amp czar (kind of like the soup Nazi on the Seinfeld Show).

Enough dry stuff for now. Living on a boat is very possible and fun. It is also a more responsible life as you are a self-sufficient unit. So what if it takes half an hour to find the pan and the rice you want for dinner!

How about going to the bathroom? Well while we are in rivers and canals and most harbors along the coast, all waste products go into holding tanks in each of the heads (bathrooms). Peaches, who always had racing boats, never wanted to use the holding tanks on her boats as they would stink, would be heavy and might clog up. Racing is only about two to three hours and then you're back at the yacht club and nice bathrooms. On our boat, she still feels the same way, even if we can get the tanks pumped out. The maxim on all boats is, do not put anything into the heads unless you have eaten it first! Enough said!

Now, your noses and sensibilities are probably wrinkled, but picture telling this to Burt. He came to me a week ago while we were still in the canal and asked what he should do if he "really" had to go to the bathroom. I explained the above in my best clinical language. His eyes got big and he started backing away from me like I was a leper or something worse mumbling about medical people being so weird. He held it, I assume. From that moment forward, he is very animated in asking for nice marinas, clean restrooms and showers. A man needs that sort of thing first thing in the morning. I bow to his reasoning.

One more story. At breakfast the other day, John asked us which way was East. Burt and I, in our infinite reasoning and our unerring sense of direction pointed in two totally opposite directions. Peaches and John were under the table holding their stomachs and laughing until they cried. Both directions were wrong. We tried to talk our way out of it but they weren't having any of it. What happens on the boat stays on the boat, unless you are a blogger.

**Burt Smith and John Pettis leaving us in the
Cohansey River, New Jersey**

21

Chapter 8

Cape May and Delaware Bay

09/15/2009 Cohansey River, New Jersey

Today is Tuesday, September 15th, a simple statement but one that took me a long time to figure out. As I stepped down onto the dock at the Greenwich Boat Yard on the Cohansey River a furry-faced fellow was walking toward me, his three-legged dog following along. You can't make this stuff up. As he walked, he alternately scratched his beard and his nether regions. He seemed harmless as he mumbled under his breath. Peering into my face with hope, squinting in the sun, he asked if I knew what day it was. I stopped walking and realized that I had no idea what the date was. I knew it was September but that was it. I used my mental fingers and toes to come up with a date, the wrong one I now know. I told him three different dates saying I was sure it was one of them. He dismissed me with a wave and as his dog gave me a last friendly look, he said "Man, I only wanted to know what year it is!" I felt like saying hey, I could have done that with one hand tied behind my back. This must be how retirement is.

We've been some great places since we talked last. Slipping through NY Harbor with our mouths open in awe and then the unexpected perfection of Sandy Hook set us up for our first ocean experience. The sun was out, the humidity low and there was nothing between us and Cape May but easy four foot swells. Commander Weather was right on the money! We went down the NJ coast within sight of the beach, following the buoys in about 40 feet of water. The guide books gave us the names of all the little towns along the way. We took turns at the helm. Fishing boats for hire were all around us. I wish I had an old plug and a pole to see what's biting. We made great progress and intended to run through the night to make Cape May. John and Burt were dropping comments about getting of the boat at that point. Peaches and I locked eyes but made no comments.

The fuel was getting low and Atlantic City loomed. Actually, Atlantic City was visible for most of the day, looking like a glowing castle sitting way out on the water. The closer we got, the more it became attached to the shore. Following the markers we entered a wonderland for boaters and gamblers alike. We were all so taken by the lights, the huge yachts and the joy of being tied to a dock we decided to stay. As the sun set, the only available slip was where we pulled up to the fuel dock. Without electric and at only $3 a foot, it was a deal I guess. Was it going to be this expensive all the way to Florida? Our hair, wind tossed and sweaty from a long day on the water, Donald Trump had nothing on us for bad hair!

As we tried to sleep in a town where they never turn off the lights, a beautiful multimillion dollar motor yacht pulled in on the other side of the dock. Two dock hands magically appeared to catch the lines and within minutes two very cool, well rested, impeccably dressed men stepped off the boat. They made some small talk with us about leaving Cape Cod without their captain that morning and how smooth it had been at 26 knots. Remember little us at six knots and bad hair?

The guys started early and by the time I got up to make their second pot of coffee and breakfast we were back out parallel to the beach, watching water towers pass by, one for each town. Ocean City brought back memories of a house my parents rented and we all joined them, arriving from various parts of the country. My brother Bob, of the lame nautical sayings, rode a bicycle down thirty wooden steps at the back of the beach house into the hood of a parked car. We were all a couple of beers into the afternoon and it seemed like a reasonable trick to all of us standing at the top with him. I can't remember for sure, but I think it was sometime in the 60s.

Wildwood, NJ was easy to pick out with its wooden rollercoaster. Cape May lighthouse was next and we all came to attention. Going around the corner was awesome. The water changed immediately to a hard chop on the bow and wind in our faces. Delaware Bay can be tricky according to the guidebooks. We could see the Jersey shore but the entrance to the Bay was so wide we couldn't see the Maryland shore. We found the shipping lane and set the chart plotter for enough distance to get a feel for where we might spend the night. Our first really big fully loaded tanker bore down on us and, you guessed it, Burt was at the helm. These tankers and container ships come down the shipping lanes like freight trains. You spot them, look down at your navigation screen and when you look back up, you see the water being pushed up into a big wave by the bulb-shaped prow. Then, the shadow caused by the metal sides of the ship flashing past, darkens your view. Nothing can describe how small we felt, but Burt never flinched and hung onto the wheel. He might not have been breathing but he didn't bail out either. Not a hair out of place. Not a twitch of his eyebrows. Not a word slipped from his mouth until the behemoth passed. He merely asked if it was time to turn on the coffee. A true old salt has been made in under a week!

There were crab pots dotting the shallow waters everywhere outside the channel. We turned after the Skip John Shoal Light and started the obstacle course to the Cohansey River, about 25 miles southwest of the C&D canal but on the Jersey side. As we came closer all we could see was tall marsh grass. The tallest landmark in sight was the 15 foot green marker at the entrance behind Grass Island. Around Grass Island, now fully submerged by the tides, we entered a swift outflowing river. The Cohansey wound like serpentine curves at Watkins's Glen through the yellow grasses. It should have been about 2 feet deep with a muddy bottom to catch our keel but the river measured 50 to 75 feet on the depth sounder.

Crab boats and small outboard boats stacked with empty traps and their brightly colored buoys passed us. The river widened at a big gentle curve and two marinas appeared. We pulled into the Greenwich Boat Yard where a white-haired gentleman came out the short dock to help us with diesel and water. I asked him some questions about the tides and he managed not to smile while he patiently answered my stupid questions. The tides where suddenly the most important variable since we left Buffalo. He didn't even crack a smile when Peaches came off the boat with the water hose and asked the same questions only 5 minutes later, but his eyes were sparkling.

Peaches and I were shocked when the guys were packed in under 2.3 minutes and ready to find transportation, any transportation except another boat. John is an easy going guy who runs his business in Buffalo and helps out anyone when they ask. We asked and he not only came through the Erie Canal but ran his business by phone while he ushered us to the Delaware Bay. He needs a bigger shirt to hide his huge heart. You know I love you. Burt wanted an adventure and got one. He is such a support, takes kidding well and is a master storyteller. You can't beat that combination. Thanks, Burt. We hear they took several taxi rides and in desperation finally got a Greyhound bus to Buffalo. I bet no one offered to make a pot of coffee for you when you needed it.

Peaches and I cleaned the salt and muck off of the boat, cleared out the debris and somehow another car carrier bag ended up on the foredeck (mostly dock lines and scuba stuff). John, please don't read this! The dark came and it was so quiet here on the Cohansey. We were all alone. Charts and guidebooks littered the table and uneaten leftovers dried out on the plates as we decided where we were heading in the morning. Morning came without the sounds of the guys getting on and off the boat. No laughter or clinking of coffee mugs this morning. When I went in to settle up our bill, the owner offered the use of his golf cart to go into town for supplies. Our destination of Delaware City was only a couple of hours away so we took the cart and the verbal directions to town and set off with our bags, money and high hopes. We wound through the boatyard of large but mostly derelict wooden boats of every shape and size. Off we went on the main highway in a green golf cart. Cars slowed as they passed, it was only about a lane and a half wide. Houses were small, surrounded by large fields of corn, yellowing in the early fall.

After 20 minutes at a lot less that 6 knots we stopped and asked a woman how far to the grocery store "Well you can go straight ahead to town but keep going when you are done and see all the nice old houses. It's a circle, only a mile all the way around to get back here. Or, you can go the other way around if you want to." We smiled, nodding our heads in understanding and continued another 500 feet around the corner to the general store/post office/Deli. No miracle mile here, but plenty of milk, bread and conversation. And, you can go both ways around the loop if you want to.

Up Delaware Bay, ducking ships and crab pots, we found the markers leading into Delaware City just after the C&D canal. I was at the helm with Peaches spotting markers as we entered a gradually narrowing river leading to the Delaware City Dock. By the time we came starboard side to the face dock, the river was only 6 feet deep and only as wide as Star of the Sea is long. I thought, John, we made our fist trip without you but how, oh how am I going to turn this thing around to get out of here tomorrow?

A low front is passing through here tonight and tomorrow so we will stay another night before leaving. We are looking forward to walking on dry land, window-shopping, eating anything made out of crab and free internet. There is so much history here; the maritime museum, Civil War era homes and the War of 1812 markers. Charlie Obersheimer is right, we need a good American History book on board so we can know more about where we are. He said on a boat there are long periods of easy times punctuated by occasional moments of extreme fear. We have managed to have at least one adrenaline rush daily from some big ship or a tricky docking. I'd like to keep it that way; simple fear, not complex. We're on to the C&D Canal after the low front and the high winds go by.

As we started out to explore the city, we met the two French Canadian families Burt and I talked with at Haverstraw. They were only 9 days into their 2 year voyage when they were both struck by lightning on the Hudson River. All their electronics were fried to a tune of $40,000 each. They'd been at the marina for three weeks waiting for the insurance to pay for the instruments and labor to reinstall them. One couple was middle aged and the other there with their three young children, home schooling them and trying to keep them occupied during the interminable wait. They got underway two days ago, taking the NY Harbor to

Cape May run in one long piece, changing helmsmen every 2 hours. They were here, a bit bedraggled but proud of their accomplishment. They are heading to the islands and the Panama Canal and on to the South Pacific. What a big dream!

The peak sailing season for the locals is coming to an end, with many sailboats at the docks but few of them being used. We are at the leading edge of the snowbird migration of cruisers aiming for the Florida Keys or the islands beyond. Oh John, a nice fellow at the marina used the six foot tides and currents in the narrow river to flip our boat around facing out, all just by holding the lines and letting the water do the work. Who knew?

Extreme high tide at the Bohemia Vista Yacht Basin
Trying to push the water back into the river with a front loader!
Chesapeake City, Maryland

Chapter 9

C&D Canal and the Bohemia River

09/18/2009 Bohemia Vista Yacht Basin Chesapeake City, Maryland

Day # 14. I think I mentioned that we are like chickens, up with the sun and in a heap when it goes down. Now, I need to add that we are one with the weather. On beautiful days we travel and when it is cold and raining we stay at the dock and regroup. Um, I need to add one other thing. We are at the beck and call of the tides. For those of you in the Great Lakes, tides may have made you walk down a really steep gangplank from your cruise ship or found you at a pier in New England where low tide revealed mud flats and small boats canted over waiting for the tide to come back in. We are now one with the cycles of the moon.

"I don't know if we can get in there, it is low tide." Or more famously "Which way do you turn this damn wheel to make the rear end come into the dock!" We've had quite a few volunteer tutors (never been in one place long enough to have a mentor except John). They all start out by saying go slow and you won't run aground too bad, or go slow you'll feel how the boat should go. In the Bohemia Vista Yacht Basin on the Bohemia River, it went like this,

"Throw me your stern line and I'll drag you (read it your sorry ass) in here. By the way, that's a big boat, just you two ladies on that? Usually a boat that big has a man on it somewhere." I declined to reply but did hit him square in the chest with the (wet) stern line.

So tides, weather, sun up, sun down and now I'll add shallow water all control us. The Bohemia River isn't more than 9 feet deep in the center. We are sitting in the marina with a foot of brackish water under our keel. I managed not to hit any of the boats in there but I sure did an amazing thirty-point turn to back into the arms of the above named and now wet dock hand. Thanks for all the backing lessons, John! One more tide item and then I'll be quiet about it. They had such a big high tide with the new moon today (neap tide) that it went over the fixed docks and into the parking lot of the marina. A kid in a back loader and wearing a life vest was running at full speed, bucket down through the parking lot pushing the water back into the river and it was working. If he ever gets tired I would really like to give it a try. He's having way too much fun and getting paid too!

Our travels are full of coincidences. When we walked around the flooded parking lot, we entered the main building and met the owner after we registered (a dollar a foot for those of you who might want to stay sometime). Curt Sarac is from Buffalo and the only one of his family not in medicine. His father was the chief of surgery at Peaches' old stomping grounds, Deaconess Hospital. On the way to her office she passed a plaque to Dr. Sarac every day for 16 years. Curt was most gracious and made sure that one of his employees delivered a bag of fresh fruits and vegetables from the farmer's market to our boat before the day was done. Pure ambrosia.

I skipped over the part about getting to the Bohemia River. The C&D Canal turned out to be anticlimactic. It was wide and deep and the clouds were spitting rain. There was a tug and long barge coming up behind us that passed without slowing down a bit. Peaches did really well. I tried to get her to look behind our boat at the barge gaining on us. She preferred to watch it on her navigation screen. Must be it is less threatening that way. We got through the whole 12 miles with only barges and tugs, no huge ships that could slap you against the banks of the canal with their wakes. Whew!

Tomorrow, on to Havre de Grace on the western shore of Maryland from the Bohemia River. It will be about 60 nautical miles, just about a full day of sailing. It's in the mouth of the swift-flowing Susquehanna River. The town is, according to our guidebook the duck decoy capital of the WORLD. There will be lots of Victorian homes and another maritime museum. Captain John Smith founded the town at this location in 1608 and it was eventually named and settled by the Marquis de Lafayette in 1782. George Washington probably slept here too but I cannot corroborate that story.

This will be our first attempt at anchoring outside of the Great Lakes. We hope to do a lot of this along the coast and the boat is finally orderly enough to do it. The Zodiac (the dinghy) is straight on the davits at the stern and the anchor locker is free of hoses, garbage bags and other stuff we have been throwing down there to get it off the deck. We are ready (it is high time we started anchoring and stop paying the sometimes astronomical docking fees).

We are two weeks out of Buffalo and finally Peaches seems more like her old self. She had a hard road retiring on Friday and off the next Friday for who knows how long. I give her a lot of credit. She planned on sorting her paper at her leisure. Well, her leisure was definitely getting in the way of us going from the front of the boat to the back!

The two days in Delaware City were perfect, raining all day with nowhere to go. Peaches worked without stopping from dawn to dusk, moving paper piles from one place to another. She entered information on her computer and on her ever-present iPhone. By last night, it was a miracle. The Nun-card was not needed.

I am closet OCD (obsessive-compulsive disorder) as are most of my friends. I have this insatiable urge to make order out of chaos and when I am in need of medication for this, I try to organize things that don't need to be organized. But I digress. Thanks, Peaches.

My world was tilted a little off kilter since we left Buffalo on the boat. After the sorting-miracle, my world is again centered on its axis and all is well. We can do anything. I am sitting in the cockpit of the boat with a glass of bourbon on ice next to me. The sunset is all baby pink and blue clouds. The osprey nest near us is as big as an upside down VW Beetle, the gulls are on top of all of the dock posts and the only sound I hear is the sound of the water lapping against the hull. Thanks for following our adventure and commenting. We love it!

Havre de Grace Lighthouse, Maryland

Chapter 10

Havre de Grace MD

09/21/2009 Havre De Grace, Maryland

We have a long string of "first time ever did that" moments. We came from the Bohemia River to Havre de Grace on Friday. It wasn't such a long trip but it was so shallow that we had to go very, very slowly. There was also a veritable quilt of crab pots covering everything but the marked channel. The small buoys are all different colors and some have flags. We haven't clipped one yet, but there's still lots of time for that.

Let's see, our string of firsts. We anchored for the first time and my brother will know it was a fluke. It stuck the first time. (from lame nautical sayings, "Fluke: the portion of an anchor that digs into the bottom, holding the boat in place; also any occasion when this occurs on the first try.") We still got up a couple of times the first night to see if we were dragging. As of today, we've gone three nights without moving. Another first, getting the Zodiac dinghy down off of the davits into the water and the Honda motor running for the first time.

Everything worked great and we made it into town to walk around. Book stores, clothing stores and a marker saying that George Washington.......marched through this town. No sleeping I guess. Peaches went into the Art Room Store where the owner was like the Welcome Wagon Lady. By the end of a half hour she knew all our plans and we knew where to buy anything and who to call if we get in trouble. She was at the top of that list. Peaches got a sketch pad and I hope she uses her great talents to sketch some scenes.

Another first time is running the Honda generator. We've been at anchor for three days using our battery banks. It's been all debits and no deposits if you remember the analogy to a financial institution. We ran the engine to charge the batteries using the alternator but then thought why not the generator? Where to put it? The generator and the resulting carbon monoxide should go at the pointy end of the boat, away from us. This entails dragging a heavy yellow marine power cord from the plug at the stern of the boat to the generator 40+ feet away. Okay, done. Start it and then watch the monitor in the aft cabin. It sort of worked but I still used my call-a-friend card and talked to Andy at RCR back at home. He said we're doing fine. I think so too. I didn't know enough to ask more questions.

So, we are on an adventure and not on a vacation, but there are some similarities. One is have you noticed how fast your finger and toenails grow when you are away from home? How about your hair is perfect, it's perfect, it's a little wild and then, totally out of control? We are in the wind and weather so much I don't even bother combing my hair with anything but my fingers. By the end of this voyage we will be like the children raised in the forest by wolves; few clothes, hair everywhere and nails long enough to use as tools!

I've read a couple of books already and Peaches is in the beginning of Michener's *Chesapeake*. I read it just before we left and already the river names are making me recall the Indian tribes and their wars. There is so much history in each of these little towns. I think everyone who attended the first Continental Congress left their footprints here. Yep, even George.

I needed to get one of my prescriptions refilled and so, not unlike home, I found my purse, got the boat keys, needed help getting the dinghy off of the davits and took the short boat ride to town (with all our accumulated garbage bags). I tied up at the dinghy dock. I almost took a header as I stepped out of the boat onto the dock but saved it and bowed to the guy getting his huge cabin cruiser ready to go out fishing. I meant to do that three steps and stand movement.

I walked the six blocks past windows showing everything from oyster and crabbing tackle to antiques to French pastries. I came into the pharmacy and showed my Rx and walked around and walked around and around again. The pharmacist finally came out from behind the counter and said my insurance wouldn't cover the med but he could give me a month for $9.95. So, I got three months and he got......some stories. I reversed my steps and found the bakery had closed while I was telling stories. I took my sub-compact Zodiac back to the Star of the Sea (home). It only took an hour or two and I got a couple of nice boat rides and a walk out of it too. How cool!

People are so interested in our trip. We went into an antique book store and the owner had a lot to add to our understanding of this town. It missed being the nation's capital by one vote. He had some great stories of his travels too. Our waitress at lunch said she was from upstate PA on the Susquehanna River and now she works and lives at the other end of it where it meets the Chesapeake. Everything here is tied to the rivers. The barges that go by are filled with stone from a quarry up river and are headed all up and down the east coast. The trains rattling on the bridge behind us go from Washington to NYC and Boston and back. I've never felt quite so connected to this country as I do here.

I almost forgot to mention the last "first time I did that" incident. We filled up with diesel and water today and so we pulled anchor, motored over to the marina and laid the boat up against the face dock like real sailors. I was crawling all over the deck opening the fuel cap and closing it, opening the water cap, oops, the other water cap and PLOOP. This is a sound heard only by boaters. It indicates that something as valuable as gold has been irretrievably lost to the muck at the bottom of the bay. Ploop went the two specialized wrenches (spanners I subsequently learned) to the water tanks, the holding tanks and the fuel tank. They had a few token floaters attached but not enough to slow their decent enough so I could catch them with the boat hook.

Peaches was very gracious and I have been wearing my guilt like a pro. We can use the winch handle to open the water and a jury-rigged curved-tipped needle-nose pliers to open the fuel tank. Hopefully we can pick up another spanner at the Annapolis Boat Show in October. I will buy two sets and a helium balloon set-up to keep them afloat.

We leave tomorrow for a place called Middle River, then on to the Patapsco River and then the Baltimore Inner Harbor where we'll meet my Dad, the youngest 87 year old on the planet. I hope he has room for a bunch more "first time I ever did that" moments on his dance card. He will use his unlimited bag of trivia to tell us where we are, what happened there and who made history at any given spot we pass. Can't wait.

31

**Peaches on the bow with her iPhone,
Maryland Yacht Club, Maryland**

Chapter 11

This and That

09/25/2009 Patapsco River, Rock Creek, Maryland

Today we traveled from Havre de Grace across the Chesapeake to Middle River on the eastern shore. It was a 45 nautical mile day with no wind so we used the iron jenny (engine). Peaches was hooked on watching the blue herons who were everywhere. She said they looked prehistoric, like a house on stilts but with graceful curved necks. The mist was still on the water as we left the Susquehanna River and the cormorants were all drying their wings. They make me think of the gorge at the base of Niagara Falls where they perch on every rock and bush. Peaches is becoming bird wise. I'm so glad she's looking outside the boat and away from the charts occasionally. The large red and green buoys are a problem or should I say the birds are a problem. All buoys are numbered in white paint. All birds poop white. So, an 8 looks like an 3, a 4 looks like a 1. If it is a double digit, you might as well just close your eyes and guess.

As we got out to the main shipping channel, we got intimately involved with the minefield of crab traps. Peaches was at the helm as we crossed from the west to the eastern coast through the traps. In Peaches' words "I ducked and wove my way slowly through them only to find that I was all off course by 30 degrees. Chris came up with the sandwiches for lunch and I was shook. We had to sail to a mark to find out where I took us. Chris, of course drove her section like Mario Andretti. She needs to go slower, slower, slower." Who me?

We anchored near Bowley's Marina in Galloway Creek. Anchoring is like going through the locks. Each person had a job and it worked. Peach is on deck with the control for the anchor and I'm at the helm. We have walkie-talkies and she directs me. I follow the best I can. It is not a well-oiled machine by any criteria but I can see that it will be. We had a well-deserved rest after the field of crab pots. There is a pattern of long lines of pots laid by each crabber but often this magic line does not lead to where you are going.

Peaches and I moved the boat from Middle River, Galloway Creek around several islands and into the Patapsco River, Rock Creek. This is the home of the Maryland Yacht Club. It is a child in the listing of yacht clubs in the US at 105 years. Buffalo Yacht Club is ready to celebrate 150 years of continuous service in 2010.

We made dinner reservations for tonight. Holy crow, I have to put on clothes. No, not so quick, I wear clothes, my standard shorts and a T-shirt. I often put on shoes when we get off the boat. What I'm getting at is I have to find real go-to-the Maryland Yacht Club- clothes. I am talking about as big a transformation as Burt did when he got off the boat to go home to the safety of his wife and home in Buffalo. One minute he was comfortably grubby like the rest of us and the next he looked like he came out of a Ralph Loren advertisement. I rummaged through my hanging stuff and put something together. How quickly we forget something simple like wearing good clothes. Peach did a good job finding clothes, exclaiming that she was going to wear socks with her deck shoes. What will we be like in six months? What about after a year in the islands (reference: raised by wolves)?

The weather has been hot with scattered rain showers. We both got up last night to rearrange the lines holding the boat in the slip. We were rubbing some on the starboard side due to a shift in the winds. Sleeping on a boat is like sleeping in a house with your children in the next room. You can go from comatose to problem solving mode in seconds.

Problem solving is a good topic for today. We are setting up a pre-flight check list to use before we depart any moorings, anchorages or slips. It looks long but is mostly common sense. There is always that one thing you forget once, forget it again and then something breaks. Here's an example of the list: close all the hatches (yes, batten the hatches); turn off everything except the refrigerator; turn on the instruments, electronics, engine start battery and the fuel pump; make sure that you pad the really important breakables down below like the coffee maker, the toaster and the flat screen TV (I just blew our cover didn't I? I didn't say we were camping, just going for a simple adventure). Oh, first check the oil, transmission fluid, raw water pump, on and on and on. So, when you put the key in your vintage BMW, back out of your garage and turn right into Tim Horton's for your coffee, pat yourself on the back for not having a list.

We are tied up to a dock at the Maryland Yacht Club with over a hundred boats; some sailboats and some that wouldn't look out of place in Trump's Marina. There's food, water, electricity, laundry services and lots of people who love to talk. Peaches talked with a couple in a trawler who have done the Great Loop. That is going counterclockwise from the Great Lakes to the Illinois River. They go down the Mississippi River through Mobile and turn right along the Gulf of Mexico and around Florida and up the East Coast. Some go all the way to the St Lawrence Seaway to the Great Lakes. Others cut off 1500 miles by taking the Erie Canal. It is quite an accomplishment. This club is a stop-over for the Loop people (Loop people sounds like it's out of a diagnostic handbook, how about Great Loop Adventurers?).

We've been anchored for several days before coming here. The battery banks were down even after a four hour motoring trip. They should have been charged fully with the alternator. I reread the Inverter book, the Link 2000 book and finally called Andy Lopez, my friend and electrical guru at RCR Yachts under the Skyway in Buffalo. I got him at the end of the day when occasionally a beer might be in the hands of the yard guys. I gave him my story, the numbers on the Link and how long we had been 'off the grid'. He said again we were fine. I took a deep breath and we just talked about our trip, his summer projects, gossip. I told him at least 14 times what a great trip we're having, mostly because he wants to do the same thing soon. It must be hard for him to set up all these boats perfectly and then get left behind to do another.

I spent today topping off all the batteries with distilled water. Sounds easy? It used to take me about 2 minutes to top off the battery for my Kubota tractor once a year. Something Andy said to me about higher temperatures made me want to check all the batteries on the boat. Batteries should never be stressed, should be used often and be respected for their potential kind of like good horses. So, armed with a little Solo bathroom cup and a gallon of distilled water, I attacked the batteries under the stairs, each 260 pounds. They needed several cups. Done!

Next job, the batteries in the back of the boat that are only accessible by crawling down into the two corner lazarets in the cockpit. They pass as comfortable corner seats during the day while you are sailing but today they look like coffins on end. They are only large enough for me to insert myself with my arms tightly at my sides into the small open end. The deal is you have to do a deep knee bend, wiggle your arm out of the hole to flop around and find the cup and the gallon of water you couldn't fit in when you jumped in. I filled all the red-topped openings of the two golf cart batteries. I didn't drop any of the caps into the well under the battery shelf. A lot of big pokey things caught on my shirt and shorts, but I survived. I got out and did the other side but there is less room there because of the big inverter and the swim deck shower set up.

The batteries took more water than I thought they would. The warmer the temperature, the more water that evaporates away. I'll watch them a lot more closely now. I stumbled down the stairs into the main salon and Peaches asked me if there was any water down under the batteries. What? I just did a magnificent Houdini imitation and lived to tell the story and she is asking me a question like I'd been leaning on the counter in the galley making us a cup of coffee. I know I was incredible today and that's enough for me. I didn't look under the batteries.

Before Peaches reads this, I need to say what a wizard she was today rescuing a line tied to a post at the stern of the boat. It was looped irretrievably and it took loosening all the lines all the way around the boat, extending the electric cords and looping another line around the post with the Landing Loop (a big Y-shaped extendable pole for reaching to the dock with your bow line). Then there was a lot of manipulation with the boat hook to drop the line. It took us an hour but we'll be able to take off early tomorrow morning without help from the dock staff. One of the signs of confidence is to do your own work, solve your own problems. It doesn't hurt to be two 62 year old women taking off from your slip without a hitch, smooth and perfect. And people think we spend our afternoons sipping margaritas under the shade of our cockpit canvas. We wish!

**Chris and her Dad, Bill underway from
Baltimore Inner Harbor to Annapolis, Maryland**

Chapter 12

The Baltimore Inner Harbor

09/26/2009 Baltimore, Maryland

Peaches has a few things to say about our trip to Baltimore. She doesn't often do a blog but when she does, the content always surprised me. We are in the same place at the same time, see the same things and feel the boat moving under us the same. Well, maybe not just the same! So, Peach is writing today

Last night our plans were to rise early to get the water tanks topped off, pack up and depart the Maryland Yacht Club without incident. My iPhone rang its wake up alarm at 0600. Did you know at this time the iPhone has 76,000 applications, the wake up alarm the most simple? We both heard the alarm from opposite ends of the boat and ignored it. Chris finally had the coffee grinding, filling the boat with good smells. Our hope was to beat the heavy rains coming east from Pittsburgh. Another reason, the free or nearly free docking of the inner harbor of Baltimore is usually gone by 1100. We talked through which lines to release first as we leave the dock and when to start backing out of the slip. We moved out of that slip perfectly. Where are all the applauding masses who should see this perfection?

Exiting Rocky Creek we passed a conglomerate of craggy white rocks. It makes you feel good the boat-rending rocks are just where the charts show them. We started up the Patapsco River heading west to Baltimore. The winds were up and the swells were moderate. The noise of the AIS was like music in the air, alerting us to boats larger than 100 feet coming and going from Baltimore Harbor. It is a pain to keep pushing the accept button to silence the alarm on the navigation software but knowing where they are and which direction they are going is worth a million. I made a cheat list last night of all the red and green buoys we would pass on the hour and a half trip to the inner harbor. It worked. We ticked the buoys off right on schedule.

We went under the Francis Scott Key Bridge with a clearance of 186 feet. This is one of the few bridges we ducked under where we had no concerns about being demasted. I know we take a lot of bridge pictures but how many bridges have you seen the underside of and marveled at the beauty of construction?

Continuing down the red and green buoys we see Fort McHenry and the entrance channel to the right. Large ships were everywhere, anchored, tied to commercial docks, making their way out or into the harbor. One set of piers had rows of grey military looking ships without any markings on their sides. We saw the Red Cross ship HOPE being loaded. History is everywhere. Fort McHenry is what inspired the writing of the Star Spangled Banner. Key was a prisoner on a British barge and while looking at the American flag at the fort, he wrote the famous words.

We passed the fort, turned to the right and entered the channel to the Inner Harbor. Skipper Bob's Guide recommended anchoring right in front of the World Trade Center Building. Knowing we were going to pick up Chris' Dad we docked adjacent to the Baltimore Aquarium. We called the harbormaster and a kid in a red shirt and driving a golf cart showed up. He said we were fine there but there were slips across the harbor near the schooner, The Spirit of Baltimore II. We paid him for a night and proceeded across the harbor. We had to dodge the harbor taxis going back and forth with tourists. We were so lucky to have a chance to hook up to electricity again for about $50 a night. You couldn't possibly get a junky motel room for that on the trendy waterfront of Baltimore.

The crème de la crème today is that Chris used her newly acquired skills, learned from John Pettis, to traverse the Baltimore Harbor backing the Star of the Sea into a dock shared with the Spirit of Baltimore II. It was like she had done this all her life. A couple was waiting to go onto the Spirit of Baltimore and helped us to tie up. Gigi and Chris from Philadelphia were so happy to be away from their children for the first time while celebrating their 10th wedding anniversary. They handled the lines well and were really into our trip when we started sharing stories. They even commented on what a nice job Chris did backing up the boat. Star of the Sea is about 44 feet but with the dinghy hanging off the davits in the back it like docking a 49 footer.

When we got settled, tied up just right and hooked into the electricity, we sat in the cockpit and dropped our jaws at the same time. The people and the boats and the colors and the fact that we came in here safe and on our own made us giddy. The harbor was alive with boats of every shape and size: the Spirit of Baltimore II, the submarine near the Aquarium, the USS Constellation (the last all-sail warship built by the US Navy) near the Harborfront Place, the gondolas near the World Trade docks and a motorized pirate ship shooting water cannons. The kids were doing the limbo and laughing as the Pirate Ship tears across the harbor, music blaring. The building just behind us is the Intercontinental Hotel. It's like we are at the drive-in movie with all the history and tourism going on in front of us. We see Oriole Park at Camden Yards poking above the first line of buildings. We hear the Star Spangled Banner played to open the early evening game. How perfect!

A bowl of soup with oyster crackers tastes good while we wait for the rain. The new side curtains for the cockpit keep out the rain and the winds. Chris called her Dad, Bill Flanders, to say we were docked. He comes into the Baltimore airport tomorrow around 3 PM. Only a father could say that the crime statistics for Baltimore are very high and two women shouldn't go wandering around at night. My Dad, if he were alive, would have said exactly the same thing, exactly. We stayed onboard tonight while the 2 inches of rain fell.

The sounds of the harbor are phenomenal. The church bells chime the hour, the horns of the tourist boats blast and you can hear the commentary as they pull away. The music from the baseball game is completed but the sound of the rain continues on our deck. Someone walked by the boat a couple of minutes ago. I hear them say "Buffalo, how did they get here from there?"

Baltimore Inner Harbor, Maryland

Chapter 13

Lost and Found

09/28/2009 Inner Harbor Baltimore, Maryland

Have you ever gone into a room and stood there wondering what you went there for? That doesn't happen on this 44 foot boat. What does happen is much harder to explain. It isn't a senior moment or even plain forgetfulness. It is misplacing your keys or your phone in a space 13 feet by 44 feet. How hard can this be? I don't know how many times Peaches, in complete frustration, asked me to call her phone. We are standing a foot apart in the main salon. She can hear it and locate the precious iPhone and be complete again. I smile.

There are several things I haven't found since we left. The D-cell batteries and the bags for the shop vac have disappeared. They are on the manifest list but not in their place. I have things squirreled away in the smallest indentations of the hull, under the floor in the bilge (wine cellar) and under every cushion and mattress. It may be years before they are found, a small irritation of my everything-in-it's-place syndrome.

The absolute best lost item happened today in the National Aquarium. We bought the tickets to let you into the exhibits, the dolphin show and the 4-D nature movie. Peaches, when we were planning our trip, ordered a khaki vest with 20 pockets. It looks vaguely like a safari-in-Africa vest but in her defense we were planning to go to some way-out uninhabited islands. She wore it today and as we got to the entrance for the dolphin show she grew pale, patting and opening all of the pockets. She opened them twice and then a third time. No ticket. The people behind us were craning their necks to see what was wrong. Dad and I moved subtly away from her, distancing ourselves from the show. She finally found the receipt, not the ticket, and they let her in. So, even in a 20 pocket safari vest, things get lost.

Let me tell you what I think about 4-D movies. They are technically very attention-getting, but after the first spray of real water in the face (coming from the back of the seat in front of me) and the first time I was poked in the rib cage, I sort of lost my enthusiasm. Only when the lights came back on did I notice all the bells and whistles attached to the back of each seat (squirters, bubble machines, air vents, oh, and rumblings under your seat). I never found the pokey thing that got me in the ribs. We sit there with 4-D glasses on, I think, just so we won't see what is going to splash or hit us next. No, I'm not a grump, but the animals jumping out of the screen and the waves seeming to crash over us all was enough techno stimulation for me. My only heads-up to you is to check out the place before the movie starts, then sit back and enjoy. The photography is so cool.

Baltimore harbor is exactly what Buffalo should have done 20 years ago. It is beautifully laid out, safe, colorful and bustling. The structure of the harbor and the city and the available military and locally made boats to show off are the same in Buffalo NY. What an awful shame it is for us not to have this type of attraction, yes for tourists, but for us too. Off the soap box. This morning we walked most of the length of the harbor walk on Monday. It was much less crowded that Sunday but no less fun to people and boat watch. We note each boat outfitted for cruising like ours who come in looking and hoping for a place to anchor or dock.

The National Aquarium was topnotch. The jellyfish exhibit was outstanding. The local Chesapeake exhibit just echoed our new love for this part of the country. There was an Australian exhibit for Dad who had been there and seen most of the marine animals, bats and birds.

I hadn't gone to a dolphin show since my sons were little kids. They are in their 30s now. We sat behind the splash zone with the other grey haired-senior citizens but hooted and laughed as loud and long as everyone else. There was a part where the dolphins spoke to command and an infant behind us made the same noises while sitting in her mother's lap. It made your hairs stand up on end at the connection between the child and the dolphins. They did their jumps and splashes, a lot of fish treats, but also did some really subtle imitations of the trainer. I was sorry when it was done.

My Dad, Bill, flew down yesterday from Buffalo airport. He found the light rail connection to Camden Yard, walked over and found the boat without a problem. Baltimore is a well-known spot to pick up and let off guests because of the good connection from the airport to the inner harbor. We had a great time talking but he kept getting this expression on his face like "hurry up, I already heard this part." I didn't get the connection until we called my brother Bob. He said he hadn't called because he had such a good picture of what we were doing that he didn't need any more information. I think we've shot ourselves in the foot with this blog. We still love doing it.

We talked with a couple of women who came in on a small day sailor from Georgetown, further down the Chesapeake. They were pleased to see a larger boat being captained by a couple of women. (I'll bet she used the word old women in her head). She was so familiar with the area that she gave us a lot of good suggestions for lower down in Chesapeake Bay. They suggested, when she found we had the Chesapeake Cruising Guide, we read a few more pages ahead in the book when we were planning so we don't sail right past something great. It is called planning a_h_e_a_d.

She suggested we go up the Potomac River to Washington DC after we go to the Annapolis Boat Show early next month. My friend Lee spent a lot of time on the water down there and has been trying to get me to commit to the time it will take to do this trip. I just hope you don't read about us being boarded by the CIA or Homeland security looking for weapons, bomb making material or subversive blogging!

Cooking on the boat hit a new high last night, docked at a dock, hooked to electricity and with Dad here. I dug out my Spanish FAGO pressure cooker to do a Cuban pot roast. I'd planed this months ago. I've been having mixed results over the last year learning how to use the pressure cooker. When it was good it was very good, but when it wouldn't seal and pressurize, it was a burnt mess. IT WAS PERFECT! The seasonings were subtle, the meat tender, the sauce perfection. I almost didn't get this done because, in my striving to have every kitchen tool known to man or God, I couldn't find the simple can opener. I needed canned diced tomatoes or it was just going to be plain meat. It took the whole time browning the meat, dropping a whole bottle of dried oregano onto the floor and praying to the pressure cooker goddess while on my knees to finally find the opener. Lost and found!

We're off tomorrow to the Megothy River to anchor for the night and explore a bit in the Zodiac. We did read ahead in the book and know that our short term goal of Annapolis is the next river down from the

Megothy. Small steps. I can't wait to show Dad all the ships in the outer harbor on the way under the bridge and out to the Bay. He'll tell me who they are, where they are from and probably what they did during the war. I'm catching the history bug from him and it's the only type of book I want to read. When you travel this slowly, there is a lot of time to see how it might have looked to others centuries ago. The old buildings hide among the new. The shape of the bays and the fishermen's working docks are practically unchanged. I have the freedom and the time to find out who and why.

Cadets at the US Naval Academy, Annapolis, Maryland

Chapter 14

Just Transportation

10/02/2009 Annapolis, Maryland

I'm sitting in the cockpit of the Star of the Sea. The marching band from the Naval Academy is practicing for the Navy vs. Air Force football game tomorrow. They sound sharp. The drums carry out over the water like they are in our dinghy behind the boat. It is overcast but not raining with a pretty significant weather front coming in so the harbor is anything but flat. I am rolling back and forth and trying to hold my hands still to type. We have been on a mooring ball in the entrance of the Annapolis Harbor off of the Severn River since early Wednesday afternoon. We left the Inner Harbor of Baltimore on Tuesday about noon and anchored in the Megothy River on Tuesday night. More about that simple statement in a bit. Whether by land, sea, air or, after today, Segway, we are all about transportation.

Until now, I've never really thought about any of the sailboats I have sailed or owned as a means of getting from A to B. Sure, we went to Youngstown from Buffalo to race and completed the Erie/Dover race, but that was set up as our race course, not our idea of a destination. My point is that Star of the Sea isn't just a sailing vessel or a home or a motor boat. She is transportation, and a sturdy and forgiving boat she is. We haven't had to utilize a lame nautical saying yet to save us from the briny deep or the more frightening coastline, but keep them coming Bob. You ever know when it will be the kingpin to our survival.

Dad and I went for a quick walk before leaving Baltimore Inner Harbor while Peaches talked at length with Raymarine about her computer program that integrates with the navigation program up at the wheel. It's never fun to listen to all that geek talk so we took off for the Barnes and Noble. We got lots of fresh air, stretched our legs and got the coffee beans we needed to fuel the next leg of the trip. Gee, that was quite a blast of wind, I thought. We walked back to the boat and cast off our lines. There will be lots of big ships to see on way out, lots of commercial piers and many slips full of military transport ships. We made our way out to the Francis Scott Key Bridge, rubber-necking all the way. Golly, the waves are getting bigger and look at that chop, just like on Lake Erie I thought. On we went with me at the wheel and Peaches calling out the numbers of the green and red buoys as we passed them by. It's green on the right as we go out into the Chesapeake Bay.

We continued on what was to be a short trip. After about 4 hours of wallowing in big swells with waves splashing up over the bow, we made the turn into the Megothy River. The entrance was narrow but well-marked. It was overcast but not raining yet. Even in the river the waves were formidable and the pesky wind kept rising. First the gusts were 20-30 knots then back to a baseline of 10 knots. Then, gee, the baseline is 30 knots and that last gust was 40. We aborted a couple of tries at anchoring behind Gibson Island and gathered ourselves to face into the wind until we came to a lee shore where the wind wouldn't make it impossible to anchor. It was easily ¾ of a nautical mile before we ended up in a small bay near a marina and a yacht club. We managed to avoid the youth sailing program of about 20 small sailboats as we made for a closer spot to shore. We watched the depth meter to find the right place to drop the anchor. The kids were sort of distracting when they flipped over those little sailboats every other minute. They flipped them back up and continued the race like it was nothing. I was impressed the race committee didn't haul them into the yacht club because of the big winds. We anchored and the wind started to die. We rested comfortably in about 13 feet of water and started dinner. I asked Peaches if she'd looked at the weather before we left the Inner Harbor. She said

"No, I thought you did." I did not. I think we need to get that preflight list printed and stuck to the wheel of the boat. Any day that I say "Gee" and "Golly" more than three times should trip something in my brain other than early dementia or a return to childhood. We got through by the seat of our pants this time, never unprepared again. Oh gee, my Dad was with us!

The following morning we took off for the short trip to Annapolis. Seas were flat and the sun was up. If you folks in Buffalo think that summer is done and winter is setting in I want you to know we feel it a little here too. Nights are in the 40s but days remain in the 70s and not nearly the rain you've had this past week. The big winds hit you the day before us. Someone sent pictures of the Buffalo Yacht Club Basin with all the boats riding up over the docks! When the wind blows right up Lake Erie, the water really stacks up at our end.

We entered the Severn River and made out way up to the Annapolis Harbor. It didn't look the same to us. We've always been here by car when the boat show floating docks filled the harbor. We went for diesel through the empty harbor while Peaches called the Harbormaster who offered us a slip as well as a mooring ball in the harbor. It was a no-brainer when he said we could take one of the mooring balls and keep it through the Sailboat Show starting on October 8th. A perfect solution. We'll be able to watch the big boats coming in to be shown and, even better, watch them build the docks and walkways of the sailing venue village that suddenly appears floating in the harbor once a year (all from our cockpit).

We dropped the Zodiac into the water and went into the small inlet called Ego Alley. This is where

the large hot-shot boats go to be seen turning at the city end near the Alex Haley (of Roots fame) statue. The Harbormaster had already stopped at the boat when we tied up so we were free to scope out the town. We got the information booth brochures and had a cup of coffee at Starbucks while we planned tomorrow. It rained a bit so we stayed until our window of opportunity opened. We toured the harbor by Zodiac and took some pictures. I moved us under the three-masted schooner Arabella's bowsprit to take a picture of the silver figurehead. Back to the boat for some rest and to work out how we're going to keep the batteries charged for almost two weeks. The generator is out and working so well that we let it run all night. It is all about the amp hours.

Thursday was a walk to the Naval Academy and a tour of most of the buildings and grounds. It was a lot of walking but both Peaches and Dad breezed through it with only a couple of sit-downs on historic benches. The undergrads were all in their full uniforms and we had the good fortune to see them muster for formation. They were all in navy blue except for the seniors in kaki. They filled the yard, stepping to the bagpipes and drums, hundreds of tall, lean, perfectly sculpted men and women. I was very moved. They filed, in matched pairs of brigades, up the ramps and stairs to the main hall for lunch. We loved that the bagpipes and drums played on until all were in and then filed in themselves.

We went on to see the crypt of John Paul Jones. He never lost a battle on any ship he sailed. Before he was fighting for the colonies, he was a privateer for the British. I didn't know that. He's not the pristine father of our Navy as I thought. His sarcophagus was carved black and white marble. It was over the top with large columns, dolphins spouting water, carved seaweed covering the top and crabs on the supporting pillars. My first thought was that any man who commissioned something like this must not be very generous of heart and possessed of a swelled head. This was confirmed by the tour guide who mentioned that John Paul had a bust made of himself in his 40s that pleased him so much he had 30 copies made to give to his closest friends.

We went into the museum to see the history of the Navy as well as the Naval Academy. The ship models upstairs were unbelievable, especially the ones carved by British prisoners from the bones in the soup served to them for dinner.

Signs were everywhere for Navy to beat Air Force. It's a big rivalry. There is a football game going on right now with Cornell and a non-Navy team. We'll have another front row seat on the boat for the game. We'll probably be watching a lot of things from the cockpit tonight as the boat is rolling back and forth like a hotdog on a grill. Going below for much will guarantee a good case of mal de mere.

It is Friday and we changed our plans some by taking the water taxi into town. It is a service from the Harbormaster for those boats on city moorings. They come up to the side of your boat with two railings for you to grasp and go down the steps into the taxi. So easy! They come with a phone call or a hail on channel 9. The captains jockey these boats around like nothing, stopping on a dime, lining up their gate with yours. I know the job must get old for them but they are my new docking heroes.

Walking to the bookstore for another city tourist map we decided to take a Segway historical tour of the

old part of the city. Peaches said she was game. My surprise was my Dad said yes, he definitely wanted to do it. As far back as I have memories, he has never expressed a firm opinion without mentally polling the others involved. Always soft spoken but smarter that anyone I know he is not usually so quick to say yes. I was thrilled. Around the corner the tour storefront was full of empty Segways. After we talked a bit with the owner and signed all our rights away including, if we died during the tour, he got Star of the Sea. The training started immediately on the carpeted floor of the store, first Peaches, then Dad and then me. We learned to mount, dismount, go forward and back and turn. All moves are very subtle. A sharp movement causes big troubles. We all did well. Off we went with helmets and wired for sound so we could hear his instructions and the tour. He put me in the middle so I couldn't set the speed for the tour.

Down brick sidewalks, brick streets, weaving in and out of traffic and pedestrians, we conquered bumps, cracks and tree root lumps under our wheels. We were amazingly able to listen to his good talk about early Annapolis. It was the capital of the colonies for a time and is centrally located in the middle of all the history you may or may not remember from high school. The Segway became second nature except for the times he had us stand still on them. That was a real trick! There were a couple of ugly dismounts but I will not name names. We returned well informed and shot through with adrenaline. On the way I saw people smiling at us, three 10 feet tall ducklings following the leader through town. I also saw true fear in some eyes (well founded) and a couple of thumbs up. One 8 year old school boy made the ultimate compliment by saying "cool" under his breath to the equally impressed kid next to him. All it took was a Segway for two 62 year old ladies and an 87 year old gentleman to cut through the generation gap.

So, transportation can be anything from your feet to your yacht. It could be a Segway or just your mind. We've tried them all in this first month of our adventure. All have been more than our expectations!

**Annapolis Boat Show, taken from the porch of the
Annapolis Yacht Club, Maryland**

Chapter 15

Sailboat at a Sailboat Show

10/12/2009 Annapolis, Maryland

We woke up this morning to Peaches iPhone warning us of high winds building to gusts of 50+ knots. We calmly made coffee, ate our oatmeal and raisin bran, talked about our plans for the day, checked the amp hours used overnight and then we got busy.

The sun is out and the temperature is climbing out of the low 60s. We could see the wind coming in the cloud patterns (old salts, are we). Both battery banks have floated (makes me smile). It means we can have electricity without guilt. We cleared the deck of loose items and tied the generator down on the foredeck. We tied the dinghy to the davits and the boat with a bird's nest of knots so it wouldn't become a flying object. The gusts were blowing us in wide arcs, so wide we saw the starboard side of the boat moored in front of us (usually we are parallel so not a normal sight).

Even a week ago we would have been in full-blown fight or flight stress over the high winds and the boat. We would have plummeted to the lowest survival level of the Maslow Scale, but we didn't. We didn't leave the boat and we didn't make ourselves work all day long. Our iPods and Kindles came out of storage and we just relaxed.

The busy Annapolis we enjoyed last week with Dad is a cyclone of activity (no pun intended). Monday morning long snakes of floating docks hauled by harbormaster and volunteer boats entered the harbor. There were two barges driving in the pilings. All sorts of sailboats were hovering in the harbor, waiting for their spot to be built. When it was ready, they were built into the matrix. Because of the wind gusts, the delivery sailboats were heeled over with their rails buried (even without sails) and minutes later bobbing upright in the harbor. Lots of dollar signs were flashing in the skipper's eyes as they struggled to keep the sailboats in one piece. When the day was done, the docks came all the way out to our boat. The new boats left over looked for spots to anchor for the night. The boat and people watching was fantastic.

Tuesday when the winds subsided we went into town to do the laundry and have showers at the harbormaster building near Ego Alley. We finally saw the Annapolis we knew from the boat show; banners everywhere, delivery trucks unloading and backing up traffic at the traffic circle for hours. There were handsome young salespeople from the yacht builders and marine equipment companies walking through the pedestrian traffic with their iPhones to their ears and serious looks on their faces. They were going a hundred knots while we (old salts, remember) were strolling through the rush, clean and comfy from our showers with our laundry following us in our red box on wheels.

Being on mooring ball #25 has been more than just a good seat for the show, but during the show is a place to entertain friends. I could list them all because they mean so much to us, especially on the trip, but I won't today. The exception is John Pettis who actually came back on the boat to share dinner with Vince Dunn and us. He even spent the night. What a great time we had. I had to tie my hands behind my back after I made and served dinner, drinks and desert so I wouldn't point to parts of the boat I've had questions about since he left. I managed to control myself. We can figure them out ourselves now.

Now that the city blocks of docks with the most beautiful, sleek, fast yachts are floating in the harbor, I think that the sales pitch this year is "mine is bigger than yours." There is a sailing mega-yacht tied in front of the Marriott that is taller and wider that the building! There are vendors from all over the country and some from Europe. Boats are for sale but in booth after booth they sold everything from the tiniest piece of hardware to wine glasses. There were books by adventurers like us and masts with seats to climb to the top of them. We wandered through the booths between lectures and clinics muttering under our breaths "no room on the boat, no room on the boat." Peaches said "we can just talk to them. We'll learn something new and we won't buy anything. Come on!" Well, that mostly worked for us. We talked to a lot of vendors and learned some "pearls" about equipment already installed on our Beneteau. What we got was a lot of encouragement for what we were doing and for where we were heading. What did we buy? Stay tuned.

The lectures are sponsored by Cruising World and the Coast Guard Auxiliary. Jimmy Cornell, a multi-circumnavigator, shared his knowledge and pictures with us and is also on his site www.noonsite.com. Beth Leonard has written the bible of cruising and lots of her good advice is on www.bethandevans.com. Their books sit on our bookshelf, dog-eared and full of bookmarks. Don Street with his disheveled dress and gravely voice is a legend among sailors. All of these speakers are like heroes to us. We were so surprised to see them in person, not just read their books or look at their DVDs. Beth, for instance, looks like she could be a check-out clerk in a grocery store or a secretary for the mayor. Instead she is a hard working author and intrepid sailor with her husband Evans. They are not ten feet tall or people who can turn heads in a crowded room. They are like us.

So, what did we buy? We bought a tri-sail that is used as a stay-sail to stabilize the boat at anchor. It will

keep the boat from swinging in wide arcs at anchor in big winds. We bought magical fender grippers that hold and quickly adjust the fenders (bumpers) that protect the boat when we are up next to a dock or in a slip. The new replacement spanner with floats was my best purchase (see picture)! Peaches got us a set of nesting stainless steel heavy-bottomed cooking pots. The all have lids that strain out water, have removable wrench like handles and all fit in the room it took for only one of my good heavy cooking pots (I promised to ship the others back home). Cool! The down side of the boat show, a new box of papers, brochures and freebee stuff from the show is on the sole of the salon, waiting to be sorted or to trip me on the way to the shower.

Dr. Liz Hatton and her family among the friends we saw this week. We mention her because she brought us a great present from home, two flu shots. Picture us all huddled around their car in the dark in the parking lot of the Annapolis Yacht Club. Liz is drawing up the serum by the light of a pen light. We go one by one to get our injection on the dark side of the car, unseen by the hoards of people walking by and the security guard 20 yards from our location. I can only imagine the headlines, in the morning paper, of our arrest for drug abuse, trafficking, endangering underage children and much more. But, we got away with it!

Tomorrow we're off to St. Michaels across the Chesapeake. It has been a wonderful 13 days in the harbor starting with my Dad's visit and completed as happy but tired drug abusers. We are so lucky.

**The Thomas Point Shoal Lighthouse
Near Annapolis, Maryland**

Chapter 16

A Swim in the Chesapeake

10/15/2009 St. Michaels, Maryland

We arrived in St. Michaels late afternoon on Tuesday. We called ahead and secured a slip at Higgins Yacht Yard. We motored out of Annapolis Harbor and looked forward to unfurling the sails on the way across the Chesapeake. The mainsail came out most of the way from the mast and then hung up on one of our vertical battens. We tried to get it in then get it out but it wouldn't budge. I climbed onto the deck to try to jerk it loose but it didn't work. We raised the main halyard a bit, nothing. Finally we made a dozen big circles through the wind, letting the boom go strongly from side to side and the batten came loose. We furled it and will check it for damage when we get to the dock. The rolling and swinging we did in Annapolis Harbor must have knocked the battens out of kilter. It happened at the beginning of a race we did in Erie last summer and we almost didn't get the main out and set to make our way across the start line in time.

The Thomas Point Lighthouse marking a large shoal off of the South River came into view, the most photographed lighthouse in the Chesapeake. Now that we were safely on the eastern shore we entered Eastern Bay and the Miles River. St Michaels reminds me of Niagara on the Lake, Ontario, both quaint, welcoming shopping spots. It is the home of the Chesapeake Bay Maritime Museum. St Michaels is the town that fooled the British during the War of 1812. The town was being bombed in 1813 when the residents placed their lanterns high into the trees making the British aim too high to do damage. The only cannon ball to land in a home came through the roof and bounced down the stairs next to a mother carrying her infant.

Tuesday when we were settled onto the face dock, we checked the Sirius Weather and found a Nor'easter on the way by the end of the week. A low front is also coming through to add rain and wind. Gale force winds are predicted for Thursday and Friday. With the waves already 5 feet and the winds gusting to 40 knots out on the Bay, we are glad to hunker down. We are getting good at hunkering.

Sandy, the yard manager, gave us a great deal. We are 44 feet long and got a free night and a rate of $1.50 a foot for the week. We promised ourselves we wouldn't head out in questionable weather, so, what a beautiful place to be stranded. Our goals are to get haircuts (children of the wolves), explore the museum, shop in a real grocery store and find the source of a frustrating small leak (more about this later).

The yard crew helped us move the boat to a slip with

our bow facing into the wind. I backed the boat around the end of a large dock and into the new slip. My heart is in my throat all the time but it is getting easier and easier to do. It was windy, raining and getting colder. I went back to retie the dinghy and close the curtains to keep out the rain. Peaches was on the port side setting fenders and spring lines. Peaches stepped off the deck backwards, the safest way, onto the dock not realizing that we'd gone from a fixed dock to a floating dock. It was much lower and so much further away. She slipped, hanging one leg up on the life lines the other down in the water. She was holding on for her life, calling my name. I got down on the dock and the first thing I said was "I can't lift you up, you're too far down!"

"I'm going to drop down, get the swim ladder down." Peaches grunted.

"Help, help us, she's in the water!" I yelled to the guys on the opposite dock.

I clambered awkwardly back up on the boat and realized immediately that the dinghy needed to be dropped into the water before the swim ladder could come down.

Peaches was working her way to the stern and the swim platform. We both kept talking to each other. The lines to the dinghy kept tangling in my hands. She got to the back swim deck and was hanging on, obviously cold in the sloshing black water. The others jumped onto the boat and with three of us got the dinghy down, out of the way and Peaches up the ladder. She was dressed in a heavy fleece jacket, a sweatshirt, jeans, shoes and socks, and a wool watch cap. Peaches said she was okay and was grateful when the water was warmer than the air. It must have been so hard to swim with the clothes and shoes pulling her down. She headed for a hot shower.

The guys who helped asked me why I didn't throw her a life ring. I don't know except that she is an excellent swimmer and I thought I could get the dinghy down quickly. Peaches said that at least she didn't hit her head and I got there quickly (two points out of three isn't enough). She was sore and had a large bruise on her inner thigh. Peaches was lucky, but we both agree we need to have rules.

China Light Racing on Wednesday nights in Buffalo Harbor had rules. Ours on the 36.7 Star of the Sea went like this: Stay on the boat, don't bleed on the decks and don't rip the sails. It worked. Everyone had their life vests on and nobody worked alone. Ask our friend Sharon Carlo what the rules were and she would say "Stay on the boat, stay on the boat, stay on the boat!" You are so right, Sharon.

We've been hunting for the source of a small leak for weeks. The bilge pump goes off at night and when we walk across the salon from one side to the other. A minute is a long time when the bilge is running. There's never much water and it is clear. The other night we pulled up all the flooring, checking the thru-hull fittings and using the shop vac to suck up the water. Peaches said she would taste the water if I would. We did and thought it slightly salty. We've tightened 100 hose clamps on salt water and fresh water connections. How frustrating. We sure know the boat better in and under everything. It's raining and might snow so the heat is on in the boat for the first time. We have time to read boat schematics, instruction books and think. We will find the leak.

Did I mention how cold it is here and how few heavy clothes we brought with us? If this is early winter and fall is done, we are out of here. Peaches got an email from her cousin Burt who helped us the first two weeks. She was whining about the rocking of the boat at Annapolis. He wrote "Peaches get a hotel room." His reply to us whimpering about the cold would be just the same.

**We are out from under the rain clouds and on the way
to the Solomons, Peaches at the helm in the Chesapeake**

Chapter 17

The Sun is Out, Come Out From Under Your Rock!

10/19/2009 Solomons, Maryland

This is an awesome day for our adventure after freezing for five days in St. Michaels. It is a beautiful place but we can come out from under our rock. We are free to move about the country.

St. Michaels was a good hunkering down place for us, inside time mostly but we got our list done except for the laundry. I heard at the beauty parlor that the one Laundromat in town was owned by a couple who had a horrible divorce last year. Horrible because this town is very small and they were gossip for the whole year. Our haircuts, despite the long, long walk in the rain, were perfect. We no longer look like children of the wolves. The bonus was a freely offered ride back to the boat from the lady in the next chair. She and her husband are cruisers and she took Peaches swim in the Chesapeake story and injuries to heart. It was 38 degrees and raining.

We took a serious look at the leak and did some computer research and polled the readers of the Beneteau 423 Owners site that Peaches subscribes to on her iPhone. We used all our wildcards as lots of you made suggestions, thanks. We've been under all floors, down those tight lazarets in the back corner of the cockpit and under every seat and cupboard. We found no water, except in the bilge. So, we rebalanced the boat by moving the considerable wine cellar and canned goods out of the galley and under a seat of the smaller couch. We moved the three full diesel cans and the three gas cans back to the port side of the foredeck. Maybe some of the thru-hulls on the starboard side were underwater and back flowing? I can't prove it, but we hope we're done (I'm done!).

We packed up the boat and made sure there were no flying objects in the cabin. We filled the empty water tanks, threw out the garbage, said our goodbyes and got some sleep. The sun came up while I brewed the morning coffee. I spent last year before we went shrink-wrapping one pound bags of our favorite coffee, Brazilian Santos. Today we opened February 12th. It was a very good batch! The weather was cold but clear when we got up on deck. As I motored out of the harbor, Peaches was dealing with all the fenders we had out to protect our hull from the dock in the high winds. She had all the soaked deck lines, still dripping from the week of rain.

With all the curtains down, we unfurled the sails and attacked the strong 20-25 knot wind and waves on the Eastern Bay. Our mainsail checked out without rips or worn areas and unfurled effortlessly. We sailed in just jeans and sweatshirts (oh, how I miss my shorts), warm and cozy without the need for foul weather gear for the first time all week. Lots of other sailboats were out, but few were as lucky as we felt with our full enclosure. They were huddled by the wheel in their red foul weather gear and looked miserable. Our 7 hour journey was made pleasurable with the addition of music from our iPods, warm beverages and lunch. We seem to be able to relax enough each day-trip to add another comfort item like the music.

The Solomons, not to be confused with the Solomon Islands, is a small town, actually a small island attached to the main land by a short bridge. John Smith mapped it in 1607. It is at the mouth of the Patuxent River. The Chesapeake has so many Indian names the residents probably wouldn't even flinch at our local western New York names like Tonawanda, Chautauqua or Cheektowaga.

Before we turned into the river, before Cove Point Lighthouse, there is a large and tall set of what look like oil rigs, a large metal spider poised over the water or as Peach said, like Stonehenge sticking out of the water.

We saw it from forever away. As we got closer, we heard someone on the VHF radio warning boats to stay out of the "zone" and as we got closer (drew parallel to the rig) we saw the patrol boat. There is a biological research center and a large nuclear power plant on the hills behind this rig. They are so big I used the funnels as a mark to steer to for most of the afternoon. The guide said nothing about this heavily guarded and sort of threatening structure. We need to find out more in town tomorrow. Hey, he is yelling at us by name! I veer away and our imaginations go wild with what this place might be. It's very hush, hush.

It is dark and cold again but it's the last night that is supposed to be bad. We took a mooring ball about 4:30 this afternoon. The generator is set up (I wonder why the batteries aren't floating after a full day of motoring?), closed up the boat for the night and relaxed. Chicken over angel hair pasta with hot tea and sliced apples makes us feel snug and pampered. We don't look forward to sleeping in the boat in 30 degree temperatures without the heat pump. The single generator can't do it, so we are only toasty warm in this early fall cold when we are at the dock hooked to shore power. Soon we'll be more south, warmer, cruising with the hatches open, the curtains up and worrying about bugs rather than snow!

We couldn't walk away from the otter tank at the
Calvert Marine Museum, Solomons, Maryland

Chapter 18

You Otter Know About This Place

10/20/2009 Solomons, Maryland

Today was golden and wonderful. I know that I said this about yesterday but remember, we've been half-frozen and sensory deprived by the Chesapeake Rainy Season of 2009. When I looked out the window this morning the sun was coming up, the water flat and there were ducks everywhere. Dad, this is your best tip on where to go yet!

When Peaches got up to the cockpit after breakfast, she saw a schooner, The Sultana, out of Chesterton MD. When I got up top it looked like a Chinese fire drill. Young people were coming out onto the deck, peeling off foul weather jackets and sweatshirts like they were on fire. They were so glad to get warm in the morning sun and get some of the wet layers off. The vessel came up from Norfolk, VA during the night on their way home from the Great Schooner Race. This is a replica of a cutter built in 1767 in Boston for King George III. It was a royal revenue cutter and dispatch boat. Today it is used for educational purposes for school children and for visitors all up and down the east coast, but primarily in the Chesapeake.

We met the captain and one of the crew in the laundry room late this afternoon. They were dragging in heavy bags of wet clothes to wash. They'd been dressed in wet layers for days in the rain and the nor'easter. The captain, a woman in her early 30s, answered a lot of our questions and asked just as many of us. When she left for a hot shower, Erica said it'd been a lot of hard work. No, they didn't have heat below, the wood stove was only used for show or for the owner's parties at the end of the season in November. So, once you are wet, you just stay wet. Our cold, but comfortable and dry boat, doesn't seem so bad any more.

We started out in the Zodiac today with our laundry, soap, red box on wheels, cameras and garbage. We checked out the dinghy dock at Zahniser's Yachting Center.

Our friends Gail and Don emailed us that the heads (bathrooms) here were the best on the Bay. We concur. With the laundry done we ventured out to look for the Calvert Marine Museum. It wasn't where we thought it should be so we moved out into the main channel and talked to a fisherman who pointed us back to where our boat was moored. Our attention spans being short in new and interesting places, we continued beyond him to a dock with all sizes of tugboats. We are fascinated by them. We redirected ourselves and headed back to our boat and to the big red museum right behind us. Coming into a maritime museum in a boat is so perfect.

Walking into the back door from the river, we started looking at the boats, lighthouses, old restored outboard motors, much like the museum at St. Michaels. It came to us in a flash that we hadn't come in through the front and didn't pay so we fessed-up and started again. We wandered into the children's section and immediately got lost in the skate nursery. Skate and rays are similar, both flat with kite-shaped bodies. The small skates are much smaller than rays and both may be relatives of the shark. Live skates were in a circular low pool, going round in a slow but steady parade. On the wall, a strip of aquariums showed the skate egg cases back lighted so that you could see the unborn skate frantically moving around inside the purse. We've all seen 'purses" dried up and brown on the beaches from Maine to Florida. We could hardly walk away. Around the bend in the museum an exhibit caught Peaches attention and she was gone. We finally met in the fossil section.

Calvert Cliffs were visible as we came close to the turn-off for the Solomons. I thought at first they were cliffs or maybe houses. Peaches thought they might be condos. They are cliffs made by millions of years of the ocean rising and falling during the ice ages. There were short video presentations in the museum and, sitting on benches, large fossils you could touch and explore. We came upon a window where an Oriental man, dressed in a dusty white coat, worked on a fossil. It was sitting in a tray with an array of dental tools and brushes. Peaches started talking to him, saying she had a complete set of dental tools on the boat to remove stains, drips of varnish and bird poop. He nodded wisely. We asked him a lot of questions and he gave us the answer to the "what was that" mystery. More later.

Two sleek and very well fed male otters were in a large outdoor tank filled with water, stone, sand, trees and driftwood along with a dry backyard to play on when they got tired of swimming. They swam and corkscrewed through the water at warp speed. I initially thought they'd be impossible to photograph, but they got very curious and started swimming at 90 mph and stopping in front of me, pausing before they pushed off and were gone. One of them was really posing and trying to please. We ate our apples and granola bars while we watched them from the benches in the sun. They never stopped swimming fast, flip turning and pushing off with their back feet. They are orphaned brothers, the keeper said as she threw them their afternoon treat of milk bone dog biscuits. One of them was shaved and had been recently spayed because of his aggressive behavior. Postoperatively, all was right in the world of otters again. We dragged our feet, looking back as we moved on.

The woodworking shop was on our way to the dinghy dock so we stopped to talk to the men working near the open double doors. You could tell they loved to talk and so do we. These gentlemen are long retired from other more corporate type jobs but are living their dreams covered with sawdust and wood shavings. They maintain all the floating exhibits, restore old boats donated to the museum and sell them. They help people build their own canoes for a price, all proceeds going to maintain the museum grounds. The sun was setting and we got into the dinghy with the clean laundry smelling fresh and warm from the sun.

Back home, while I am writing this, Peaches is reviewing tomorrow's journey to Sandy Point near Reedsville. We are not planning to anchor in Reedsville as it is the main packing plant for menhaden, an oily fish used for fertilizer, pet food and Omega 3 fish oils for human consumption. The boats that are used to harvest them use purse seine nets. These boats are everywhere, always heavily laden on their way in. The guidebooks use both the word malodorous and upwind so we are staying away. Today, during our 50 nautical mile day, we passed the entrance of the Potomac River, a decision we had to make because of the cold weather delays we've experienced. We'll take the month to do this trip to Washington on our way home.

Oh, the mystery facility with the guards and the patrol boats. The wise Oriental man at the museum said, "Oh that a major East Coast pumping station for propane. Lot of ships come to offload here." He went on to say there are huge fines for crossing the invisible line around that station with your boat. The fishermen in the area try to slip through because of all the fish in and around the pilings. This could still be a cover up. Wise man might not know all!

Navigation involves lots of markers, buoys and, yes, birds

Chapter 19

Navigation How Do We Do It?

10/23/2009 Portsmouth, Virginia

Point A to Point B can be a problem whether you are driving to the grocery store or cross country to visit friends. There can be bumpy roads, lots of traffic, your car can break down or the weather can be horrible. Since the Solomons, we have luckily encountered none of these problems. In a boat there is one other variable: you can run out of water over the bottom (less than skinny water). I did put us softly aground before docking in Portsmouth at the huge Tidewater Marina on the Elizabeth River (first shallow water reference). This was after winding our way through more commercial traffic and amazing boats and tugs than we have ever seen in one place. More later.

I want to talk about how we know where to go every day when we get up, after we have some coffee, and pull up the anchor. There are spiral bound books on top of spiral bound guides for each area we go through. The guides have small charts, written navigational hints and history on the towns and rivers we are going to explore. We also have paper charts in big chart holders, folded charts in protective covers and information from the internet on specific places we want to go. At night when we plan, the table is piled high with papers. When we packed the boat and went into the Erie Canal, I thought we were way oversupplied with guides and seemingly redundant charts. As we left the Chesapeake today, I look at the ragged corners and marks in the margins of our trusty guides and realize that it is truly never enough. We used it all.

The night before we leave, we go over the maps and guides and, with our experience, judge how far we can make it with tomorrow's weather forecast (that will make our trip easy or maybe shorter than we would like). Peaches is bent over the charts as I cook dinner and get the galley cleaned up. We sit and pour over the books, one often complimenting the other. Buoy numbers are written down in sequence and occasionally a plot is made with the parallel bars and the dividers. The conversation in the Chesapeake is about the depth of the water in the bay where we will anchor at night and what direction the winds are blowing overnight at our destination.

When we left our two day stay at Solomons, we got diesel, filled up our water and retraced our steps back out of the harbor and into the shipping channel of Chesapeake Bay. This is a broad highway of buoys to follow. A new pair of buoys comes every nautical mile. As we leave the harbor and head toward the sea, the green is on starboard and the red on port. Because we are new to cruising, but feel a little braver, we sometimes, with careful research or knowledge from locals, will go outside this imaginary highway if there are no shoals or obstructions. This saves time but it shouldn't be taken lightly unless you grew up around the area and know innately where the land might come up too quickly to meet your hull. Bob quotes "people inside the boat, water on the outside" (second shallow water reference).

There are large 50 foot tower-type lighthouses that loom on the horizon for 20 miles, like thruway signs announcing Binghamton or NY City. There are buoys, lighthouses at the end of shoals and on points of land, and red and green shapes on tall posts. Buoys come in all shapes and sizes. Nuns are short and sort of nun-shaped (sorry Peaches), without bells. Others are tall, lighted and with or without bells. There are also cans, like oil drums. All have numbers or letters on them and all have birds roosting on them. They are watching for fish, sunning themselves, resting and pooping on the letters and numbers making them undecipherable. Some smaller markers say "No Wake Zone" or give a speed limit in knots.

Enough of this dry stuff, but it does take both of us to get navigation right. Whoever is at the helm watches everything outside the boat as well as the navigation program at the wheel. Ours is a Navionics and has been very accurate so far. It also announces the presence of large ships through the AIS program. It went off all day today!

The other captain, in this case Peaches, is following along in a guide or a chart or both. Because it is Peaches, she is also using her iPhone to get weather, buoy and tide data and where the nearest West Marine is for our destination. She is also taking pictures, sending emails and text messages.

It was a beautiful day going from the Solomons to anchor in the Great Wicomico River at Sandy Point. The bay was flat so we put the boat on autopilot (cruise control) and ate lunch, talked and generally had a great time. The anchoring was smooth (anchoring is like a free night in a motel except it is in your own house). It only costs us the price of one gallon of gas to put into the Honda generator to recharge the batteries. Peaches sister Susanne said we should take into consideration the real cost of each daily trip (the cost of the boat, all the bells and whistles we put on later and fuel). Well Susanne, we had the most wonderful $10,000 sail today in the Chesapeake. Our night was quiet with only three other boats scattered near but not right on top of us. The anchor didn't budge an inch.

From Sandy Point, where the water was so flat and still, out to the Bay the water roughed up to 2 foot swells with white caps and chop. There goes our day on autopilot, eating lunch and reading books like tourists. We thought we might not make much progress slamming into the wind and need to stop sooner than we planned. Peaches called the Deltaville Yacht Club to see if they had room for us and they said it would be free because of reciprocity between our yacht clubs. Good deal. We started to turn in and none of the buoys numbers matched the charts and the coastline looked odd. Peaches took the helm while I did a second opinion with the paper charts, and for once, this was a good mistake. We were way past Deltaville and close to our intended long day's stopping point, Mobjack Bay.

We anchored in tiny Chrisman Creek, off of the Poquoson River off of Mobjack Bay (did you get all that?). If it sounds like we had to wind our way into this spot, you are right. The winds died down late in the

afternoon but we needed protection from building southwest winds during the night and this creek did it all. The sunset reflected in the still water, doubled the beauty. Tomorrow with be a short day as we leave the Chesapeake for the ICW.

We started today after reading all the new books we pulled out on the ICW (Intracoastal Waterway) last night. The rules and signs are different and it would be all motoring from Portsmouth on down. Mile Zero of the ICW is in the Elizabeth River running between Norfolk and Portsmouth

VA. We pass the big shipyards, the even more impressive Navy Yards while the menhaden fishing boats stream by us. Tugs, super-fast ferry boats and other cruisers like ourselves were all in the area called Hampton Roads. The bay also includes the entryway to the James, Elizabeth ad Nansemond Rivers. The towns of Newport News, Hampton, Virginia Beach, Suffolk and Chesapeake are all right here. If it sounds bustling, it is. Also the tides, currents and wakes from all the ships are a challenge. We were lucky. Going through at noon, we weren't held up at all by commercial traffic. We followed the red and greens into Elizabeth River and when it made the split into east and west, we finally found the marina with some difficulty.

Tidewater Marina is the largest marina you ever saw but on serious steroids. We couldn't get into the gas docks on the first try. The current was too swift and the winds were about 15 knots (and the opening was so narrow). We reserved a slip last night and, when called, said to come into the slip, they would refuel us there. I circled as Peaches changed the fenders over to port. This is the part where I suddenly ran out of water (third shallow water reference). Peaches came back and wiggled us off, making me take it back to dock Star of the Sea. Through a very narrow lane paved with 100 foot motor yachts, I slowly motored looking for the dock staff waving to us from the slip pier. We started seeing more vessels like ours and then with a lot of maneuvering on my part and help from the guys on the docks, we stuck it in. Tides, currents and winds sure make docking hard in big spaces. In a narrow lane (felt like a grocery store aisle) with a 49 foot boat, it was hard. It'll be easier next time.

This is the Wonder Wash, known on our boat as the
Whuppa Whuppa, along with the centrifuge dryer

Chapter 20

Whuppa, Whuppa, It Works!

10/24/2009 Portsmouth, Virginia

Peaches and I worked all day getting ready to leave tomorrow morning. We washed the salt off of the deck and the sides. The water tanks were filled and I walked over to the main fuel dock to get the generator gas can filled. Looking at the fuel dock I was trying to get into yesterday when the current carried my bow south made me shudder. I'd be worried bringing the Zodiac in here, the dock is so small! John would have had a tough time of it.

Peaches was particularly interested in getting the green slime off of the waterline. I think it's a combination of green algae and salt. Very ugly. She was contented when it came off easily in the one place we could reach and we'll do a proper job later.

The winds really piped up today, 35-40 knots. We were rocking in our slip, protected by acres of fiberglass boats and floating docks. Since we are here until tomorrow and I've been sleeping with our "washer and dryer" since leaving the Cohansey River, it's time to try them out. Anything we particularly want on the boat for ourselves must be stored in your stateroom. You sleep with it for the duration of the trip. Peaches has been making jokes about my machines since I put them on the boat. Now she is complaining that her fleece jacket, recently worn by her in her swim in the Chesapeake, smells like something died in it. So, new gadgets, a challenge I need to answer. I have time to burn, perfect.

The washer is a Wonder Wash. You fill it with 6 quarts of warm water, a tablespoon of detergent and your clothes (4-5 T-shirts and your underwear just about does it). You close the pressure top by screwing down the lid and then crank the handle about once a second for 2 minutes. It sounds like this.........whuppa, whuppa, whuppa. You get the picture. It creates a vacuum drawing the warm water and soap through the clothes as they agitate. A hint if you purchase one, don't twist on the drain going into the sink unless you release the pressure top first, it sprays water at high pressure everywhere. Rinse the clothes the same way with a tablespoon of softener. You have a pile of dripping clothes to hang out on your line.

Enter stage left, the amazing centrifuge to dry the clothes. I've done a lot of lab work in my studies and this it one of the most powerful I've ever used. Put your dripping clothes in a few at a time, turn it on for a minute (yes, at anchor you need your inverter to provide AC power). The clothes come out all but dry. Hang them in your cockpit for half an hour and you have sweet smelling dry clothes (yes, even the fleece jacket). My arm was still fresh and I'd already created somewhat of a mess in the galley, so I decided to wash our rags, most of them smelling of diesel. I washed and rinsed them and as I pulled out the last handful from the centrifuge, there was a pair of my best underpants! They smelled of diesel, whew. I showed Peaches and she agreed with me, they needed to be washed again. How gross. I had enough Whuppa Whuppa for one day so I did it the old-fashioned way, by hand, but I ran them through the centrifuge for good measure! A good day all around.

After the laundry I needed a walk so went to get the gas can filled. While I settled up our bill for the two days and the fuel, I asked the clerk what the big Carnival cruise ship was doing out in the river, just beside the marina. He said they come into the river one after the other in the spring and fall. He said if I wanted a good show, go out and watch this one turn around. The Elizabeth River gets too narrow and shallow (I am so sensitive about that word) beyond this point.

Back at the boat I got Peaches up to watch as the ship's horn blasted three times. It looked, from where we stood, like it completely filled the river from bank to bank. It stopped and started to turn on its axis. It uses bow thrusters to do this, not a tug boat. Every eye in the marina was on it as the boats nearest to the Carnival ship were particularly vulnerable if the maneuver went south. People were on their decks and lots went over to the closest dock to watch. This ship was taller than most of the buildings of downtown Portsmouth or Norfolk across the river. He made it. He's a captain, just like Peaches and I, but he must be 10 feet tall, have a lot of ribbons and decorations on his white coat and scrambled eggs on the visor of his cap. Did I mention brass_____?

Fall on the Albemarle Sound, Edenton, North Carolina

Chapter 21

The Intracoastal Waterway

10/27/2009 Coinjock, North Carolina

We've made the conversion from sailors to ditch and swamp runners over the last two days. We left Tidewater Marina in Portsmouth about 0930 Sunday morning. Neither of us slept much Saturday night because the winds were roaring and there were scattered strong rain showers. We studied the books on the waterway and felt good about where we were going. But, how were we going to get out of the slip we occupied without slamming into our nice neighbors, or even worse into one of the 100 foot motor yachts? We separately tossed and turned all night. When the morning came, we just did it.

The dock crew came to help us out along with our neighbors from Texas (their heat exchanger had a hole in it so they weren't able to go with us today). I backed out slowly and all was well until the wind blowing down the channel took my bow the wrong way. I went down and turned around in the only empty space available (think about all the expensive fiberglass around us). I couldn't get the boat going in reverse strongly enough to make headway against the wind. Peaches, interested in saving us as well as the other boats, took the wheel and blasted the throttle as we shot backwards, slowing when she got control. We both did our best Queen's wave as we passed the startled dock hands and our friends and didn't stop until we were out and turning down the ICW at Mile Marker Zero.

The Elizabeth River continued to produce Navy ships, tugs galore and pretty soon, lots of bridges. We went through swing bridges, lift bridges, railroad bridges, tall and short bridges and bridges that weren't there anymore. The ICW played like a movie of what we'd read in the guides. We started a section that was a narrow canal through swamp and brush, touted as a wildlife treasure trove. We saw 30 miles of nothing, no boats, birds, turtles, fish, trees or even a common house fly. Red markers are on the right now that we have started the ICW. Red-Right-South doesn't work as well for me as Red-Right Return.

We came out, after all the bridges and one lock, into the North Landing River in the Currituck Sound. This is a very open area with a very narrow channel for us to follow (10 feet in the channel, less than 2 feet deep outside). The channel shows as a white line on the Navionics program. Follow the narrow white line....

The person at the helm has to watch the white road, look up, steer, check marker numbers and hope for the best. The Currituck Sound is just the narrow barrier islands away from the Atlantic. We traded off at the helm to get our heads clear after concentrating so hard. Our canvas enclosure was down to keep us warm and we had some hot tea in the afternoon to keep warm. A new type of learning curve, ICW style.

Oh, the lock, we are such lock-meisters! We come in slowly, no other boats in sight. The Great Bridge Lock was run by a lock tender from Cheektowaga, NY. We tied up and talked and told stories for about 10 minutes when he threw our lines back to us. With matching puzzled expressions on our faces, we reeled them in. We'd dropped all of 8 inches (inches?). I am so glad we had a zillion fenders out.

We didn't know what to expect for mileage this first day, when the number of bridges was so high and the dreaded lock might hold us up. Well, we were scooting along and where we thought we'd anchor looked like a dried up mud puddle or worse, so on we went. There was a good marina at the 50 mile mark. Because of a nice bridge tender who held his bridge open while we put the metal down and blew through it, we knew we could make it to Coinjock Marina, mile marker 70! The current pulled us along all day.

Three burly guys from Coinjock Marina were waiting for us as the sun slammed down behind the trees.

I thought I was a better docker than that until I turned into the current and could hardly make it up to the dock. They said to stay a bit out and let the wind and current pull the boat to the dock. It worked. We filled the diesel tank and it only took 7.8 gallons. We usually use up to 2 gallons an hour and this was a 7 hour day. What a beneficial current, 5 knots.

Peaches' Dutch friend Vero Brentjens came to get us Monday morning in her little red Toyota. She used to race with Peaches on Citation, another previous boat, and they did a bare boat trip in the Islands with her several years ago. She's lived on the Albemarle Sound for 12 years, practicing as a dermatologist. Her original practice was in West Seneca. Her son, Matt, has taken over her practice in Edenton and it has grown over the past two years. Peaches told me may stories about Vero and her family, but hadn't said much about her driving skills. We took off at breakneck speed and never stopped screeching around corners until we reached her beautiful home in Edenton, an hour away. There was rain, fog and wind clogging the Albemarle Sound so we decided Vero should pick us up at the marina rather than us spending a day each way in misery on the boat.

We had a lot of separation anxiety over leaving the boat overnight. We've been out 2 months, sleeping and living on Star of the Sea. The marina manager, Louis Davis, looked down on me from behind his counter in the marina and patted my hand. "We'll take real good care of her." I continued to stand there, not sure of what more to say. My mind kept thinking I should say the things people say who leave their children with a sitter for the first time (She likes her back rubbed and loves animal crackers before you carry her to bed). How stupid.

I finally said "Want a phone number or two?" So we exchanged some numbers and a key and off I went.

Vero entertained us completely. Her home is beautiful, just off the Sound with a large pond right behind her home with porches and large windows all around. The furniture is eclectic, books are everywhere. The two very well-kept cats had a yard most cats only dream of. The plantings were perfect. Vero is retired but not idle, keeping her fingers in politics, family and also the greening of Edenton. She makes to-scale furniture for doll houses, reproduction/replicas of old homes (and one of a Danish modern home). Her workshop has every tool in miniature that I wished I had normal sized. During afternoon tea I find out she is a quilter. Another room was floor to ceiling shelves full of brightly colored fabrics lighting up the room. Everything she does, she does full out, my type of person. It was easy to become fast friends in the 24 hours I spent with her. She just loves Peaches.

Vero has worked long and hard to make Edenton a green city, setting up an annual Energy Conference. Her home is heated and cooled by geo-thermal deep holes in her backyard. Solar panels also feed amps into her batteries. She watches her monitor as much as I do my Link 2000. I hope I get as good as she is at staying off the grid.

An historical trolley trip through the town was great to take our minds off our learning curves. Edenton was a major shipping port with Britain until the cut through the barrier island shoaled shut. Charleston became the commercial port of the Carolinas. The pirate Blackbeard plied the waters, interfering with the shipping and is celebrated here a hundred years later as just a naughty young troublemaker. His bloody sinking of commercial ships has been minimized. I bought a couple of books at a museum and according to our boat rules have to read a couple of books on the boat quickly because: one off for every one onboard. It's all about weight and balance. I am very interested in a comment made during the tour. The docent talked about the Underground Railroad for runaway slaves and said there was also a maritime underground route to the North. Vero said she was going to find out about it for us.

It is Tuesday night and we are back home on the boat with some fruit and vegetables, clean bedding and a wish to come back here when we head north on our return. The boat was fine, and in our absence, the staff turned her around at the dock so we can just loose the lines in the morning and join the current south.

When we left to stay with Vero we left an experiment running on the boat. We closed the thru-hulls in the bathrooms and for the heat/air. We took all the water out of the bilge with the shop vac, closed it up and left. The bilge was dry when we returned, so I think we got it. Now what to do about it?

Maybe 50 miles more tomorrow I hope. I'll think about the water another day.

Part of the fishing fleet in Beaufort, North Carolina

Chapter 22

The Swamps of North Carolina

10/31/2009 Beaufort, North Carolina

We have been in another world, faraway and even long ago. We've been to the swamps of North Carolina and survived, nay, prospered. We have been moving at six knots with no other boats, houses, lights or people in sight. Worst of all, there is no AT&T wireless coverage for Peaches' iPhone. She is having severe withdrawal from it, holding it and trying over and over to get bars. Hear more about that later, I know you will understand.

We left Coinjock but the current was against us as well as the wind. Not good fuel mileage today. There are no tides here, just currents. We crossed the Albemarle Sound without big waves, Peaches at the wheel. The stories of wind driven high irregular waves on the shallow Sound are in all the guides. We of the Great Lakes could have taken the waves in style. On the other side we funneled into the wide and shallow Alligator River. The depth of the water is our main concern in the ICW. With a six foot keel hanging down and only a foot or two under it as we fly along at 5-6 knots, Peaches is constantly shouting at me to slow down, "Hey, slow down." A large swing bridge let us further into the Alligator River and that's where we entered the swamps for two days.

The brackish water is the color of tea when you leave the teabag in your cup too long. It's everywhere, staining the bows of all the boats like a mustache. The moustache is a badge of courage for boats going through the swamps. Ours isn't dark enough yet. We entered the Alligator-Pungo River Canal late in the afternoon, 22 miles long with no place to stop along the way. We felt confident we could make it through before dark, but Vero's warning about when the sun drops it is instantly dark rang in our heads. We soldiered on with only small spikes of adrenaline as the sun moved toward the horizon. Our chosen spot in a bend of the Pungo River finally appeared, we dropped the anchor and it was dark before we could put on the anchor snubber! We didn't mean to but we went 78 miles.

Peaches had a very bad week for iPhone coverage. At first she just held the iPhone in her hand, hoping for a satellite to come over or a distant cell phone tower on a hill to shoot a signal. There are no cell phone towers in the swamps because there are no towers or people here except us. Occasionally while she slept and it was snug in its charger, an email or two would slip through on half a bar. What a terrible tease. No weather data, no GPS of where we were, no comforting email, no feedback at all. I occasionally saw a tear slip from her eye. I had to stop making jokes, it wasn't funny anymore.

Without help from the iPhone, we managed to make it to Belhaven where we motored in to get diesel about noon. The dock was unusual, around behind a break wall where it didn't look like there was room for us to go. I felt like the bow was going to hit the shore when the guy caught our lines and I reversed and stopped. When the fuel and water were onboard, I walked through three parking lots to the lobby of a huge white colonial mansion to pay the bill. The historical marker claims everyone slept here, even Washington.

A retired professor from Syracuse University was at the dock when we got ready to cast off. He thought we were well set up for cruising and his assessment meant a lot because it came from years of he and his wife going to the islands from here. He made the same comment so many others have as he handed us our lines, "Don't try so much in the first year." Hmmmmmm…well, we have an agenda and need to get moving.

We started out onto the Neuse River that merges with the Pamlico Sound. We are just behind the barrier islands and Cape Hatteras. The waves are just as you might expect, so lumpy going parallel to the wind and then when we turn, some of the best surfing with the wind at our backs that I've ever experienced. The anchorage we planned last night isn't suitable because there's no protection from the N-NW winds so we headed to the far eastern shore, away from Oriental and into the Southern River. The anchorage was best near the shoreline in the company of several other sailboats. It always makes you feel better about your critical thinking skills if others have come to the same conclusion and the same anchorage. We checked the anchor several times as the snubber was making a lot of noise, but all was well. We came 50 nautical miles yesterday.

Peaches iPhone is still silent, but that didn't deter our high spirits today. We motored through swamps, the brown water splashing high on our bow. We hope to make it to Beaufort NC (pronounced Bo-furt), a mere 20-30 miles away. We took a lot of pictures trying to show the colors of fall in the leaves and shots of the brown water alongside the boat. What else was there to do in the swamps?

Closer to Moorhead City I thought I saw a large fish jump, but no, it was two dolphins. Peaches finally saw them too, but after many attempts hanging outside the canvas bimini she gave up trying to get a picture. We've crossed the Mason-Dixon Line of marine life (from the Doyle Guide to the ICW). South of this line: dolphins and manatees are present, cod and northern fish peter out and other warm water fish start appearing like the grouper. I don't care about the fish, the dolphins are here!

We passed Moorhead City (sorry Burt but the guides say all the motor boat people go here because of the bars and restaurants) and went to Beaufort where the shops, bookstores and the museums are. Tra la la. We rounded the big curve just before going out into the Atlantic and found a beautiful but very full anchoring field between the main street of the town and the sand spit between us and the ocean.

We tried twice to anchor but it dragged each time. We went down further and found a deeper (14+ feet) place with more space and stuck it on the first shot. It was a good thing as we were both dead tired, more so than any time in the last two months.

The current was very swift, more than the Coinjock 5 knot current, so we decided to try the anchor buddy. It's a heavy weight that you let follow the anchor chain down and tie off about one foot above the river bottom. It keeps the boat from pulling on the anchor and dislodging it as the boat bobs and rotates around with the winds and tides. Now, whoever invented this instrument of torture was sadistic and probably laughing all the way to the bank. It is a heavy, heavy weight you hold at the end of your arm as you lean way out over the pulpit at the bow. You swivel it onto the chain and "just" reach down with the other hand and swing the lock shut to keep it on the anchor chain. It almost pulled my arm out of the socket and wouldn't feed down the chain so we got down in the dinghy and did it from the water level. Whew!

After sleeping soundly for 12 hours our outlook on life was greatly improved. We were eager to get into town and explore. Getting the dinghy down for the trip is getting to be old hat, like going out the front door and jumping into the family car. A few feet away from the boat we saw one of the wild Shackelford horses grazing by the water. I was driving the dinghy and despite little cooperation from the waves or wind, Peaches managed to get a couple pictures. We motored past the main street docks to where the fishing boats were docked and took more pictures. It was sunny and fairly warm and we weren't working hard to make time down the ditch (ICW), finally. We were just tourists. Boy, the dolphins are sure a lot bigger from a 10 foot rubber dinghy! Still no dolphin pictures, just empty water shots.

The town of Beaufort is geared to cruisers with nautical bookstores, gift shops and good lunch restaurants. We walked through the North Carolina Maritime Museum where we saw some artifacts from Blackbeard's ship, the Queen Ann's Revenge. It was found on the bottom near here in 1996 and is still being catalogued. The PBS film is playing in the museum about how they recovered the cannons. I bought a book, don't tell Peaches.

As we came home to Star of the Sea, I noticed 10 white birds feeding at the edge of the water near where the horse was earlier today. I got the binoculars and hoped for swans but got snow geese instead. How beautiful they were. We hope to stay here through the weekend and rid ourselves of the fatigue that has been building over the last few weeks. We didn't even know we were tired until we stopped. On we go to Myrtle Beach and some time with Peaches' friends Frank and Valerie.

We have been on the boat two months and we are alive, well and still best of friends. We are doing a great thing for us by being on this adventure. We are growing in confidence, trust, and keeping our brain synapses snapping and the Alzheimer's bug away. A couple stopped at our boat after seeing we were from Buffalo. They were from Ithaca and on their seventh trip down from Ithaca NY to the Bahamas and back. They were full of information and some hints about places to get provisions and engine parts in the islands. They visited just after we anchored yesterday and Peaches and I couldn't get out of our own way with fatigue. One thing he said was to slow down and enjoy it all. This was the first time this was said to us when we were so tired. Go to the Bahamas this year and really explore them. Come back to the US before June and work out a place for your boat to be during hurricane season. Don't run through the islands a break-neck speed to get to Trinidad before June. Trinidad is not out of reach, we could get there by June, but it seemed a sentence rather than our dream.

We are going on, happy to be doing this but maybe in smaller bites. For us, it is on to West Palm Beach or Miami and then across to the Bahamas sometime before the end of the year. We can't wait to go, our sentence to hard work has been commuted. Oh, and Peaches' iPhone is working like a wizard again.

Anchor Buddy stuck on our anchor, Beaufort, North Carolina

Chapter 23

No Buddy of Mine

11/02/2009 Swansboro, North Carolina

Our day began with the alarm on Peaches' iPhone going off at 0600. I could hear her screaming that she had coverage all the way back in my berth with my head under the warm covers. By 0730 we had our second cup of coffee and were on deck to raise the anchor and depart. You remember the anchor buddy I think. According to the abbreviated instruction booklet, it should glide up the anchor chain (like butter) but it seemed stuck.

We brought up the anchor chain 10 feet so we could get a look. It appeared that we snagged onto a sunken white mooring ball. Remember the currents and the tides have swung our boat 180 degrees four times with the tides over the past two days. We could have knit a sweater or woven a commendable fish net with all the wrappings and unwrapping going on under the water. Peaches thought we could get the old mooring off our anchor chain if I got the dinghy down and take a second anchor out to hold us while we pull our first line anchor up and sort it all out. I nodded agreement while she was talking and then thought there would be nobody at the helm if this second anchor broke loose. Where are John and Burt when you need them? I suggested we use our gold get-out-of jail-free-we-will-do-everything-for-you card, Tow-Boat US, to help us.

Boat US deployed a boat just minutes after our call. There were two fellows, a young man named Ian who knew what he was doing. The other guy, Albert, was from Brockport NY and retired from working at Kodak and looked like he might be in training. They tied their red boat onto the port side to support our boat with their powerful engines then stepped onboard and had Peaches pull up the chain to show them the problem. They tried to push the sunken ball around the chain to detangle it but the sweater was already knitted. Peaches was thinking of all our options: 1) drop the new 250 feet of anchor chain in the water tied to another floating ball to recover at a later date. Or, 2) we could bite the bullet and she could dive on the anchor chain in her scuba gear and do the work herself. She took another look at the swiftly moving black water and the cold wind raising goose bumps on her arms and said, how much for you to dive on the chain? It was $150 for the first hour, not covered by the gold everything card. She said, "Where do I sign?"

The wind blew and the tangled mess lay beneath us. Ian put on his diving suit and used a long hose and regulator instead of a tank so he wouldn't get wrapped up in the lines too. He went down, freed up the sunken mooring ball and then the chain. While Albert held the boat steady, Ian backed away as Peaches pulled up the anchor until it broke the surface of the water. Ian shouted for her to stop, the anchor buddy (I use that term loosely) was firmly impaled on the shank of the anchor. A problem, you might think? It was.

We couldn't move the boat for fear the swinging anchor and buddy would hole the bow of the boat. They gathered their equipment, Ian dried off the best he could and they towed us ever so slowly into the large city-owned face dock. They hauled the anchor wad over onto the dock and began to beat it with a hammer until the buddy cried uncle and separated away. We stored the anchor, took the anchor buddy back, much against our better judgment (it cost us about $400 at the Annapolis Boat Show) and we paid the damages. I'm thinking about sending this story to the inventor wherever he is hiding. We shook hands all around, these guys were so nice (They could hardly wait to get to the café to tell the story to the other locals while they warmed up.).

We left Beaufort Dock at 1030 after a pretty full morning. Listening to the VHF Coast Guard weather report we were just about on time as the small craft advisory ended at 1000. I was at the helm, trying to make some decent time (Peaches telling me to slow down, "you aren't allowed to call Tow-Boat US twice in under an hour!") The day stayed dark and dreary and was getting colder by the minute. We thought we would anchor at mile marker 248 tonight but the late start messed up the timing. Peaches called several marinas and most of them didn't answer and those that did were too shallow to take us into their dock. The channel is narrow today, the buoys close together with the shallow water fanning out on either side, large beautiful summer homes lining the shore.

Dudley's Marina was the first place we could get fuel so we pulled in off of the white line on the navigation software (ICW) to get diesel. Three guys were out on the dock to catch us. It was just the 6 feet we draw at the end of the dock, but we made it. There are shoals everywhere but we were lucky. Nothing in the charts or guidebooks told us this but the waving arms and the shouting by the dock guys certainly did. Since we were so lucky to get in we decided to stay, hook up to the electric and recover from our eventful day.

We got an email Saturday night that one of our crew-members, Larry Beck, who sailed with us on the other Star of the Sea in the Beneteau First 36.7 National Championships in Buffalo, 2008, passed away suddenly. There is a plaque in our galley that says "You cannot change the direction of the wind but you can adjust your sails" (-unknown-) Larry has adjusted his sails. We'll miss him and think of him often. Our prayers are with Sharon and the family.

One more story today to cheer us back up. I went into the Dudley's Marina office, really it's also a gas station along the main highway parallel to the ICW. I looked around at all the fishing boats and sport fishing boats, traps, and the huge launching skids for the commercial boats as I walked in. We are half a mile from Camp Lejeune and their firing range, sort of an idea about the area where we were spending the night. I walked into the store and a wave of hot, dry heat hit me like a wall. We were so cold all day today, even with the canvas curtains down and zipped.

The guys were all friendly, especially the heavy set balding fellow behind the big desk. The store had a large counter with candy and bags of chips. The rest of the store, as big as most of the grocery stores we've been in since home or the welcoming Wegmans we always used, is full of fishing gear and the biggest assortment of bait and lures I have ever seen. An entire entourage of good old boys, dressed in camouflage were hanging out, waiting to see what was up with me. I filled out the forms to stay and paid for the fuel and some chips (the only non-bait item near me). I asked for a splitter to hook up our two electric cords to the 50 amp receptacle. I said it so sweetly and with such pitiful puppy dog eyes that the lady at the counter whispered "You did that just right." I done good. The splitter was at the boat before I was, but back to the story.

The owner, behind the big desk came out and said "You're on that sailboat out there, aren't you little lady?" I didn't stop him, he was being so very kind. "I once saw out there (pointing to the bridge a half mile down the ICW) a sailboat just like yours. I was with my lovely wife and that fancy boat was getting ready to go under the bridge." The good old boys drew closer to hear the story better. "It was about 500 feet from the opening of the bridge when it suddenly tipped over so we could see the whole bottom and it slid under the bridge like a limbo dancer. You could have knocked me over with a feather!" Since he didn't call me little lady I said I thought it might have been a boat with electric shifting ballast or a swing keel. I also said, so he wouldn't call me little lady again, that even if it was a fancy boat able to do the shift, it took brass balls for the captain to do it so close to the bridge. He smiled a big grin and said "You took the words right out of my mouth." We all laughed, me and the boys, and as I walked out, he called after me "Now, you have a nice night, little lady, and a safe trip tomorrow." I waved, smiled weakly and left. Score one for the old guy behind the desk.

Peaches and Frank on the Star of the Sea, Myrtle Beach, South Carolina

Chapter 24

Christopher and Columbus

11/08/2009 Myrtle Beach, South Carolina

I know, I know, it has been a long time since we wrote in the blog, it's not lack of interest, just lack of time. We reached the sanctuary of Osprey Marina on Friday afternoon into the open arms of Peaches' dear friend Frank and the dock master, Miles (emphasis on the master part).

Let me take you back through the past couple of days in the Intracoastal Waterway adventure of Christopher and Columbus. Yes, we now have a nick-name given to us by Susanne's mother-in-law, Melva who is 98 years old. She's referred to us this way since we left Buffalo and somehow it feels like a good way to think of this adventure. We know there is an island paradise somewhere far off the coast of Florida. We've heard stories and have sailed in some of those waters on borrowed boats, but not in this boat and not entirely under our own direction (mentally and physically). We are explorers.

We left Beaufort NC after a great save from the dreaded Anchor Buddy. Somehow I will find a way to leave it with Frank as we sail away. On 11/02 we motored for about 5 hours in bitter cold weather, all canvas curtains down to protect us. It was overcast but good visibility. The wind was bitter and the high of 61 was rapidly falling as the scant sunlight faded about 4:30. We headed into Dudley Marina where I had the infamous "little Lady" encounter with southern hospitality. The next morning it was off to an unknown anchorage. It's always a little stressful when you are going to anchor because the guides and charts we have are outdated before they are printed. Shoaling happens with storms and traffic through these areas, changing the bottom.

We ended the day early as the only place we could possibly spend the night was coming up, Topsail Anchorage, a small cut to the left of the ICW. A cute miniature green trawler who was running with us most of that day radioed us saying he was also going to try it, although I thought he only drafts a couple of feet and we draft 6. He called out the depths as he went in through the markers while we followed tentatively behind, 8 feet, 8,8,7,7,8,9 etc. We turned through the second set of marks in this salt marsh, probably no place for a keel boat to be. We saw 10 feet, and then 8 feet, then 6 feet, then we were softly on the bottom. Peaches took the wheel and twirled us off and back to the 10 foot deep curve we just rounded. We plunked down the anchor. The salt marsh was beautiful but we were concerned with the predicted 25 knot winds from the northeast and we were only a bare, narrow strip of sand from the open ocean. The anchor held but the water under the keel kept dropping with the tide. We set our alarms to check the depth, wind speed and location every two hours through the night. We held, slept badly, and made it out in the morning, looking back at the cute green trawler snuggled up against the far sand spit.

Peaches called ahead, as we started out Thursday morning, to South Harbor Village Marina located just after getting off the Cape Fear River. The owner said "Come on down!" just like on The Price is Right. The Cape Fear River area was large, busy and had confusing markers for us. We were glad to know we had a safe place to rest later that afternoon. The marina was waiting to help us with the incredibly swift currents going by their face dock. They directed us to the inside of the face dock, causing me a bit of an adrenaline rush because the space to turn around inside and come up to the dock was so small. Peach was on the bow, I'm at the wheel and we just went slowly and laid our starboard side up against the dock like we knew what we were doing. We hooked to the electric and filled the diesel and water. We'd used almost no diesel the past two days because of the swift currents pulling us along, what cheap fun. We learned a neat trick for getting off the dock in the morning; keep the stern lie on and back against it softly. Your bow comes right off the dock and away you go!

Now, in case you are bored with all this ho-hum down the ditch we go stuff, we headed off to our next stop, the Myrtle Beach Club in Little River, SC. We thought in our hearts that we could get all the way to Myrtle Beach and Osprey Marina in one day, but with all the bridges we needed to go through and possibly wait up to an hour to pass, we decided to take our reciprocity card out again and try the Yacht Club. Our day would be relatively short, stopping about 3:00 PM in full daylight. Peaches pulled up the aerial shot of the Yacht Club and that was my first taste of adrenaline of the day It was a right turn off the ICW into a narrow channel that opened up into a large puddle with, count them, four marinas enclosed. It looked like wall to wall boats with little ribbons of water to slip through to the Yacht Club against the back wall.

As we found the opening, I went just beyond it because the current was so swift against us and then made the turn. I was okay, okay, okay and then the bow swung and I was going just on the wrong side of the red marker. I thought we'd be in worse trouble if I tried to fight the current and struggled to come up to the left and abort so, despite Peaches yelling "No, no, nooooooo.." at the very top of her voice, I squeaked by the red marker with it just left (wrong of course) of the bow. We came up hard on a shoal, not nice sand this time but mixed with rocks. You could feel them rubbing the keel. The waves generated by the strong current and the wakes of the large boats transiting the ICW caused us to rock and bump the shoal even more. Peaches took the wheel and tried to move us off, but to no avail. The keel was stuck, the rudder wouldn't turn and we needed help. We called the Yacht Club who hadn't mentioned there was a monster lurking at the edge of the opening and they called Tow-Boat US for us. We also talked to Tow-Boat US directly and after about 15 minutes, very long minutes I might add, he came. Peaches was worried that the keel might slip off of the shoal and we would be washed into the shore by the wakes from the other boats passing by. While waiting for help, we emptied the fresh water tanks to lighten the boat and possibly let our engine pull us off or at least keep us from going up against the shore.

The familiar red boat, this time driven by Brian and his eager black lab partner, panting and wagging her tail in the bow, arrived and took over the problem. He asked us questions to find out on which side of the shoal we were resting and whether our engine was running okay. He had me hook the tow rope to the large starboard bow cleat and said he would pull us straight to the shoreline of the opening (it was a very narrow opening). I was to reach down and detach the line the moment we moved so he wouldn't run his boat into the shore. He pulled and pulled and nothing. Well, nothing except at loud sharp sound like a large gun going off. I looked down after I found I wasn't shot and bleeding from a hole in my chest, to see the heavy teak toe-rail had split and the cleat was unsupported. We broke free of the shoal at that point and I threw off the line.

Peaches had us moving forward. Brian asked us to follow him into the maze of marinas and boats. I took the wheel and Peaches got out the fenders. The steering worked fine and we'd checked earlier for water coming into the bilge from outside and there was none. There were no sailing vessels in this wall-to-wall fiberglass palace. It was shallow going, just before low tide. The fuel dock was flat against the back wall, with us turning into it and managing to stop before we hit the side wall with the bow. There is too much adrenaline for me to see any humor in this situation, even now as I am writing it, not living it.

Brian said that a lot of his towing business comes from this shoal, so who better to rescue us? He works down here in the summer and works as a ski instructor in the winter. He and his dog are reverse snowbirds. We filled out papers and talked a bunch. The female black lab had gotten out of the tow boat, quietly moving along the dock until she was trying to make eye contact with anyone who would invite her onboard. Brian saw her and smiled but didn't acknowledge her. He said, between stories to us, "Go back to the boat". She whipped her head around and immediately looked down, averting her gaze. "Go back to the boat." She turned, walked three steps and laid down on the dock. He said she has always shown good intent but never made it all the way back to the boat. What a nice team. We were safe, but wondering under the pleasant banter, what unseen damage we might have. Probably some scratches to the keel. The rudder and steering seem fine. We need to replace the toe rail and check the deck to hull seam under it and the integrity of the cleat itself.

I felt horrible that I'd done this to us and to the boat. Both Peaches and I used the normal work of setting up the boat, filling the tanks, getting the shore power hooked up just right, closing the curtains to keep in the heat of the day, cooking dinner and cleaning up to avoid conversation. No talk between us except a couple of comments about how nice Brian was and a gulped "I am so sorry" from me somewhere along the line.

After dinner we had what Peaches described to Frank and Valerie, our hosts here in Myrtle Beach, as a "come to Jesus" meeting. I hadn't heard the term, but it makes sense to me now. Something was wrong with us, other than being overtired. We'd each been doing our best not to hurt each other while maintaining our own strong personalities. We are both capable, motivated professionals who got on a boat and thought we could run a democracy.

Our sailing experiences were different, mine mostly seat of the pants lake sailing since I was about 6 years old, only recently as a team member racing on large boats. Peaches experience is 30 years of sailing and racing a series of larger and larger sailboats on Lake Erie. Frank sold her the first sailboat and became her mentor for sailing and for life. Even before we left home, friends had come up to both of us expressing concerns that we might not be able to get along during such a long journey in such a small place. We thought we'd be fine, after all we'd been a good team racing the Beneteau First 36.7 to the National Championships the year before.

I didn't abort the turn and thought I could rescue a bad situation. I was so sure of it that I didn't follow her command soon enough. I did it out of spite, having felt like she wasn't giving me enough credit for what I knew ad felt under my feet, and the considerable amount of success I had getting the boat in and out of lots of dockings, and anchorages. She does have more big boat experience and had every right to tell me to do something and do it now. We talked and cried but there was no shouting, no permanent injury, no damage to our goals for the trip wherever it takes us. Out of this came a couple of things, hopefully things that might help others in this situation.

Peaches came from a background of many years of high level administrative health care facility management. She had incredibly huge responsibilities for patients, employees and the buck stopped with her day and night. You need a tough shell for this and a level of commitment seldom needed in most jobs. She was very good at what she did and deserves her retirement adventure. I was also a professional, but at the patient care level, direct hands on, and dealing with life and death in an intensive care unit. I managed/worked alongside a team of caregivers/colleagues, helping them to not burn themselves out. Similar but so different, what to do?

We both decided there was more stress doing the ICW than we thought there would be. Because of the shallow waters, it takes two to make it. Peaches was watching the charts, guides, occasionally looking up to catch a mark number with the binoculars. She seldom saw what was going on outside the boat, seldom if ever took any joy out of our journey day to day because of the responsibility she felt for our safety (remember the buck stops here stuff?). I finally stopped saying "Hey, did you see that bird on the post?" or "Look at that half sunken fishing boat over there." because she wasn't looking up. When she finally admitted she wasn't having any fun, I said why don't we change the trip or even just stop?

"Not a chance!" she said quickly. Then again, what to do? We need to lighten up, take things in smaller segments and continue on after a rest here in Myrtle Beach with friends.

I admitted I felt more and more pushed around by her and really almost wrecked the boat out of defiance. The more focused she became on the safety, the less she realized her every sentence was a command. It might have stopped if I had said something sooner, rather than hoping it would stop. So, a come to Jesus meeting was had and everything was better understood. Maybe nothing is actually fixed because you can't truly change people (either one of us) who have successfully navigated 62 years of living, being who we are. At least the communication lines were open and we were both being more considerate. There was respect going both ways again.

We took off from the Myrtle Beach Yacht Club after much checking and rechecking of the high tide predictions for Friday, November 6th. We got off the dock with the new trick we learned, was that just yesterday? We made it out of the packed pond of huge boats. Turning right in the ICW we were quickly in a narrow, high-walled channel cut through fossil rock deposits, past a floating log the size of a telephone pole, two bridges to wait for and seven to go, golf course after golf course (one even had a gondola over the ICW for the golfers and their clubs to transit to the back nine) before we stopped. This all made the short day seem like an obstacle course.

I pulled into Osprey Marina, a left hand narrow channel off of the ICW with a hefty load of adrenaline, another narrow turn into a man-made puddle of unknown depth. I squeezed the boat around two tall free-standing poles and into the fuel dock (no currents thankfully). Miles and Frank were there smiling, making today and yesterday seem like nothing and today the start of a new adventure. After fueling, we had help turning in less room than the boat was long. As we went around the outer docks, Miles kept asking us what our beam measurement was. After asking the third time, and after we pulled into our slip that touched us on both sides of the boat, zero room for fenders, we were home.

We are resting and making progress at getting the rail fixed, maintenance done on the boat and reprovisioning for the next part of the journey. We are having a great time with Frank and Valerie. Great food and conversation, meeting their friends and walking on the beach with their black lab is the best medicine. Last night they gave us tickets to the Winyah Rivers Foundation fund raising dinner. Frank said it was not a dress-up affair, just dinner and some fun with the "River People." It was a lot more than that.

Valerie has been making up theme baskets for a year to donate to the auction. Most of the funding the river people need comes from this function every year. She goes to household sales ad shops to fill the many baskets. Frank takes little credit for any of this, just drives Valeria and her friends around to the sales and sits with Chloe, his black lab, and waits for them to get done. I imagine he does a lot more than that. The foundation is made up of volunteers who monitor the river water for pollution and teach others about the importance of conservation. www.WinyahRivers.edu

Frank and Valerie showed us their Petri dish incubator for the water samples, located in an outbuilding behind their home. This is serious volunteer work. They said, with pride, there are no e-coli growing out of the river water at this time. The Waccamaw River is recovering. Without the watershed health projects, the waters could become dead and unable to protect the nature depending on it and the people depending on this source for clean water. Off the soapbox, but I wonder if other organizations like this one have been watching the other rivers and creeks we've traversed down the east coast?

The dinner was fun, but mostly it was the people who were a tapestry of occupations and personalities, all colors and textures. It took place at the Ripley Aquarium, a magical place where the fish, sharks, turtles, eels, rays, jelly fish, octopi and even the piranhas seemed comfortably close. Peaches went crazy with her, you guessed it, iPhone camera. We'll resume our trip in about a week. I'm looking forward to more ICW if you can believe that. Coming up is Georgetown, Charleston, Savannah and more. There is a rumor that many more swamps await us in Georgia. Hope the iPhone keeps connected. Updates in a couple of days.

Post Script by Peaches. The come to Jesus meeting, moments of truth, were not in anger but in love and respect for each other. I too, felt responsible. I was not enjoying the trip. The bottom line is we are slowing up the pace of the trip, what's the rush?

For those of you who might not know, Frank and Valerie (Dr and Dr Moliterno) are from Amherst NY, both racing with the Buffalo Harbor Sailing Club from its origin. I purchased my first boat after getting out of the convent from Frank, the Bluenose. The other boats Frank and Valerie raced were Penn Central and Megawatt. The deal when I purchased the Bluenose from them was that Frank needed to teach me how to sail, so he did. What a wonderful time we are having sharing many old racing stories from the Tuesday night races. The best one, Val was on the helm of Penn Central, I was in the pit and Frank was mistakenly lifted six feet off the deck, holding onto the spinnaker. He took his ball and went home, retiring early from the race. What is life all about if it is not the people we share it with.

Lee and Christopher helping us fix the broken toe-rail, Myrtle Beach, South Carolina

Chapter 25

Osprey Marina

11/15/2009 Myrtle Beach, South Carolina

Today was the day everyone expected us to have, each day. It was sunny, warm and I was sitting on the pointy end of the boat sanding the new teak toe-rail with iPod music coming in my ears. Perfection. Here is a job that wasn't hard, didn't hurt, get me wet or cold and was one that was going well. Then, I took a shower and we went to an oyster roast and pot luck dinner with Frank and Valerie. So very good, these Southern cooks make perfect comfort food. Peaches even tried a little bit of an oyster, but just one and just once. As you might have noticed, we took a week away from everything, even the blog. We are doing fine and appreciate the time here so much.

When we arrived we were pretty battered and tired, even a little disappointed in our slow progress through the ditch (as the locals call it). With the help of Peaches friends, we have recovered well. We have a car we can use for the time here from their neighbor Sam, so we've provisioned and traveled to West Marine at least three times for pieces and parts. We've also seen a lot of the tourist area in the off season, when the 29,000 locals can actually drive around without any traffic problems. We are posing as locals, of course. Frank says that Peaches is still talking too fast for the locals to understand her.

A lot of you called and emailed us about the storms all along the east coast. It rained here for about a week, inches and inches, and was cool verging on cold. Most of the big tides and winds were about 100 miles north of here. I'm just looking for some sun and warmth to continue the outside repairs on Star of the Sea. There is a term I heard from another cruiser here about Myrtle Beach, not just Osprey Marina. They call it Velcro-harbor. People come in from a long time in the ditch or "on the outside" in the ocean and get rested and comfortable. They make friends, find out where the stores and post office are and have a couple of favorite restaurants. Then they can't rip themselves and their boats away from the dock to continue their planned trip. I kind of understand it. We have made a lot of friends here, but we are getting itchy again to go south, where the sun shines and where sails can be unfurled. We are still in a river with wonderful river people but we are getting ready to go.

Star of the Sea Update

The broken toe-rail: A fellow named Richard came over to help us assess the toe-rail and check for possible interruptions of the integrity of the hull to deck seam. He said the seam was fine, the cleat was strong and that we just needed the new teak piece. The piece arrived from France via Beneteau USA in three days. It was cracked at one end. They refunded our money and will send another one in............six to eight weeks. We repaired the cracked one, installed it with the help of our friends Lee and Christopher who were visiting from Chautauqua NY. They were a huge help here with the boat and certainly emotionally. I missed my buddies from up north. We worked, played, visited the aquarium again and ate royally for a couple of days. We shamelessly used their pool and lazy river at the condo, as close to a bathtub as we had come (since the hot bath at Valerie's home when we first came here).

The Leak: Peaches asked Richard to help us think through the leak. She went through the steps we've taken. You were there. He looked at the water intake in the bottom of the boat for the reverse heat and air conditioning and found it was loose where it went into the filter before the pump. It was sealed with plumber's putty and had dried out. The plastic pipe could be twirled around it was so loose. It has Teflon tape and does not leak a drop. As soon as we prime the system we can have heat again, although it is a lot warmer than last week.

The Battery Banks: They are in fine shape because we have been plugged into shore power for the past week. We pick up our second Honda generator tomorrow and then will have the option to hook them in tandem to produce enough amps to use the heat and air conditioning as well as the TV and coffee maker (the big amp-draw appliances) when we are at anchor. I, as the amp-czar, will feel empowered (no pun intended) to always be able to keep the big battery banks charged.

Peaches computer and the Raymarine Navigation Software: Christopher, our friend, helped her to clear up some problems that kept her from using the software to put in the possible anchorages or marinas on our E-80 at the helm. It'll be so much better to have them in the navigation system rather than on a piece of scrap paper or a Post-It.

Peaches wants me to talk a little about Osprey Marina. I certainly will as we have been kept here with welcoming arms and smiles since we came through the channel. We were astonished when we found out we could stay here for $1 at foot for the first two days and $0.25 a foot for the rest of the time. We have paid up to $3 a foot x 44 feet for just one night in the ICW. She loves the main marina and the grounds with the sheep grazing as we drive out. We heard owls in the woods at night. There is a 500 acre zoo next door and people say you can sometimes hear the lions roar. The docks are floating so there is no changing of lines when the tide goes up and down. The grill is open for breakfast and lunch, free coffee all the time. The laundry room is so nice I am giving the Whuppa Whuppa a break. Cruisers we've met here say they leave their boats during the hot months of the summer while they go home. They come back here again and again. (watch our, Velcro Harbor). Valerie and Frank say they could put another turkey in the oven if we want to stay (VELCRO HARBOR!).

There is one problem in this location, poor cell phone coverage for both of us, Verizon and AT&T. You know how Peaches gets when she doesn't have iPhone coverage. Not pretty.

Peaches was hoping to dive under the boat to check for damage while we were safe in the marina, but Richard told her the coke-colored water (all those tannins from the trees) and the alligators make this a really poor idea. We will try and get the boat hauled up in a lift in the next few days when we leave to check for damage. The nearest lift to here just dropped a boat, and the jungle telegraph among the boaters is strong. We will look elsewhere.

I have one more story. We needed to refill the propane tanks on the boat, used for the stove and the oven. They are a smaller size than for your backyard grill, and few places will fill them. I was directed to the Socastee Hardware not far from the marina. I stopped in the hardware store after a trip to West Marine and a great hair cut (thanks Guy!). I walked in with one propane tank and a man came out to grab it from my hand. You guessed it "I'll take that heavy ole thing, little lady. You wait right here and I'll bring it back to the car for you." This "little lady" took herself into the store and started to look around. This is a great place with everything from supplies for butchering and making jerky to small appliances, paint, hardware and boots. I spotted some Fabreze Max and got one to complete the cleaning of Sam's borrowed car. (It's a second vehicle for her, 224,000 miles and only used to haul her dogs and occasionally Valerie on one of their yard sale trips without Frank)

Oh, the story. The man comes back in with the propane tank, places it carefully at the door and smiles. "It's so small, don't you want one of these out here?" He points to the row of black barbeque grills outside. I said no, it just fits in the compartment in the 44 foot sailboat where we were living. He was tongue tied. I went on to say we were leaving in a couple of days to go down to the Bahamas. As he carried the tank and the bag with the Fabreze he said he hoped my husband really appreciated me doing all these errands for him. He opened and closed my car door, smiled and said "drive safe little lady." I'm getting a lot better about this southern hospitality thing. It just makes me smile now.

Hazard Marina, hoisting Star of the Sea to assess for damage, Georgetown, South Carolina

Chapter 26

Georgetown, South Carolina

11/19/2009 Hazard Marina

This has been a very interesting day. The sky is blue with lots of cumulous clouds. There is no rain, unlike yesterday, and it is warm enough to be out in just shirts and shorts. You heard how hard it was to wiggle Star of the Sea into Osprey Marina. I didn't lose a moment of sleep over getting the boat out this time. A 10 day rest does wonders for your stress level. We had help from the dock staff backing out, another 34 point turn with my dinghy brushing the sterns of the large motor yachts in the next row. Success, we were almost out of the marina, people waving goodbye from a lot of the boats, when a small blue motorboat turned into the canal. This is where bigger is much better, he quickly backed out and we moved out into the Waccamaw River. Frank took Christopher, Lee, Peaches and me for a ride a couple of days ago so we could see where we were going today. It was fast, fun, and very cold. He showed us it would be a lot wider and deeper from Myrtle Beach down. We pulled out the books and turned left towards Georgetown.

There was lots of floating debris from the storm yesterday. There were a few logs but mostly detached green plants. They weren't lily pads but something like it from the marshes. There were few other boats today and that was fine. I liked it with just our little ripples behind us in the perfectly still waters. There were total reflections of all the clouds and trees all the way along the river. It felt like Indian summer weather, warm but with a lot of color in the trees.

In our extra day at Osprey yesterday, because of the rain, we got a lot done. I couldn't varnish but could do 4 loads of wash. Peaches made one phone call after another to follow up with the bank, insurance for the boat, friends and Raymarine looking for a chip we ordered that didn't come. We greased the big wheel at the helm so the grunting and squeaking would stop.

While at Osprey, we learned so much from Erik and his wife Pam. She's from Honduras originally and he is a professional captain who has worked in the islands. We talked to them about their previous 6 trips down the ICW. I thought to myself, I might do parts of it again, but certainly not the whole thing from Buffalo down and not in a 6 foot draft boat (maybe in a trawler though). They gave us great information about moorings in the Florida Keys. We are considering going down there for December, waiting for the

Christmas winds to calm in the Bahamas. Andy Lopez from RCR is going to be there over Christmas diving and relaxing. Maybe Peaches could have some company while she dives. I only snorkel.

Georgetown came up on the chart plotter at the helm much earlier than we expected, at 1:30 PM. After some discussion about which side of the red and green marker was the safest approach to the Hazard Marina turn off we went right and anchored in front of the lift where we'll be hauled out in the morning. Peaches called ahead and they were very gracious to fit us in first thing. There were shrimp boats at the end of all the docks and anchored in the river, most of them just getting back from their very early start this morning. It's obviously one of the main industries in this town along with the paper mills.

A grumpy guy crawled out of a beat up small white sailboat without a mast (read this a grumpy troll who came out from under his bridge) saying in a gravelly voice "Your anchor won't hold there, you're in mud and you're too close to me!" In my ears he was saying "Be gone with you, be gone with you!" Our anchor stuck just fine. We sat out in the warm sun, watching the boat's position and thinking we were seeing dolphins. I changed into something to revive my tan while I sanded the new teak rail for another coat of varnish. After I was done I brought the two Honda generators to the back of the cockpit to put them in tandem for the first time tonight. They went together easily and as I finished, Nick, my oldest son, called from Columbus OH asking if we'd used them yet. He is an engineer at Honda Research and Design as is my other son James. They can get me a deal on anything Honda. As I waited for dark, pelicans swooped and dove over the river. Some more shrimp boats came in to unload and a couple more sailboats joined us and the troll at anchor for the night. But there is more.

Like everywhere in the south along the coast, it was 5:12 and the sun set like a stone. Total darkness. The generators are ready so we start the generators, plug in the cord from the boat and everything goes so perfectly. We carefully close up the parting boards. Peaches has even taped the vent holes in them and the seam between them in case the wind might blow some carbon monoxide down into the salon. We started slowly turning on the lights, then the fans, then the TV. I cooked dinner and all was well. The generators purred like a large cat perched on the back swim platform. We each took showers with the hot water heated by the engine running for the half day trip. I pulled out my computer and settled in to start the blog. I was downloading a bunch of pictures from the camera and just started writing when there was the loudest beeping, like a home smoke detector, but louder and more insistent. I dove for the doors to the cockpit. Maybe it is part of the new tandem generator system. No, the sound is behind me. Peaches is tearing out stuff from around the navigation station where the sound is the worst.

Did I mention that with two heavy generators to carry we were so glad we could start working with them in the cockpit and not haul them to the bow every night? We want to anchor as much as possible from now on (you got it, for financial reasons and because of the generators). It seemed like a sound decision to have them there because the bow of the boat is always pointing into the wind, and the breezes will carry the exhaust out the back of the boat. All the canvas is up and there is lots of wind. So where were we, oh, in the salon watching TV and working on the computer. All the windows forward of the cockpit are open with screens inserted, fans on. What could happen? Carbon monoxide, that's what. We finally found the source of the sound on a shelf under the navigation station, right where I put it when I packed the boat, a CO monitor. What luck we had today.

The generators are shut down, relegated to the bow from now on. We sit on the bow outside under the new moon, trying to shut up the detector in our hands and filling our lungs with clean air. After half an hour, we return to the salon, put the battery back into the CO detector and it was silent.

So, it was quite a day of beautiful sun, great clouds, an easy trip, a troll and somewhat of a miracle. Our hard preparations prior to leaving Buffalo paid off. Months ago Peaches put a new battery in it and sent it with me to the boat. I just barely remember placing it in just the right place so long ago. Teamwork.

Well it's morning and without any noise from the troll jumping up and down on his deck, cackling at us, we pulled anchor and poked the bow into the lift at Hazard Marine. We watched with fear and a big dose of curiosity as Star of the Sea came up, inch by inch out of the dark waters of the lift channel.

There wasn't much green goop and the VC Offshore paint was all there below the waterline except the bottom of the keel and a little on the bottom of the rudder. Neither one of us remembered that the rudder was almost as long as the keel. A few scratches on the bottom of the keel just in the bottom paint. and one ¼ inch scratch in the undercoat, Interprotect 2000, on the rudder was all there was. Because the rudder is fiberglass, it was repaired, resealed ad repainted. We hug around most of the day waiting for it to cure (excuse the pun).

While Star of the Sea was in the sling, I hand cleaned the waterline with Culinite by moving a ladder around and around and going up and down. When everything was clean I repeated the cycle with a couple coats of wax as far up as I could reach. She looked like new (and I am going to have to get Peaches to comb my hair for a couple of days until I can raise my arms over my head again)!

Peaches was over in the lounge talking with some of the workmen at the yard and some of the people working on their boats, getting ready to go south. She got some great information about the next 20-30 miles. The tides are about 9 feet deep and some of the cuts through from one river to another are only about 3 feet in the center of the waterway at low tide. After we launched, Peaches used all her iPhone apps on tides and currents along with our guides and charts to figure out when we can safely leave tomorrow (rising tide) and how far it would be to the next shallow cut. We can only go about three hours tomorrow because the falling tide stops us after that time. Can you imagine us going into the next stretch without this information? Too much blog material for me to write! We get our first range markers tomorrow, used to line you up as you transit a particularly high current area that is also shallow. Steep but not an unmanageable learning curve.

I'll end on a really good note, fresh shrimp. Those of you who have not cooked shrimp off a boat just coming in off the ocean and cooked them within the hour, listen up! It is not your mother's fried shrimp, it is not even your favorite restaurant's shrimp scampi. It is heavenly fresh shrimp taste, requiring only some lime, salt, pepper and panko bread crumbs. A quick flip in the pan and you have flavor running all around your mouth. Peaches is not much of a seafood eater but she went from chattering to me about today to dead silence with her eyes rolled up into her head while she was chewing. Wish you were here.

It was a dark and stormy day and…..

Chapter 27

It Was a Dark and Stormy Day...

11/26/2009 Beaufort, South Carolina

The day was stormy and very dark. I awoke feeling like I shouldn't crawl out from under my blankets and start the day. Alas, it doesn't work like that in the world of southward bound sailors. Every day is another slog through the swamps of the eastern Atlantic coast.

The smell of strong coffee faded quickly from the cold, damp salon. We were up in the cockpit, Peaches with her notes and charts, binoculars at the ready and myself at the wheel.

There were few other travelers on the ICW this morning. The birds were in hiding under the leaves of the marsh grass. Not even an insect stirred (not even a mouse).

We ran out of conversation quickly, only keeping track of the depth of the river and the marker numbers. Suddenly, around the bend in the river, right in front of us, came the sound of large boats at full speed. Our curtains were down and closed and it was still loud! We couldn't see them but I was already looking for places to duck the obviously huge crafts coming our way. It seemed like an hour of holding our breaths when they came at us, boat after boat.

They were all camouflaged, small, fast boats, low to the water. They were festooned with corn stalks, hay and branches. The men were in heavy clothes of green and browns, some with masks covering their faces. They were heavily armed and heading right at us!

I was frozen at the wheel. Peaches had the camera in her hand from taking pictures of a barge-building yard we passed a few minutes ago. Instead of dropping the camera and running below for her sawed-off shotgun, she just started shooting. I kept the boat in the middle of the river, wondering what was to become of us. It was like a bad dream, our worst nightmare. We had to save ourselves somehow. Our adventure couldn't come to an end like this!

The first flotilla split and roared around us, heads down and looking like the terrorists they were. More came from around the bend in the river, each more frightening than the ones before. Peaches cried "I got them! I got them on the camera." I was thinking what was going to happen if they got us; offer them our money, our guns, our jewelry, our dinghy? What could they possibly want from us? I thought we both needed to take this situation and turn it around, grab the guns and show our strength. No one else was here to do it for us. All the warnings and concerns of our friends and families at home were burning holes in my mind.

Three more boats passed, none of them acknowledging us as is the custom in the ICW. Each seemed more sinister than the last.

Then, common sense took over. Why would there be pirates or terrorists on the ICW in the middle of the swamps of South Carolina? Why would grown men who weren't commandos or thugs dress like that? Why would any men travel in open boats in the rain with the temperature in the 40s? Why the hay, cornstalks and the masks?

It was a dark, cold and stormy day in the South Carolina Swamps and we were just passed by a bunch of duck hunters!

The inviting river walk, Beaufort, South Carolina

Chapter 28

Toogaloo River to Beaufort

11/26/2009 Beaufort, South Carolina

Another good night at anchor. We were warm, safe and finally found we could have the heat going in the boat as well as the lights and the TV. Life is good. It has been so cold and damp during the days that we need some comfort at night; warm dinner, hot tea and a warm boat.

Peaches has been combing over the guides and the charts and contacting the navigation Gods on the iPhone about our going through Charleston Harbor. There is one bridge near the harbor, the Ashley River Bridge, which has a vertical clearance of only 56 feet. She has nightmares about this and goes into long winded dissertations about our exact mast height added to our antennas and instruments on the top, added to the distance of the waterline to the deck mounted mast. No matter how many times we add them up or debate the validity of the guessing part (the instruments and antennas on top) we come up with 58 feet. We would have to pass under that bridge at the lowest of low tides and would still be an ass to try it. With all the rain this past week, the water level is most likely to be higher than normal water levels.

We went over the guides together finally and, as it turns out, the Ashley River Bridge is not on the ICW. Peaches confirmed this by calling a marina on the other side of the bridge from the harbor and gave them our measurements as if we were coming for a couple of days. "You can come if you feel confident enough" the guy said, in other words you can come if you are feeling lucky! So, we cruised through Charleston Harbor in the rain and fog without any bridge worries at all. I think we got through this with the help of the iPhone Gods and probably the use of the Nun-card. I wonder what she'll worry about now!

We took off in the pouring rain this morning. We hadn't done this before because we are already driving the boat through these shallow and deserted rivers and creeks, looking through plastic windows that make the outside look like it is being seen through Vaseline. Now add rain that makes it impossible to tell the color of the markers until you are next to them. Luckily, it lightened up and quit raining about mid-day. It was still cold and damp and a day of duck hunters.

We really picked our way, Peaches watching the markers and me watching the depth meter, trying to keep the boat in more water than the depth of the keel. It seemed endless today. We got to the deeper part with lot of current and Peaches took the helm for a while, doing well with our first range marks. We caught up with three other sailboats who were obviously having the same troubles we were. Suddenly the red Boat US towboat went streaking by. At least this time we didn't call them. We had some concerns about coming up too close to a towing situation in an area with no water depth to move around the other boats, but they were pulled off quickly and we will make it through. A line of sailboats formed going into Beaufort, all of us looking for a comfortable place to spend Thanksgiving.

It was slack high tide when we got to the Downtown Marina of Beaufort. We took our turn at the fuel dock for diesel and gas. A good docking, and then another good docking at our assigned slip. We are starting to get compliments when we slide into small spaces with Star of the Sea. More teamwork, Peaches out on the deck ad me under the blue tent.

Beaufort (pronounced B-e-u-fort) is a town perfectly suited for the transients coming down the ICW, going south for the winter. It has a handsome waterside park with benches that are like porch swings all along the high breakwater. The most magical trick since we came is the sunshine. It dawned warm and brilliantly sunny this morning, Thanksgiving. We were told there were two free dinners today, one in Hemmingway's and another in a church. They don't call us homeless but transients who need a home to come for dinner. How cool. I find out that this is The Place for Thanksgiving. I agree.

We slept so late this morning that we weren't hungry enough to go for dinner, but the others all said it was wonderful. While our small turkey breast cooked, I took a long walk this afternoon and talked to a fellow from Savannah. He comes here to see the historic architecture. It's a real temptation to go on the horse drawn historic tour, maybe if the sun continues to shine.

We are working hard but having fun. I was pretty sure that they couldn't happen at the same time. Come join us if you want to give it a short try. Happy Thanksgiving!

Historical tour of Beaufort, South Carolina

Chapter 29

Galley Fare

11/29/2009 Beaufort, South Carolina

Projects are keeping us in Beaufort for a few more days. We can stay for a week for the same price as three days, so here we are. We've marked the anchor chain every 30 feet with day-glow yellow paint to help with anchoring in Georgia where the tides run 7-9 feet. Peaches marked the chain so that she knew how much chain she had out compared with the depth of the water. We're also tracking down the (yes, it is back) persistent leak of salt water into the bilge. Still no more than a gallon or so per day but we can't find it.

The other minor problem is I have no electricity to the watermaker. I started re-pickling it (not a culinary feat but a preservation of the valuable membrane until we start making water in the Bahamas) and couldn't run the pump no matter the number of times I climbed in and out of the locker in the cockpit where the watermaker is located and went down the ladder to the rear bunk where the defective switch is located. You know when you are so sure you know what is wrong, you keep going over it and over it and then you change one variable and do it again? That was my yesterday. I tried the voltmeter but didn't register any DC current at the switch. A guy named Joe is coming over tomorrow morning to test for us, both the electricity and to take a shot at finding the leak.

While we've been waiting, we haven't been idle. The marina has a car we can use for short one hour trips. We bulked up on bread, milk, fresh fruit and vegetables. Our freezer is still full from Myrtle Beach. So, how do we go for sometimes a month in-between grocery stores? A good question for sure. I read books, blogs, attended lectures and just plain used my common sense to have foods on the boat I could make just about any meal out of.

Before leaving Buffalo, I used a Food Sealer by Sunbeam to seal packages of foods to protect it from the worst enemy of boaters, moisture. This was the machine most often mentioned by people who have spent years cruising all over the world. I have everything from prepackaged soups (mostly Knorr Leek Soup) I can use to make anything. There are prepackaged instant mashed potatoes for my Irish friend, Peaches. Coffee beans are shrink-wrapped and will last over a year without refrigeration. You just need to pad the packages as the coffee beans rub holes in the bags as they move with the boat motion. Dried mixed mushrooms, herbs, dried pasta, sun dried tomatoes, dried beans, flour in 3 cup bags and sugar in 1 cup bags, premixed bread mixes in one loaf bags, pancake mix in one-breakfast amounts, on and on are shrink-wrapped and stored. This machine is probably the best money spent for the galley. All of this is stored under the V-berth where Peaches sleeps. Under the bed is also all our OTC meds, Rx meds, personal needs like toothpaste, shampoo, razors, zip lock bags in great quantities and sizes, TP, paper towels, and much more. Peaches' scuba tank and related equipment is in another storage place under the bed. Don't tell Peaches but I have two boxes of paperback books shrink wrapped in the way front compartment.

Under one of the seats of the couch in the salon are all the canned goods, (chicken, tuna, corned beef, stewed and diced tomatoes, canned tomato soup, chicken broth, soy, teriyaki and chili sauce). There is a wine cellar (a big selection of wines and ice wines all wrapped in bubble wrap and on the port side in the aft state room). All cans and wine bottles were in the galley, but we couldn't see the starboard water line so balanced things out.

In the galley, at the right when you come down the stairs, there is a cupboard over the sink with dishes, coffee mugs, wine glasses, silverware and cooking utensils (like spatulas, lime/lemon press, basting brush,

knives). There are a couple of narrow shelves over the freezer with bars to hold in the spices, teas and condiments that don't need refrigeration. The refrigerator is below the counter, has four shelves and unless you know just where something is, you drop to your knees and pray to the refrigeration gods. The freezer is in the countertop and has a bunch of baskets so you can move layers more easily. Frozen meats take up most of the space with a couple of Bartoli ready-made meals in bags.

Under the sink is the garbage can attached to the door, cleaning stuff and way back at the end of my arm reach is the carbon filter we use for all the drinking and coffee water (a separate spigot on the sink). Everything we have and buy is taken out of the cardboard containers and stored in zip lock bags. Cardboard contains cockroach eggs and that is one passenger you don't want in your home.

There is a counter where the most important amp using equipment is stored, the coffee pot and the toaster. They are used every day and are worth every amp they take. Under this is a drawer for knives and bottle openers, Kelly clamps and bag clips. Under this are three sliding baskets for fruits, vegetables, rice, pasta and some cans. Under this (makes it seem ten feet tall, but is only about three feet) is a cubby hole for the pressure cooker and the nesting pans. Rolls of paper towels are shoved in between everything for padding.

How do I cook? Just like at home except I watch the amp meter a lot more. I have to throw more switches to enable certain things like lights, the pressurized tap water, the outlets, etc. To cook dinner, it goes like this: take something out of the freezer and let it thaw in the sink or the refrigerator depending on the temperature. You need to be so careful not to touch the meat or food as you package it or after you remove it from the package. Also, don't reach into the pickle or olive jar with your fingers. Germs love, absolutely love an inattentive cook and they seek out damp places like on a boat. I monitor the thermometers in both the freezer and the refrigerator all the time. I am the amp and the germ czar on the boat.

We stop the boat when we are traveling about 3:00 PM as the sun sets so fast. After we are anchored we start the generators after dragging them and the heavy yellow electric cord to the bow. While Peaches checks our position and the anchor, turns on the anchor light etc, I start the chicken or fish in a pan, low and slow heat and covered for the best flavor and moistness. Lime pepper, rosemary or maybe garlic is used from the spice rack. I might do a rice mix or a homemade risotto and a vegetable or salad.

This all sounds ho hum, but think about this. It requires a lot of up and down to get the pans (sit on the floor and unstick the stacked pots, pull out the baskets to get the rice and the chicken broth). Then, to your knees in front of the refrigerator to get out the butter, milk, pickles, cranberry sauce (we hadn't been to the store for a while) and then back up to check if we have moved at anchor. Peaches is now at the table planning ahead for tomorrow's trip through the shallow twisting rivers of Georgia. We'll talk it through after dinner.

When we are underway, I usually make us a sandwich. Cold ham or turkey doesn't look good a couple days out of the grocery store so we use tuna or canned chicken to make a spread/salad that morning. It pays to switch off driving and hope for a period when it doesn't take two of us to move the boat through the shallows so I can duck down and make lunch. We are both losing weight even eating like I describe above. It is a busy and a healthy life for us.

So, that's the galley, except for one more thing. We sometimes need a little liquid libation, especially after a hard day and even more so after a good day. This is part of the galley fare aboard Star of the Sea.

A dock along the way to Kilkenny River, Georgia

Chapter 30

Georgia on My Mind

12/04/2009 Kilkeny River, Georgia

The weather was so good in Georgia, I wore shorts a lot in Beaufort, at least until the sun set at 5:00 PM. We stayed an extra day in Beaufort because of a weather alert about strong winds, heavy rains and tornadoes. Only one day after the official end of hurricane season, a major storm. It hit late Wednesday night with heavy rains, not much for winds, but man, were we prepared. A tornado did touch down inland about 20 miles, hurling double-wides into the trees. We were right to stay.

A great week of R&R in Beaufort was the best thing we'd done for ourselves. Joe came to look at the boat and fixed a burned out switch for me. His teaching on the voltmeter and labeling some of the wires under the aft bed was priceless. Peaches talked to him, after he was trapped in the boat with us, about the upcoming transition into Georgia and our relative inexperience with tides. He mentioned several places to watch out for by name, a huge help. He's a sailor and knew what he was giving advice about when we told him our keel was 6 feet. He couldn't help with the leak.

We left early the next morning with a lovely flip turn off the dock using the current to turn the bow (old dog, now an old trick).The temperature went south with us, not getting higher than 40 degrees. It never got warmer and in fact decided to rain. We were chilled to the bone, riding in the cockpit with all the curtains down and zipped. We were in layers of clothes, not having brought a lot of cold weather duds with us. Thermoses of hot coffee were clutched in our cold fists. As the morning went on, Peaches went from just layered sweatshirts and a fleece hat, to hot water bottles (tonic bottles) and winter arctic gloves. It was that cold. We couldn't wait to anchor, set up the two generators and get the heat pump started. We patiently waited for the batteries to charge and float, and started the heat pump. Whew. It made us comatose to be that warm!

You can't believe how much we've thought about Georgia over the past three weeks. We are now firmly inserted into the twisted rivers and creeks of the Georgia ICW. One comment before we get started, the state of Georgia no longer maintains the ICW except near the major ports.

We first thought of Georgia as merely a clean shot to get into Florida until sailing friends we made in Myrtle Beach mentioned that the ICW goes 300 miles for every 100 miles south you go. Another comment was "go outside (in the ocean) if you can wait for a weather window, it's really shallow in Georgia." We were still in South Carolina at the time and it didn't seem like the time to worry yet.

Peaches has been glued to her iPhone for the tide tables and current readings, making out elaborate grids of all the creeks and rivers we'll pass through or possibly anchor in. She is wearing her head lamp at the table while she looks at the charts and tables. The LED lights we replaced the ceiling lights with are not great for reading (but almost no amps!). She is learning the finesse of when to depart in the morning to make sure that we can clear some of the shallow cuts. The tides in this section of Georgia run in excess of nine feet, so lots of planning needs to be done. She is officially the Queen of Tides, at least on this vessel. I have no doubt she could help lots of others going through here.

Today is a good example. We stopped last night, after leaving Beaufort, in Wrights River South. We stopped at 2:30 PM in the afternoon because we were just at low tide and wouldn't make the next cut from one river to another. We left this morning about 0800 at near high tide. The first cut was Fields Cut where low tide could be as low as 2 feet, so adding 9 feet for us is a big deal. The lowest point I found was at the entrance, 10 feet. We would have been calling Boat US again if the tide was down at all.

Coming out of Field's cut into the Savannah River, I asked Peaches to see if anything was coming. She was momentarily speechless but made up for it quickly when we both saw the HUGE CONTAINER SHIP bearing down on us. I mean, if I had stuck the bow out another foot we would have been gone! While we both shouted at each other, we managed to hold position, aim at his stern, rev the engine and make it through the prop wash. Burt, this would have caused you to soil your chinos.

So, tides are everything here. As we are going through rivers and creeks, and today a couple of bascule bridges, we had company for a change. Yesterday we were in a string of three sailboats. Today we were mainly with one other sailing yacht from Annapolis. We led for the first part of the day and were glad when he picked up the lead and took us through some heavy current and lots of areas where we needed to use range markers to keep our position in the swirling currents. Range marks are a tall pole with red and white stripes with a shorter pole in front with stripes. Piece of cake, line them up with the bow of your boat and you are magically on course. It takes two of us. When the lower pole wanders to the right, you need to steer right and line them up again. Old dogs, new tricks.

On the way we've seen more shrimp and fishing boats, but far outnumbering them are the mega-yachts. As we went along the rivers and after passing the river to Savannah and we came upon the town of Thunderbolt. Innocent sounding, but the amount of white fiberglass in a one mile strip was staggering. We looked like a toy sailboat made for the pond in Central Park. So many big motor yachts were tied to the docks and piers we couldn't see the shoreline or the houses of the town. There is a lot of money in Georgia, hidden in the marshes and grasslands.

We continued on toward our evening anchorage this afternoon and along a couple of the stretches we saw sunken ship icons on the chart plotter program at the helm. We're both craning our necks to the left as we go by the spot but then Peaches looked right and there was a mast sticking up out of the marsh grasses. It made the hair on the back of our necks stand up straight. This skipper did not take the tide tables as his holy grail.

Traveling is great for a lot of reasons, some of which I have mentioned before, but here are the top ten reasons we are glad we came: 10) It beats the heck out of still working in Buffalo or anywhere, 9) The boat was packed so we might as well go, 8) We talked about it for so long, it was time to "sh__ or get off the pot." 7) It's a great way to meet new people, 6) It is one of the only ways I could think of to get Peaches' basement cleaned out, 5) It is a neat psychosocial experiment to put 2 type-A professional women in a confined space for 3 months (and more), 4) Two people who have their Coast Guard Captain's licenses need a trip like this to use all the stuff Captain Daniels crammed into our heads! Everything has come up, from plotting to the ID of lights coming at you in the dark, 3)It's like a desensitizing vacation for slightly claustrophobic and a somewhat OCD freak (me); 2) Seeing the world at sometimes less than 6 knots is not a pain, it is a privilege to see history up close and personal. Also, it is a great way to dispel your land locked prejudices (like Georgia being just a pass through to Florida); 1a) It is a myth that sailing down the east coast of the USA is a vacation where you read all the books you want to, take long afternoon naps, eat bonbons, drink blender margaritas and listen to music booming out of your yacht speakers. It is so much more. 1) Old dogs, lots and lots of new tricks.

On our way through Georgia and the 9 foot tides, we went so slowly that the birds hitched a ride

Chapter 31

Darien River

12/06/2009 the middle of Georgia

It was a cold day today, a very cold day, only 30 when we got up. The boat is heated until we go to bed, then we turn everything off. This morning when I crawled out of the blankets was about 50 degrees. It makes you glad you slept in all your four layers of pants and sweatshirts. Yesterday we spent an extra day in the Kilkenny River because of heavy rain. This morning we were up at 0630, a new record since the days of Burt and John. After pulling the anchor we continued another mile and a half up the river, away from the ICW, to get diesel, gas for the generators and water for us. It was the oldest wooden dock we'd seen, floating on rusty oil drums. You need to walk right up the middle of the dock sections so they don't flip you off into the river.

The owner of the Kilkenny Marina, in his late 70s, came down and caught the bow line for us. The current was so swift but we were able to turn in the narrow river and come up to the dock. The owner handed me the diesel pump handle and pointed to the water hose, his breakfast napkin still tucked into the neck of his long underwear. "I'll just go back up and finish my breakfast while you fill your tanks, if you don't mind?" He climbed the ramp back up to the shore and we kept moving so we wouldn't freeze in place. We filled all the tanks, washed the deck, particularly the foredeck where the mud from hauling up the anchor this morning still stuck. When I went up the ramp to the shore and the shack, I could see this place has been here forever. As I entered the building, the door wasn't standard size, just a little over the top of my head like the building was sinking into the dirt. The owner and another fellow were still tucking into their steak and eggs, a plate of toast stacked high between them. No wonder he wanted to get back in the building.

The bait tanks were mostly outside by the docks, but inside were two coolers, not for Cokes as advertised on the side, but frozen bait. I am not sure where the "fixings" for their breakfast came from, there wasn't a refrigerator in the large, low and cluttered room. At least he wasn't one of those "little lady" kind of southerners. This place must be classified as back water, I think. I paid and waited for him to call the credit card company. The blackboard sign behind the counter was just perfect. In order, it listed the specials: bait, chopped or whole, fresh or frozen, fresh hot sandwiches, oil, coffee, batteries, and fresh home-made pies (was all this stuff in with the bait?). Not kidding you, he was sweet and offered to come send us off if he could finish breakfast first. I got out before he little-ladied me.

We crossed St. Catherine's Sound, did a bunch of range markers in small rivers, then Sabelo Sound and then Doboy Sound. Georgia is like this, a bunch of very small rivers and then you duck through the open ocean stretches between barrier islands. Two great names today are Dog Hammock Point and the Wahoo River. Tomorrow we hope to get through the biggest part of what is left of the Georgia coast. We have one more day without rain so we will do as much as we can.

Darien River is our chosen anchorage spot for tonight. It is nice and wide, but as we went further into it with Peaches on the bow, it didn't get shallow enough to anchor. She was directing me with hand signals because the wind was too strong to use the ICOMS (walkie-talkies). She finally dropped the anchor, and kept dropping it, and kept….. When the boat finally caught and stopped we were pretty close to shore on the starboard side. We sat and watched a bit and when the boat veered closer to the marsh grass in the current (I'll bet about 4-5 knots) we went into overdrive. The engine was back on, the chain coming up, all of it. We went into the middle again and stuck it proper this time. Peaches is really getting to be the master of anchoring. Instead of this being hard for us to do as a team, it is one of the things we do best. We sat and watched it for a while before turning everything off. Finally we carried the generators to the front, got the boat settled for the night and went below. Peaches retired to the shower to try and get warm, she'd been on the bow in the wind for a long time. It's a good thing the engine produces lots of warm water while we motor along.

Hot tea, gingersnaps and the heater on made us relax with the warmth. Peaches comment was very concise "If I had wanted to be cold, tired and stressed, I would have signed up for an outward bound seminar!" I agree. It is supposed to warm up some this week. Frank, our friend from Myrtle Beach, needs to come along with us for a couple of days through Georgia and he would understand why we plan some R&R every week. Adventures are supposed to be challenges, but also need to be fun. It still is.

Dinghies, waiting at the Fernandina Harbor Marina, Fernandina, Amelia Island, Florida

Chapter 32

Amelia Island, Florida

12/11/2009 Fernandina Beach, Florida

The end of Georgia couldn't come soon enough for us. We made our way around Hilton Head and Cumberland Island to come into the St. Mary River, cross near the submarine facility, and enter the Fernandina Harbor. Our reception was warm, the marina set up for easy docking, and the dock staff couldn't have been more helpful. We took a spot on the long face dock, part way between two very large 100+foot motor yachts. The smoke from the paper factory south of the marina was worrisome but there was no smell. We were safe and sound again. There was a tall Christmas tree visible from the dock, near the base of Main Street, Fernandina. The streets were busy with people and cars, and the train tracks were busy with cars carrying pulp trees to the paper factories (there are 2). We couldn't wait to get into town and walk around. There were no sidewalks in the swamps and tidal estuaries of Georgia.

Today is not a typical Florida day because it is cold, rainy and windy. We were thinking of continuing further south (the operative word) to St. Augustine to have the boat leak repaired (more later). Our visit for the last few days at Fernandina Harbor Marina has been interesting for both good and bad reasons.

First the good: we've met so many veteran cruising families who have freely shared their successes and their failures. There is a captain's lounge where people congregate as they are doing their laundry, using the showers, watching TV or working on the free computer. A bonus for us is the information from people who do this every year. It boosts our courage to continue. We've decided to go to just the Bahamas and in particular to the Abacos. We don't need to go all the way to Trinidad, just because the insurance company told us to. Now that we have a plan, we are anxious to get going again.

The bad part: the day after we arrived here it was in the mid-80s and beautiful. We walked everywhere, had dinner at the Marina Sea Food Restaurant, and got stuff done on the boa.t We just loved being in Florida but, that night, the winds came and it got cold (45 degrees, the bad part). We are tied to the dock, on the outside of the long face dock, exposed to all the winds, tides and currents. Usually, when you are on a dock, you can trust that you will not be bouncing around a lot, not worried about the safely of the boat or yourselves. Well, after a couple of nights of no or little sleep because of the pitching of the boat and the heavy rains (one night I actually had to brace myself with arms and legs to keep from being tossed continually like a salad) we found the source of our leak. So, it is good and bad news. It is probably the swim deck thru-hull and also the rubber seal around the back of the swim platform and hull. A Beneteau 423 owner's blog Peaches follows said these are the most common two sites for salt water leaks in this model of boat. The bilge came on over and over as the winds and the rains forced the waves up onto the swim platform. Places in the back lazarets that were dry every time we checked them had water, not lots like we were going to sink, but a gallon or two.

What to do? Unfortunately we need to pull the boat again and have the thru-hull replaced and the rubber gasket in the back removed, screws checked, and then resealed. Peaches spent most of yesterday calling around to find a lift large enough for the boat and also large enough to lift us without taking down the mast (like they lifted us at Hazard Marina). Why the concern about a little water in the bilge? If it hadn't changed from the annoying little amount it was, all along our trip, it would be bothersome but not dangerous. Now, with the amount of water much more and it happening in conditions that will not be unusual for us as we go along, we need to get it fixed. now. So, out of the water again, probably in St. Augustine a couple days motoring from here. We are stopped by weather again today and tomorrow, but should be able to leave on Monday. They can't take us on the lift until Monday.

So, today is a day of relaxation and small projects. I used a cab yesterday to go to the Publix grocery store for supplies and to the pharmacy to fill our prescriptions in preparation to going south. When I shop I use a box on wheels with a handle. It folds to a briefcase size. When I was done shopping, I called the cab company and a guy named Jeff picked me up, a cruising sailor like myself who is running a cab until he has enough money to go the next 100 miles south with his boat. I had the box on wheels tightly packed, a small live Christmas tree sticking out of my purse, and a smile on my face, a cab driver who was jealous of us leaving and who gave me names of all the good bars between here and the Bahamas. Merry Christmas!

Because it's getting close to Christmas and it's still the beginning of our adventure, we won't be flying home for the holidays like many of the other cruisers. We couldn't leave the boat with a leak like this, especially if the batteries die and the bilge pump doesn't come on! We hear the place to go is Vero Beach, south of Melbourne. All the boaters still around have a communal Christmas dinner. They put boards across the washers and dryers, a table cloth and then everyone brings a dish to pass. Sounds great. The yard manager in St. Augustine thought our repair could be done in one day, so we can make Vero by Christmas.

We wrote a Christmas letter, even though I used to sigh when one came because, although chatty, they were impersonal. All things change as we change, so the letter and this blog are the best ways to touch the most friends and family.

One more story: when you find yourself in a room full of cruising families, bartering happens, conversations are loud and long, and frequent laughter happens. People huddle around each other's laptops to see pictures, charts, blogs, and West Marine parts lists. People tell their most harrowing stories as well as where the best marinas and where the best diesel prices are located.

One family from Quebec Canada is here at Fernandina on a mooring ball with their 28 foot catamaran, Katmandu. They have three children and, like Peaches and I, were getting as much information on going to the Bahamas as we could from generous cruisers in the captain's lounge . I didn't think much about their journey at first, but seeing their children watch TV and use their little laptop to contact their friends via face book, made me wonder how they all fit in such a small boat. Then, I thought how hard it must be to get everyone showered, dressed and happy. I overheard that they were gone for one year only and the mother was home schooling the kids. Hey, how do they all fit in a little 10 foot dinghy? The father, Stephen, said they had been here for weeks and weeks, waiting for their new mast to be delivered. It didn't sound good. It had a manufacturing defect and broke off about a foot above the deck while on the way down the NJ coast in rough weather. Stephen was with his brother, and the family hadn't joined them yet. Demasted, holy shit! He is thinking about a reconditioned mast to make their departure south sooner, it's so cold here. They seem so calm and well adjusted. I would be over the top crazy if it'd been us. I don't know what Peaches would do. I give them so much credit.

The bartering is really sharing. Someone needs some medical advice, someone needs directions to the grocery store or the post office, someone needs comforting because there are problems at home, someone needs a hug and we, like in the *Wizard of Oz*, need courage. We got a whole bag full of courage and the tools to make our voyage to the "beginners" part of the Bahamas, the Abacos possible. Connie and Ken from the sailing yacht OZ (how ironic), thank you from the bottom of our full hearts. It is like solving any problem you have, make the pieces smaller and it becomes possible. I hope we gave at least some of what we got from them. Happy Holidays everybody.

Peaches is showing the high and low tides at the Fernandina Harbor Marina, Fernandina, Florida

Chapter 33

The Tides Line Up

12/15/2009 Fernandina Beach, Florida

This is a chance for Peaches to talk about how she got the title of Queen of Tides. I'll let her continue.

What a wonderful stay we have had at Amelia Island. The stay was extended because the tides didn't line up with the daylight hours. In preparation to go south, I've made an extended tide schedule for the next 100 miles. Especially this week, I focused on District 7 Notice to Mariners. The Notice to Mariners outlines missing navigation marks, dredging and for us especially, shoaling and sandbars.

To leave Amelia Island and go to St. Augustine, we need to leave on a higher tide and anchor before the low tide. The picture we put up for you shows what the tides are like here as I stand on the dock, high and low.

As I was working through all the Mariners' books, I found a number and name for Robert Lehmann, from the Army Corps of Engineers. Yesterday I placed a call to him and he was extremely helpful. He said to me "I would like to meet this Skipper Bob fellow." He gives Robert's name out in the anchoring and marinas book and it amazes Robert every time someone new calls him. I said we live in Buffalo and he was very familiar with western NY as he was from Mississauga, Ontario, Canada.

The first thing he said was "You ought to go outside, it's a better place for your boat." I shared with him that we had a leak and just discovered the source. For the readers who might not know, the Army Corps of Engineers is responsible for surveying the depths of inland waters, Great Lakes and coastal harbors. Their purpose is to keep boaters like us safe. Just before we hung up, he said "Mark #1, don't go in the middle of the channel there or you'll go aground." He was great and told me to call him anytime.

After going through all these books, charts and talking to the Army Corps of Engineers, the fine print it says "by the way the tides during the full moon can be greater in depth and shallower at low tides." You can't win.

While looking at my grid of high and low tides, currents and shallow areas we got some wonderful news. Beneteau finally returned my call today about the leak. They were gracious and were aware that this was a frequent problem in the production of this particular boat. They wanted to arrange to have the boat repaired, at their expense.

After multiple calls this morning, we are taking the boat about a mile away to Tiger Point Marina in this same harbor. Beneteau contracted with a guy named Roger from Jacksonville to come up here to do the repair. He will repair the self-bailer in the locker in the swim platform. We are getting a gallon in the bilge three times a day.

Captain Bill, a charter fishing owner we have been talking to since coming here last week has adopted us. From day one he said if we needed a ride anywhere or needed anything we couldn't get at the docks, he would take us. Today, he stopped by and I told him about the repair. He said "Come on, I'll take you over to the marina so you can see where you will be going." So, Chris and I hopped into his 4-wheel drive vehicle and off we went. Captain Bill has a tangle of tattoos on his arms, a big smile and is referring to us as his two Aunts and that he won't let anyone take advantage of us. He has a doctor appointment tomorrow morning but will be right along to see that Robert does the work properly. He also said we should make a list of things to do while the boat is hanging on Beneteau's dime. We have an armed guardian in Florida.

We are extremely pleased that Beneteau came through as they should have so we can stop going through the shallow ICW. We will return to Fernandina Marina after the repair and set the boat up to go on the outside, sailing and motor sailing. We need to check the sails and rearrange our heads (not our toilets) to being a sailboat again. We cannot wait. The question of the hour ahead of us is where are we going to be for Christmas? The answer, wherever the wind takes us.

Our front steps while waiting for the leak repair to dry, Tiger Point Marina, Fernandina, Florida

Chapter 34

Yacht on Stilts!

12/18/2009 Tiger Point Marina, Fernandina, Florida

Check out this ladder, the front steps to our home for the last three days. Yep, 20 feet off the ground is where Peaches and I have been "hanging out." We are pleased to say that our work on the leaks was completed yesterday but we are in the "waiting for the 5200 sealant to cure" mode. We won't know whether we got the two leak spots until after we are launched tomorrow and stay at the Fernandina Harbor Marina for a day or two. If the bilge stays dry, then we are set. We won't leave for just that reason. If water still slips into the bilge, then Beneteau hasn't done enough for us.

I want to let you know the huge impact living 20 feet over the hard surface of the marina has made on me/us. Sure, there is the inconvenience of not being where our friends are and all the conveniences of the other marina, like getting off the boat and walking into town, going to the laundry or just being able to plug the boat in and have water available. But, there is more.

When our boat is in the water, all of the systems are set to operate in this wet medium. There are thru-hulls we spoke of before to either let water into the boat or to discharge water out. The reverse heat and air conditioning is one system that can only work with circulating water. The engine is another, as it is partially cooled by circulating water. So, the engine isn't important up here on stilts, but the lack of heat when it is in the low 40s at night is.

So, hot tea, coffee, soups and socks are the rule of the day. Today we are huddled inside the boat watching a series of DVDs called Water Life. How appropriate, a visual journey into our blue planet. Did you know that raccoons dip their food in water not because they are fastidious, but because they lack saliva? So much trivia.

The real impact of living up in the air for several days out of the water for me is what comes out of the boat on a normal day. By out of the boat, I mean the little bit out of the sinks when you brush your teeth or wash your hands. The soapy water that exits when I wash the dishes is one that I really didn't think about it until I saw the bubbly puddle under the boat yesterday after I'd done a bunch of dishes. I use too much soap. Maybe it is even the wrong soap to dump into the ocean or the rivers and creeks where we've been anchoring. Last night we turned on the water heater and each took the first shower in a couple of days (no comments please, we are in a different lifestyle place than you-all right now). All that soap, shampoo and conditioner tinged water is pumped overboard through the thru-hulls.

My point of reference has always been to do no harm to the environment, but in reality I have been more concerned about the amount of water we both use. When we travel, we have only what the tanks can hold before we stop at a marina or diesel stop and can refill. So, in a normal day I wash the dishes in a batch at night, washing things and putting them back into the wash water until I have a bunch to rinse at once, and rinsing over the wash water to keep it hot and deeper. When we shower, you get wet, then turn the water off; you soap up, shave your legs, shampoo. The water is back on briefly to rinse, about a gallon or a tad more used (nun-showers, Peaches calls them). You don't leave the water on while you do much of anything. Now, I need to think just as much about what goes overboard into the water.

This afternoon, I will see if better products will do as well as what we normally use. Thankfully I've got internet connection through my Blackberry to find out what is recommended. That isn't the case for Peaches, who has no bars, and you know how that makes her feel.

Another bit about living up in the air like this. When they pull the boat out it is done on a huge 35 ton lift with slings put under the boat at preset points. It lifts us up then backs over to the land where we are inspected then blocked up. This took quite a team of guys, who put large wooden blocks under the keel then started putting specialized jacks under the hull all the way around. The boat is lowered down on them and then the ones on the starboard side are chained to those on the port side. Up in the air like this is stable. We can walk around without any feeling of wobbling or movement of the boat.

The lack of movement of the boat is what is throwing both Peaches and I off. We are so used to constant movement while in the water. Our bodies are set to compensate all the time, no matter what we are doing. Our semicircular canals in our ears, where balance is sensed and signals sent to your brain, is set to constant movement. We are not moving, we know it intellectually but our bodies make us feel like the boat is still moving under us. It is easier today than yesterday, but still very disconcerting.

The other problem living on stilts is we have both gotten so used to all the normal boat noises; creaks, groans, water tinkling along under the hull, the wake of a passing boat tossing us and the hum of a boat engine near us starting up. Hundreds of noises that our brains now classify as normal. Up here, the creaks are different, the life lines around the top of the deck vibrate constantly in the winds, the pumps for the fresh water are loud and the pumps to discharge water are incredibly loud. The water coming out of the boat splashes on the concrete! There are voices of people under us. It is hard to sleep at night for two reasons, weird sounds and no comforting rocking motion to put you to sleep.

So, in our adventure there is always something new. I am just about done with this up in the air part for sure. Hope you are all well and enjoying the holiday spirit. We are, in our ever-changing way.

This is the hidden source of the leak, a split in the sea water
intake in the aft head, covered by the hose clamp

Chapter 35

Ta-Dah!

12/23/2009 Fernandina Harbor, Florida

Yesterday the Beneteau contractor, Roger, came back to reassess the leak. When we came back from Tiger Point Marina, we continued to have some water in the bilge. The bilge pump was only going off about twice a day, a gallon each time. This was only half of what we had before. Also double hull construction is made with baffles on the way to the lowest point of the bilge where the pump is, so it takes some time for the water to make its way there. This could be pre-leak fix water.

So, we were prepared for him. The back two lazarets were unloaded and hand cleaned on the inside hull and all the condensation from the walls. Peaches piled all the contents in the cockpit, leaving enough room for poor Roger to get in with us. We went down below and cleaned out under the galley and bathroom sinks. We managed to just drink our coffee before he knocked on the hull (people announce themselves by saying "Ahoy" and requesting permission to board. I don't have the pipe to whistle anyone aboard like in the Navy).

He got a thorough progress report from Peaches before he dropped himself into both back lazarets. He found about a cup of old dirty water (we'd cleaned out about a gallon yesterday). He went below and looked at the entire bilge area, under all the floor boards and we pumped it dry. Roger checked the heating system as this puts some water into the bilge when it dehumidifies the air. It was dry. Please stay with us, it gets better!

Then, and I could feel it coming, he asked me to take everything out of my berth along with the mattresses. That filled the whole salon. He checked where the shaft comes into the boat from the prop to the engine and checked the engine and all its possible fluid leak potentials. All dry. He then checked under the sinks in the galley and in Peaches' head (bathroom). Then, more thorough than we are, he had me throw everything from my head into the wrecked back berth and, voila! There it was.

The hose that feeds salt water into the hand pump toilet to flush it had bubbles coming from under the hose clamp. It was leaking ocean into our boat. It is a ¾ inch plastic hose, how significant is that? There was a slit in the hose, underneath the hose clamp where you can't see it, probably defective since its initial installation in the factory. The boat has been leaking some since we got it in September of 2008.

So, three leaks, the last one probably the most significant . Last night after we put everything away (took all day and I never want to have the whole boat avulsed again, ever!) there was about a cup of water in the bilge, not enough to make the pump go off. This morning, the same one cup was there, so with a lot of ceremony and good feelings all around, we pumped it into Fernandina Harbor. Ta-Dah!

Now, the best of the best. All of this was paid for by Beneteau, hopefully out of a sense of guilt for this boat being bad from day #1. This was the second new Beneteau purchased from them. We humbly accept their covering the bills. So does Roger, who was just as happy as we were yesterday. We sent him home with a big gift box of fancy fudge from the Fernandina Fudge Shoppe to share with his grandchildren. What a great guy. We have his call-me-for-free-anytime card to use in the case of an emergency. He knows every inch of the boat as do we, so could probably offer a valid fix for what is wrong over the phone.

Peaches and I are officially back in school again (another set of learning curves). I started rereading my Marine Weather book with coffee this morning. Peaches has set up a grid to record weather forecasts and then fill in what the weather actually turns out to be to help her start to predict what the weather is going to do. All this is to help us figure out weather widows for our hop-skip-jump down the coast of Florida to get to Lake Worth. This is where we'll pick up my brother Bob and cross the Gulf Stream to the Abacos in the Bahamas. I feel alive again and Peaches is doing little dances around in the boat because she cannot fully express her glee in words. It is like the entire weight of the boat has been lifted off of our shoulders. Finally.

Why were we so worried about a few gallons of water a day in the bilge? Without knowing where the leak was, it could have been a hidden portion of a hose, maybe a big one, that might have let go and sunk us off shore. A ¾ inch hose like the one that was leaking in the head would, if it let go, eventually overpower the bilge pump and we would have to quickly get to a marina or ground the boat at the side of the ICW to save it from sinking. It didn't get to that point, but as you know us so well, we wouldn't let it. We're going to get an A in cruising if it drives us bleeping nuts!

Become weather wise and get ready to go out on the ocean for our first overnight experience is our new goal. We've been here so long the boat looks more like a home and very little like a sailing vessel; coffee pot out on the counter, books everywhere, spices loosely sitting on their shelf, the TV sitting loose on a bookcase. Imagine your living room as it is right now suddenly turned upside down and shaken a bit. Anything loose can become airborne and be a missile aiming for your head, certainly causing injury. We won't leave until it is secure. Our miniature Christmas tree and snowmen can stay right where they are until after Christmas. Have a Merry Christmas and Happy New Year, we certainly will. Love, Peaches and Chris.

Peaches and pirate friend, end of 2009 in Fernandina, Florida

Chapter 36

Highlights of 2009

01/01/2010 Amelia Island, Florida

We've gone approximately 2000 miles; been away from home for 122 days; eaten 300+ meals, not had anywhere near one shower a day; slept 122 nights (the sleep of hard work); climbed up and down the stairs to the salon from the cockpit many thousands of times; carried the generator(s) to the front of the boat 30+ times; written 42 blogs (holy crow!); gone through 57 locks plus the one in the ICW; used $947 of diesel fuel (pretty good for a motor boat disguised as a sailboat). We have been rescued twice by Boat US and several times by ourselves when nobody was looking; we've been continuously taking unneeded stuff off of the boat; we have also brought more onboard; we listed to starboard for most of the trip until we moved the canned goods and wine cellar to the port side. We've torn the boat totally apart 15 times at least, photographing while looking for the damn leak; we've now spent a week dry as a bone, wondering what we need to worry about now. You get the picture.

Was it worth taking this trip slowly down the ICW? Absolutely it was. Would we go down the ICW again? Not if you paid us, but maybe if you gave us a well appointed trawler to do it in and book contract with a large advance. Will we ever get going on the rest of the adventure? Hold on to your hats, ladies and gentlemen, here we go!

We've decided to join up with Connie and Ken from the sailing vessel (cool way of saying sailboat) OZ. They are the couple from Mississauga, Canada who gave us courage, like the lion got in the Wizard of Oz, to keep going while gently giving us options of where to go and how to get there. We will leave Fernandina next Thursday or Friday to go to Cape Canaveral and then back inside the ICW to Vero Beach. We've been waiting for Connie to get back from Canada, visiting her sick sister who is now doing much better. So, she can take a couple of breaths and we can depart, but Ken has been well taken care of by us in her absence. We've been getting Star of the Sea ocean-ready and provisioning for the four months in the Bahamas. We looked over the charts with our new buddy-boat friends and have decided to not go the Abacos (baby Bahamas) because it will be just as cold there as it is here. We're heading for Miami to cross over Gulf Stream then north of Bimini and around to Nassau. Ken and Connie have been in the Exumas (lower portion of the Bahamas) a lot and there is so much to see and do. I would give my left hand to be warm for two days in a row right now!

To be ocean-ready we checked the sails, tightened everything on deck we could reach, set up the gale sail for rough weather and the tri-sail for anchoring and the ditch bag. This last item is just what it sounds like; a bag that will float, carrying everything that is truly important to help in our survival if the boat goes down. It is always packed and ready to grab along with our EPIRB that sends out a locator signal. Our life raft is certified ready and carries copies of our documents and some money as well as all the supplies needed to survive the sinking of our boat. That said, we do not plan to use it, although the company will give you a new life raft if you have to use yours. Nothing would tempt me to do that. We wouldn't have a boat to carry it on!

We've been working hard to get everything battened down so that if it is a rough water crossing, nothing will break. It is a work in progress, but if OZ decides we are leaving, I can be ready in a heartbeat!

While waiting for Connie to return, we got a rental car and spent a day in St. Augustine with Ken. It's the oldest town in Florida, possibly in the whole South US. We went to a business called Sailor's Exchange. We've heard about this place since we crossed the South Carolina boarder. It has all things marine on consignment and also odd lot used and new items. We got there, so excited, only to see it was closed for the week between Christmas and New Year. So, when Ken saw a car coming out of the alleyway by the store, he stood in front of it, stopping them. He started a long story about renting a car especially to come here today from Fernandina and originally from far-off Buffalo and Toronto...... The guy stopped him and said "Show me your rental car key." Ken did, and they reluctantly turned off their engine and reopened the store.

We had a giddy two hour shopping spree. Remember, we've been locked up on a 44 foot boat in the cold for three weeks! This isn't like going to Macys or Lord and Taylor. Thankfully we weren't dressed up because we were so dirty from pawing through barrels and shelves of orphaned items; from hardware to seats, from fishing supplies to books. Peaches got a couple of small, sturdy buckets made in Spain, some stair treads to replace the ones we wore out going up and down (up and down). We got a couple of spare door handles and locks to lock up our sawed off shotgun (protection from the pirates).

We had lunch and some specialty brewed beers at a tavern in St Augustine by the water. We saw the sights and the Spanish architecture and fell in love with the old/new Lion Bridge. The city built a temporary bridge while the original stone Lion Bridge was dismantled and sent out piece by piece to be sandblasted, restored and repainted. It is now being reassembled. The temporary bridge will be knocked down and the cement and road bed will be dumped off shore for a fish breeding reef. Jeb Bush must have gotten some of his brother's federal money while he was Governor.

We went on to Jacksonville and to the largest West Marine Store in the country, probably the whole world. This one looked like Macys on steroids. You can imagine how giddy we were with shopping after this morning alone! We rose to the occasion easily and Peaches got more engine filters, more charts (we are the most charted people I know), and replaced our snorkels because they got terminal internal mold sitting in the flooded swim platform locker.

What a great town Fernandina Beach has been for us. We found two wonderful book stores there, The Book Loft and Book Plus. Needless to say we supported the local economy without a problem. There was a new bakery that opened up while we were there, Patty Cakes Bakery. Their coffee and pastries are to die for. I forgot to tell you about Christmas Day. A day like any other for us except Ken, Peaches and I went to church, a promise I made to her before we left. We walked through the practically deserted town until the three blocks before the church, where the whole town seemed to be. It was full of people parking cars and helping elderly relatives out onto the sidewalks, keeping the young children from crossing the street before they got hooked to an adult's hand. It felt good to be part of this. We found standing room only in the church, both down and up in the balcony. The service started and before any singing, the priest said that there would be a service and mass for those left standing in the community building across the street. We left, hoping for a seat and found that all seats were taken there too. We scooted into the kitchen and watched through the pass-through where people are served their dinners. Leaning on the counter and singing carols and listening to the homily was just perfect at St. Michael Roman Catholic Church. We were part of the community.

New Year's Eve, we had company stop to see us at Fernandina Marina. Luanne and her daughter, the daughter's boyfriend, Michele and her daughter, her daughter's boyfriend were on their way further south in 2 cars. I worked with Luanne at Millard Fillmore Gates hospital and was so very pleased to see a close friend from home. It was New Year's Eve and they'd been driving through snow for over 20 hours at that point. I felt sorry for them a little because they were tired, but a lot because it was so cold all down the whole state of Florida. Peaches set us up for some pictures before they left and as she got ready to click the shutter she shouted "Say leak!" Every sailor and boater on the dock whipped their heads around to see where the emergency was! It was like crying out "fire" in the mall. The picture turned out great.

So, we end the year happy, warm (only because the heat pump is running) and with a dry boat. We completed the year but not the adventure. Stay tuned, "the best is yet to come."

The boat "threw up" again
Do one job and the whole boat gets tossed, Fernandina, Florida

Chapter 37

What a Mess, the Boat Threw Up Again

01/07/2010 Amelia Island, Florida

Hi everybody, long time no write. We went through a little moodiness when we couldn't leave because of the weather. Do you realize it's only 50 degrees in the Bahamas? That is a crime! It's going to be in the 20s here tonight, although it was sunny with a high of the 50s during the day. We were drunk with the sunshine.

We are also delayed for a couple of other reasons; Peaches had to have a crown done emergently (completed yesterday) and we are still waiting for Connie to return from Canada. She is as far as Kentucky and almost here. OZ will be our buddy boat going the 300 miles down Florida and across to the Bahamas. We are lucky to have them as they are nine years ahead of us on the learning curve. We have some things we could share with them from our bag of tricks and our general knowledge. We've probably had 8 ½ years of events in the past 4 months, but I digress.

The picture tells it all, the boat threw up again, everything out and nothing stored. It is an episodic gastric problem, usually caused by us, the inhabitants. It happened a lot during the dark time of the leak. The boat threw up her contents because we are getting ready to go out on the ocean like big girls and we need to get everything battened down.

John Pettis, the last of the deck bags is finally off of the foredeck. Yippee! Hooray!

We need to find places for the swim fins, the diving weights, the dozens of lines we kept in the deck bag, the shore power cords, the water hose and the gas siphon for the generators. Oh yes, the generators need to be kept down below so they don't tip over or become flying death bombs if we get tipped over by a rogue wave or our own stupidity. That done, we are ready.

We both called our cell phone companies to see if any simple modification of our plans with AT&T or Verizon would allow us to continue to be totally preoccupied and Peaches not more than a foot from her iPhone. I've made fun of Peaches' fatal attraction to her apps, but I'm as guilty as sin of texting my compadres. But, I draw the line, never before I have my coffee in the morning.

The upshot of the research is: it's horribly expensive to use the phones like we use them now. For instance, I have a plan with unlimited data transfer and use the phone toggled to my computer to gain internet access to do the blog. It was going to cost me $1.49/mb (last month I sent approximately 1500mb just on the blog alone). So, what do I do? I signed onto Skype so we could at least call home.

You can talk to other Skype people for free as long as you have an internet connection. You, if you both have computer cameras, can watch each other as you talk. So, if you would like, check out Skype. There will be internet places in the Bahamas, Connie says, but it won't be every day or sometimes every week (my heart just stopped). You clutch your computer wrapped in a black garbage bag close to your chest in the dinghy and motor to shore and the café or beach hut for internet. In a warm, sunny, small town with other people relaxing, a plate of conch fritters at my elbow and a cold beer near the other elbow, you can bet the blog will be better in the islands.

So, there will be blogs, great pictures and finally some video clips on YouTube if I can get the hang of it. The only thing we won't have is our phones turned on. Please email us. I'll have to find a suitable object that beeps and smiles at Peaches when her iPhone turns off, maybe a Gameboy.

Connie told us to provision for happy hours, so we got lots of tonic, scoops, cream cheese for dips, gin, limes and bourbon. The rum we'll get there. Anything that is fun to eat is expensive down in the islands. Yes, we have enough paper towels and toilet tissue. I defrosted the freezer for the first time and mounted all the fire extinguishers that have been rolling around at the bottom of our closets.

I dug my bathing suits from under the V-berth and can't wait to put my heavy sweatshirts and one pair of dumb Levis far away. So much cold. I thought I would wear my shorts all the way from Buffalo in September to the Bahamas in a couple of weeks. Wrong again!

Peaches is in her position at the table with her head lamp on, beeping away as she puts waypoints into the Garmin GPS. She'll put them into the Navionics program on the boat too. It is how the airline pilots go from beacon to beacon, we go from one imaginary point to another. The waypoints show up on the map along with a little boat (ours) on the course as we move along. What a comforting help to have our course show as a black line on the chart. I've read too many books of trips, expeditions and commercial ships in the past. The success of the trip depended on the wits of the captain and a sextant to find out where they were. We are so lucky to have our electronic toys.

Connie said that going "outside" on the ocean is like breathing compared with going down the shallow ICW. We can't wait, we are so itchy to go. Think about joining us somewhere along our way in the Bahamas. The problem is timing your visit with where we will be at the time. It is possible, long time cruisers say, to name the place, or name the time, but never both at the same time due to weather fronts passing through. After all, we will be on Island Time, Mon!

The dark night at sea.....

Chapter 38

We've Gone Coastal: The Dark Night at Sea

01/15/2010 Vero Beach, Florida

CHRIS: It was a dark and stormy day................. no, I've used that one before. Actually we are safe and sound in Vero Beach, Florida, but pretend you don't know that because it will spoil this great story. So, here goes.

We packed up the boat on Tuesday, took our last shower for a while, tightened down everything inside the boat so that when we are tossed around in the big ocean, nothing will come loose. Then we tried hard to sleep. We'd been snug and comfortable for far too long and kind of forgot what it was like to work, even to get up early in the morning.

We were up at 0600, got the boat ready, packed the long shore power cords and filled the water tanks. The dock guys, all friends now, came and turned the boat around and we were off by 0800. OZ was out right behind us, they assumed the lead position and out we went into blue water at last.

All was well. The boat was running smoothly, the Atlantic waters were calm, about 2 foot swells with a little chop, just like Lake Erie but with so much more water involved. We followed OZ through the St Mary's River markers, by the big jetty and into the shipping channel where we set our course to a waypoint near the St. John's River where it goes into Jacksonville. Because the seas were so benign, we skipped the St. John mark and headed diagonally (not following the coast) to Hetzel Shoal, above Canaveral. We were about 20 miles off the coast at this point, out of sight of land, and heading further out to hit our mark. Not like in NJ where we always saw the shore. The total distance from Amelia Island to Port Canaveral is about 164 nautical miles. This is the dry part of the story, the set up for the rest.

We were being tossed and rolled a bit by the waves. There wasn't enough wind to put out a sail. We were so very ready to finally sail. The navigation system was great, we knew right where we were all the time. The autohelm was steering for us. It was like heaven compared to the ICW where Peaches had to hold her breath, worrying about running aground or where the next marker was. Here we did the whole trip with three main marks to hit. How bad is that?

It started to grow dark, giving Peaches and me a few moments pause, but we put on the navigation lights. The lights from the chart plotter were warm and friendly, kind of like a fireplace is at home. You can see surprisingly well at night, although there was no moon. Tons of stars all seemed to be very close to the horizon except for the dipper and Orion's Belt directly overhead. So, all seemed well. We had a warm supper and were ready to start taking turns sleeping wrapped in a blanket in the cockpit so we could help at a moment's notice. I went down to use the head and out of habit looked at the Link 2000, our battery monitor. Battery bank #1 voltage was getting low but I knew the robust bank #2 would pick up the slack.

Gradually the lights got dimmer and dimmer and still more dim. What's this all about? Peaches was very worried too. Suddenly, while Peaches was resting wrapped up like a mummy, the lights on the chart plotter went out and I woke her up. Then the autohelm quit, causing the boat to whirl in a circle until I caught the wheel. The VHF went out too. She took over the wheel while I reread all the notes given to me by Andy from RCR who installed all our heavy duty electronics and batteries. I thought maybe there would be a way to get the second huge bank on and also get the alternator to charge all the batteries. I was afraid to put all the batteries in parallel. Andy's sheet said it could be done if we couldn't get the engine to turn over, but didn't say anything at all about doing it underway.

PEACHES: As Chris is reading the notes from Andy, I'm trying to think how we can talk to OZ. I have a handheld VHF that I got out and there were 2 backup handheld GPS that we turned on. We shut off all the electronics but the running lights, even the refrigerator. As I'm at the helm, I watch the lights dimming and dimming more. Chris takes the helm and I go down to my room in the V-berth. I get my religious medals that I got as gifts before we left, St. Nicholas, St. Elmo and I also prayed to St. Michael. I'm not sure why. St. Elmo and St. Nicholas are patron saints to sailors and mariners. I came upstairs and said "Chris, there is only a minute or two of power left. I got onto the handheld VHF and called OZ. I asked them if they saw our lights and they said that they were very dim and almost gone. So, I told them if they see our lights go out, they should call our latitude and longitude to TowBoat US.

Ken said, "They don't come out this far, Peaches. Are you sinking?"

"No" I said softly.

Ken then asked, "Is your engine running okay?"

"Yes" I said, "but it may not keep going because of the …." he cut me off.

"You're just fine Peaches, just follow our mast lights and we'll be there in the morning" He asked me a couple things about turning the breakers on and off but I was too frightened that it might cause more problems than we already had.

I told Chris, "You have a few seconds to figure this out."

Chris said she had one more thing to try, turn the Emergency Switch, the parallel switch. She did and then the lights brightened up by 90%. She was blinded by them when she came back up the stairs.

We knew we had the problem solved in the short term, but maybe the other battery bank would be used up too. So, we continued to use the handheld GPS and handheld VHF radio. We hand steered the whole rest of the long, long night. About an hour later, Chris went down and found that all the batteries were being charged by the alternator, that the switch had truly put all the batteries, including the start battery, in parallel. We still didn't use anything while they charged for the rest of the night. It was a long night (I'm going to keep saying this). We were going to try to sleep some but from 10:30 pm on, but our adrenaline was so high it was hard to fall asleep.

CHRIS: I kept asking Peaches to wrap up and sleep. She would go down for about 10 minutes and pop up again like toast from a toaster. After 5 hours, she finally slept some, and then relieved me at the helm for a while. We alternated driving until you could see some light in the eastern sky. What a relief. We were in contact with OZ off and on, what a comfort. Our only way to know where we were was to follow their 2 mast lights. It was mesmerizing but a little disorientating without a horizon to look away to in the dark. We really would have been in a pickle without them. No chart plotter, no wind for the sails, no lights to keep the big ships away from us, no radar to know that the ships were even out there. It was a horrible series of thoughts, but nothing happened. We thought our way through a bad problem and Peaches used her Nun-card over and over again.

After about 27 hours, we went into Port Canaveral. We went through a long canal where all the big cruise ships come, then into a lock. I thought we were done with locks after the Erie Canal. This was an easy one. On to a bridge that opened for us right away and then we were back in the ICW. I can't believe I'm saying this but we are back in the ICW and headed to a place called Dragon Point where we finally anchored for the night about 4 PM. We were so very tired. We came down below after the anchor was set and looked like 2 Zombies. We couldn't talk, could hardly walk, and couldn't get out of our own way. We both got showers because the boat makes a lot of hot water from the engine when underway. I made two grilled cheese sandwiches that we ate but I don't remember doing it. Peach was in bed by 6 PM, not caring that it was still light outside. She slept until 0600 like she was in her own bed at home. The boat was very still in the water, but I think we wouldn't have awakened if 76 trombones went through the salon.

We got up in the morning, much improved. You know, it would have taken us at least 5 long days of travel to get this far down the ICW, we lived through the time at sea and we figured out what to do. So, today it was sunny and much warmer when we got up into the cockpit. It looked like Florida and even smelled like Florida. Off we went on about a 5 hour trek down the Indian River portion of the ICW. It was fun, safe, kind of skinny water as they call it down here, but warm in the 70s. The dolphins were beside us a lot of the way, but we still couldn't get a good picture. We saw all kinds of birds, even white Pelicans. There were wild untamed sections and also some of the largest homes on the water we'd seen all the way down the coast. Just huge!

Star of the Sea is on a mooring ball in Vero Beach. It's beautiful here, lots of boats on the other balls. They do a strange thing here, putting more than one boat on every mooring ball, so we are on a mooring with OZ. It is kind of fun once you get the boats hooked so they didn't hit each other's spreaders on the masts and no hull bumping. We were immediately invited to a happy hour on a neighboring boat, a large motor yacht called Orient Express. They were friends of Ken and Connie's from years past and we arrived by dinghy, one of about 10 tied to the stern of their boat. People in Vero, the old salts, love a set of virgins (well maybe a bad choice of words, newbies) at cruising because our stories are so outrageous. Then, they have the opportunity to tell theirs. They were so supportive. We drank a lot and laughed even more. Back on our boat(s) we were glad to be safe. Driving in a dinghy while slightly buzzed in the dark is not too cool.

We rented a car with our Canadian friends and went about an hour south...............to a boat show in Stuart Florida the next day. We're just going to hear the speakers. If you believe that, then you believe the one about people reading Playboy for the articles. There is always more room for stuff on the boat, I guess.

Off to Fort Pierce by boat on Tuesday and then another one day hop on the outside (as they refer to the ocean) to Lake Worth in West Palm Beach. If the weather works out Star of the Sea and OZ might go straight to Miami. Both boats will wait there for a weather window to go to the Bahamas. More stories to come. It wasn't really a dark and stormy night at sea, but it was dark, we did have troubles and Peaches prayed all night t. I am not sure what turned the tide, but I am grateful.

Postscript: There are no pictures of the dark and stormy night, as it was dark.

Years of Spanish moss on a tree at Vero Beach City Marina, Vero Beach, Florida

Chapter 39

Relaxing

01/20/2010 Vero Beach, Florida

We are really in Florida, with warm days and cool nights. It's the first time I really feel like we've traveled to another climate zone. We are eating meals up in the cockpit, having people in for dinner and just hanging out with the canvas curtains up and OZ firmly attached to our starboard side. We've been so cold that all we've seen for the past month and a half is the inside of the boat. How great to be out in the air, see the sun set and talk to other people. I've been in shorts for days and Peaches has even dropped her sweatshirt and wooly socks into the laundry.

So, Velcro Harbor was a label I attached to Beaufort SC, but oh, how wrong I was. This place, Vero Beach is the original Velcro Harbor. There are lots of cruisers and boats, nice facilities, weekly happy hours with live music by some of the cruisers, and free busses for shopping, the movie theater and of course West Marine. It'll be hard to rip ourselves away, but we are already watching for the right weather window to go from Vero to Fort Pierce on the ICW then offshore to Miami. In the meantime, we are totally relaxing.

We've reinvented the inside of the boat one more time. This time we are not looking for a leak or for a missing piece of equipment. We are getting rid of all the boxes on the boat from reprovisioning. Now that the heat is off, the boat seemed a little damp so every box on the boat, some we thought weren't a problem, are gone. There is the cockroach egg thing, but dampness is also bothersome. So we have plastic baskets of full but slippery Ziploc bags. I hope I labeled them all. It's kind of like taking all the labels off the cans. I'm going to draw the line at that. Mystery crackers are sure less bothersome than opening a can hoping for tomato soup and getting cranberry sauce.

Another anti-damp attack is by using a hanging product called Damp Rid, a hanging packet of desiccant (a white water attracting pellet) with a plastic bag attached to the bottom to catch the water. We have them hanging in the staterooms to keep the bedding and the mattresses dry, the closets and the heads. I fleetingly thought about hanging them from the ceiling fixtures all through the boat but had a flash back to being in the horse business and having sticky flypaper streamers hanging everywhere in the barns (not a pretty picture).

Being on a mooring or an anchor is a little hard but we are getting there. No leak, so no need for a dock. OZ is very self-sufficient and we are learning. We use the Zodiac like the family car, to get water, go to the laundry room, the computer room, catch the bus to town, go to the happy hours on Saturday, or just to hang out. We aren't heating water for showers and basically conserving electricity so it is a little like camping, but in warm Florida (oh, in a yacht).

We aren't making water yet, because water quality is a problem in this harbor. There are too many boats, dumping water and stuff but more importantly there are dead fish everywhere. Every type of fish living in the waters here has been killed by the cold water and temperatures. They float in with the tides and you can't use your dinghy and outboard without clunking against them. Ugh. There were temperatures in the 20s here during the holidays and this is the sad result. The sea turtles and the manatees are also endangered, migrating to the outlets of the power plants where the water is warmer. An article in the paper this week said the Iguanas are falling out of the trees because they are going into hibernation, something they don't normally have to do in mid-Florida. The strawberry crop took a big hit too. This has been an interesting year to make our first trip down the East Coast. Also, it makes us think about something other than our cold selves.

Concerning the dark night at sea adventure, I talked to Andy Lopez (the electrical guru) on our way from Port Canaveral to Vero. He said he didn't mention or write down for us the setup to use for going long periods motoring with all the instruments on. He said we did the best thing, putting the batteries in parallel. We won't have to do that on the overnight to Miami, because there is another magic switch. The battery switch back in the lazaret by the inverter has bank 1, bank 2 and both. If we place this switch on both, everything will be charged by the alternator in the engine as we are underway. Funny, I had it on band #1 while we were underway and bank #1 didn't get charged. I feel like we got sent out with a very complex electrical system without some of the information we needed to be successful, to be safe. So I've asked for a wiring schematic to be sent to us. That way we can have someone help us if it goes wrong.

So, as I said in the beginning, we are really in Florida; the home of the pink and blue houses, the turquoise taco stand, the Pelicans, the Blue Jays, the native Floridians in their fur coats and snow boots (it is winter, after all), the tourists in their shorts and flip flops, and at least some warmth and sunshine during the days. We are so lucky to have come this far. We are so fortunate to be safe and not one of the statistics from Haiti or the Cayman Islands. Our happiness is diminished by these tragedies.

SV Melodeon, with Chris, Frank and Ginger Bear on their junk in Vero Beach, Florida

Chapter 40

A Junk at Vero Beach

01/26/2010 Vero Beach Mooring Ball #6, Florida

We are leaving tomorrow about 1100 to make our way to Miami. We should arrive there in the morning, barring any unusual electrical problems or other gnomes unknown to us in the bilge of the boat. We are excited to go because we are so much more ready than we were for the last coastal adventure. Peaches has been entering waypoints like mad and collecting her chart books for the trip. Now you know why I helm the boat, just watch the E-80 navigation system and do whatever she says to do. How hard is that? Our water tanks are topped off, the wash is done and we cannot get another morsel of food into either the refrigerator or the freezer. It is a monumental task to just get out the milk for cereal in the morning.

I know you Northerners don't want to hear this but it got a little cool last night after the low front went over us, dumping about an inch of rain in the morning. Poor souls we are, actually had to dig out a blanket to wrap up in. Enough said, I don't want to lose all the readers. I sat in the sun and read, drinking coffee out of my thermos while doing the wash (Peaches thought I was working so hard doing the laundry and that's fine with me).

I need to explain the title of this blog. We met, at the weekly happy hour party on Saturday, a couple from Belleville Ontario. They have been on a mooring ball close to us and I've been intrigued by their boat. It was obviously a steel hull boat, one of a kind, with three gaff-rigged sails, three masts and sails made out of striped awning material. The name on the boat is MELODEON, registered in Nova Scotia. Chris and Frank own this great ship and we had wine and a tour of the boat last night.

Here's a little background, with their permission. Chris and her former husband about 20 years ago decided to build a steel hulled sailing boat. They both learned to weld and because she was so much more into getting the ship built; Chris did most of the welding (Rosie the Riveter!). It was still a bare hull when they divorced and amazingly she didn't lose it in the divorce. She met Frank and they've been together for 20 years. This is their maiden journey in the Junk, and they have such awesome stories to tell. Peaches and my adventures pale against what they have achieved.

Over the years, they have completed their boat with donations of used marine parts and by being in the right place at the right time. The pilot house has a diesel stove, sink, lots of navigation equipment, a double bunk that pulls out of a 6 foot seat and beautiful old brass porthole windows all around. They made the large common room 6 steps down with a V-berth, a head, two long couch-like seats that could double as berths and a wood stove. It feels a little Scandinavian in the simplicity of the wood trim. A large fold-down table is in the common room and can seat 12 people. The chairs are folded up inside the table for storage. They have a hallway that includes a full bathtub (sheer decadence), a composting toilet, and then their generous sleeping quarters.

The rest of their crew is the dog, a ginger-brown Schnauzer who lives on the boat, never getting off or riding in the dinghy (although they have tried). He uses his 3 foot x 3 foot patch of welcome mat as his "head." He was so excited to see company, he went from one to the other of us constantly to be patted and told how handsome he was.

Frank pulled up the aft gaff sail so we could see how it works. They've done so much research on this type of sailing my mind was overloaded with information as he talked. The picture shows that the sails are patchwork awning material. Our boat looks so white-bread plain next to theirs.

Their plans have developed as they go along, taking a year to see if this is what they want to do full time. I think now that they have shaken out the wrinkles in their boat, they will continue. They talk of going to Panama to wait out the hurricane season and then, with additional crew other than the dog, go to the Mediterranean. We promised to meet them on January 25th of next year and plan a mutual adventure across the ocean.

I just thought you'd like to hear a cruising story other than ours for a change. I heard this story yesterday from Chris. They were going across Lake Ontario to get to the Erie Canal to start their trip and were going to overnight at Duck Island on the way to Oswego. A storm was building and they were blown into the island, against a stone wall with breakers crashing against them, driving them deeper into the wall. They have a powerful diesel engine but it was no match for the winds. Frank can't drive as he has only one eye, so Chris was at the wheel. They spent over 2 hours getting picked up by the waves and pushed over at a 30 degree angle and closer to the wall. She said it was odd that they were both totally calm, trusting each other. They figured they weren't going to die during this, but that the boat, although a very sturdy steel hull, might be smashed to pieces. Their voices were calm, she said, just conversational. They decided that they could only push the engine so much. Chris said by that time she was so pissed at their predicament so early in their trip, so she went full-bore backwards and paralleled the wall and eventually got them out of trouble. She said getting mad sometimes is the extra push of adrenaline needed in a save-your-sorry-ass predicament. If any of you want to read their blog, it is humorous, just like they are. Go to: http://www.travelblog.org/Bloggers/MELODEON They are both musicians, with a full keyboard and electrical bass and other stringed instruments stored about the ship. Great people and great stories. I'll write again soon, when we are in Miami. Hope you are all well. We are great after this nice stop in Velcro (Vero) Beach.

Seaboard Intrepid after a rough passage, docked in Governor's Cut, Miami, Florida

Chapter 41

Our Trip Smooth, INTREPID'S Rough!

01/20/2010 Venetian Causeway, Miami, Florida

You had to see this container ship to believe it. We don't know the real story, but the marine police have it surrounded as we come into the Government Cut in Miami. Yesterday, two large tugs each dragged in a container that came off the INTREPID at sea. We could have run into them and been holed and sunk, a hazard that is well documented in many cruiser's books. But, it wasn't the case this time. It is hard to believe that these huge truck containers float just below the level of the sea and can't be picked up by radar or visual sight. On the deck of the ship, they look much more benign, just like dominoes tumbling over on a table.

So, we survived another overnight trip with OZ down the Florida coast. About noon, we left Vero Beach waving the Queen's wave to all our new friends. We followed the ICW south for about 2 hours until we came to Fort Pierce. OZ made a sharp left and so did we. As we exited into the Atlantic, the swells got bigger and the wind was from the north-northeast, to our advantage going south. It was rolling and a little lumpy out there. I steered for the first couple of hours (fairly sure the autohelm wouldn't be able to compensate well) until we tried the autohelm, which did just as good a job as I was doing. This makes our trip move along with no further energy expenditure on our part. Most cruisers name their autohelm to make it a true member of the crew. I think we'll wait until we can really trust it first, then a gender, then a name.

None of you would have particularly enjoyed the ride, just like sitting on an exercise ball with someone beating you about the head with a large pillow. You had to compensate for the big movements of the boat to keep your head level, thus your stomach level, if you catch my drift. I hear this is excellent for development of your core muscles.

The color of the sea was a beautiful turquoise blue with white froth on the top, about a force 2-3 on the Beaufort scale of wind and waves. We could easily see the shoreline, lots of high-rises and palm trees, some stretches of beach too.

We timed leaving Vero with when we wanted to arrive in Miami. We needed it to not be an outgoing tide against the then easterly winds. It would make entering Miami like going through the surf line at the beach. So, our day went on. It was not a day where you sit and have intelligent conversation and eat cucumber sandwiches and drink cups of Earl Grey Tea. We talked when we needed to and could not read or do anything useful. Both of us had bars on our cell phones and somehow managed to text, take pictures and talk to friends, (imagine that!).

It was getting dark (have you heard this one?) and it was still lumpy. Lumpy is my favorite term for the kind of sea where you have to hang on when you get up to walk anywhere. Often the movement of the boat sits you back down hard, right where you started your journey. We had the mainsail out to stabilize the boat in the seas, trying to look like a sailing vessel. It was so warm we had the side curtains rolled up. Even with the seas, it was still 100% better than our last trip. Oh, and we had buckets of electricity thanks to the alternator. End of problem, knock on wood.

I managed to wedge myself in the galley and try hard to think of something that we could eat that was warm, filling and would take about 6 seconds to prepare. I did some hot dogs (Nathans of course) in a pan, wrapped them in soft tortillas with Grey Poupon and a pickle and called it dinner. Ice tea, already made, completed my time below. It was dark, but with a moon for light and all the lights from shore glittering, we didn't seem to be so alone out here this time. As always, OZ was trudging on in front of us.

We made it through the long night without putting on heavy sweatshirts and foul weather gear like the last trip. I stayed in shorts with a windbreaker. The warm weather made night travel seem less threatening. The navigation system worked well, we always knew where we were. Peaches' other two handheld GPS units confirmed our plot. The Garmin kept telling us how many hours to go until Miami.

After about 23 hours and dawn breaking, we could see Miami. From Ft. Lauderdale on down it was one high rise building after another......certainly different from going down the NJ shore over 4 months ago where there were little towns, each with their own water tower and an occasional Ferris Wheel or roller coaster.

We surfed into the shipping channel of Miami like we were surfing onto a beach. It was tricky steering, but we made it. Peaches started taking pictures galore. We followed OZ as they took us to a temporary anchoring spot. The tide was low and we would not be able to get into the anchorage at the Venetian Causeway until high tide. We motored into the ICW again and anchored in a bay beyond a bridge, right in the middle of a sailboat race. The small boats were skipping over the waves at a speed we will never see with Star of the Sea. We were tired as we dropped anchor. It was exactly 24 hours after we left Vero Beach., a trip of 136 nautical miles. We tried to sleep but didn't do a very good job because I was still full of adrenaline and found I was too hungry to sleep. I read for a while, got up and found Peaches up too, so we had a real lunch of soup and sandwiches then got ready to move the boats around 4:30 PM when it was closer to high tide.

Our transit through the Port of Miami was interesting, with some very shallow water as we entered the causeway. We anchored between two islands with our stern facing the roadway connecting the islands to shore. Then we slept the sleep of good sailors (despite having had a whole pot of high octane coffee).

So, what are we doing next? We are sitting through the weekend because of thunder storms and contrary winds on the Gulf Stream (you only cross if there are no northerly winds, including NE or NW winds. It goes against the direction of the Gulf Stream and creates mountainous waves. Not my cup of tea). Bob, my brother (infamous for the landslide of lame nautical sayings and poems at the start of our journey), is coming by plane on Monday afternoon. We'll pick him up in the dinghy off of the rocks of the causeway road behind where we are anchored. We'll have a raucous happy hour, introduce him to Connie and Ken from OZ and the family from Katmandu. We last saw Natalie and Stephen in Fernandina Beach without their mast. They are now fully masted, packed and ready to join us going across to Nassau. The Nina, the Pinta and the Santa Maria.

Our plan is to leave on Tuesday morning about 10 AM after fueling up and getting our water tanks filled. It should take about 27-29 hours total to go the 46 miles to Bimini and round the corner and go to check into customs in Nassau. We will see the clear blue waters of the Bahamas as we come to them in the daylight always a heartwarming sight according to OZ who have done this eight times before. It'll be interesting to see the Gulf Stream, supposedly quite a different color and much warmer than the surrounding ocean. The Atlantic is a very deep trench coming up from the south between Cuba and Florida. Our depth finders will go crazy trying to find the bottom until we get to the banks of the Bahamas.

I can't wait until we are there. It will be fun having a third person so we can get some sleep along the way. Peaches and I will turn our phones off as we go out of the harbor, actually Peaches will probably wait until the last second to call AT&T to shut the iPhone off. We are going shopping today and I hope to find her a Gameboy or something like that to hold in her hand.

Bahamas bound, just coming to the banks as the sun set, OZ out in front

Chapter 42

Gulf Stream Crossing

02/06/2010 Nassau, Bahamas

We left our anchorage near the Venetian Causeway in Miami about 1030 on Tuesday morning. About dinner time Monday night, Bob showed up in a cab from the airport and Ken and I went out in the dinghy to the rocks by the causeway near where we were anchored. The cab left him off after Peaches started waving our lantern when every cab crossed the bridges (one if by land two if by sea…). He clambered down the rocks, hauling his errant suitcase and jumped aboard to join us at our elongated happy hour feast on the boat. He was delayed by his luggage so we had to drink for him until he could join us. After Connie and Ken left for their boat, we could hardly sleep we were so excited about going in the morning.

Some of the other boats left earlier in the morning, Katmandu with them, but we had to wait for the tide to come up in order to slip over some very skinny water on our way to Government Cut and out Miami Harbor. While we followed OZ, we could hear a lot of chatter on the VHF from others already out several miles into the Atlantic. The containers floating out there, according to the Coast guard, were a concern, so we listened to see if anyone else found them. We motored out of the cut, put up our sails and motor-sailed into 1-2 foot seas under a brilliant blue sky, warm temperatures, winds 10-15 knots and all systems are go. Bob was really eating this all up. A little while out of Miami, a motor launch pulled up right beside OZ and questioned them while OZ continued on course at 6 knots. They pulled away from OZ and came up behind us, four men in uniforms in a powerful boat, running beside us a foot off our rail and asking us where we were going and who was aboard. It was the border patrol, our taxes at work.

As the trip continued on through the afternoon, and we didn't spot any of the loose shipping containers from the INTREPID, I was beginning to think our trip had been choreographed by Walt Disney or Pixar animators. It was simply perfect.

Our initial course was set to intercept North Rock, just above of the island of Bimini. We kept waiting for the Gulf Stream to show up a different color, maybe lighter blue, flowing to the north, but the water was all the same deep sparkling blue. We didn't have the means to take water temperature, so despite all of Ben Franklin's hard work, we couldn't corroborate his findings of much warmer water flowing in a river along the Atlantic Coast. The pull of the Gulf was felt on our course over ground.

About 5:00 PM we came to North Rock, shortly after Bob was the first to say "Land Ho" for Bimini. There is a special feeling you get when you've planned a trip like this and gone over your charts, collaborated with your friends on OZ, checked everything twice, and come out right where you intended. So very cool. Thanks Connie and Ken. The weather window was just as advertised by Chris Parker, the Bahamas weather guru on the single side band radio.

The boat was going along in 700-800 meters of water (meter is 39 inches, a little over 3 feet) and suddenly we were in 10 meters and the waters turned clear, turquoise, green/blue. You could see the bottom and everything on it. We'd come out of the trenches of the Atlantic onto the banks of the Bahamas.

One of the things that happened, along with good stories, a good lunch and just plain fun was the official naming of the autohelm. First of all, she is female as is the boat, and her name is Stella. Peaches wanted to call her next boat Stella Mara instead of Star of the Sea, but she was dissuaded by several of her priest friends.

They thought, perhaps rightly so, that everyone in Buffalo would just call it Hey, Stella! The name is perfect for our intrepid auto helm as she has behaved every bit the competent and ever-present lady she is.

The other amazing part of night sailing, other than the sunset, is the moon-rise. This was a waning moon so it didn't come up until 10 PM, looking like a big square shipping container (still on Peaches' mind) on the horizon. It finally emerged as the moon and the visibility was much improved. The waves were of no consequences most of the night. Bob got a chance to see the navigation systems, the radar and the Sirius Weather program working. There was lightning on the horizon in front of us and to the north and with the Sirius, we could tell it was tracking away from us and towards Freeport in the Abacos. Ken confirmed this with his radar. Lots of toys to play with. Lots of time to play.

But then, out of nowhere, came our only problem. Stay tuned.

I went below to take a nap so that I could man my watch at midnight. It is so much nicer to have three people on board so you can sleep in your own bed, not on the cushions of the cockpit. It is even nicer when your new crewmember is a sailor. Below, I was comfortable, not too hot, not too cold, not being pitched around by the waves when the dreaded sound came. It was loud and right under my mattress….whuppa, whuppa, whuppa, whuppa…The prop sounded like it was coming off and taking the shaft with it. The engine sounded terrible. We didn't lose power, but Peaches and Bob slowed it right down, trying to see what was wrong. What did we hit? Was there damage? Should we try to go forward or backward or just stop? What?

My bed over the shaft was vibrating; the wheel and all the instruments at the pulpit were vibrating. We have a razor sharp cutting wheel behind the propeller that is supposed to be able to clear most things that might wrap themselves around the prop. We very much counted on it working, as it was dark, unfamiliar waters, and I am sure neither Bob nor Peaches wanted to slip off the swim platform to investigate. We kept the engine running at idle, about 1000 rpm and we set all sail and continued, our speed actually better under sail than it was with the engine. OZ suggested that we keep on going toward Northwest Shoals and the Northwest Channel. If we have to dive on the prop, maybe we could dive on the prop just before the channel. After going along we decided that everything was resolving and we continued, hoping for an early sunrise. Ken thought about what it could have been, calling us occasionally on the VHF with suggestions.

So, the sun came up, beautiful. We were tired and decided that there was no reason to dive on the prop until in the marina in Nassau. We were out in what is called the Tongue of the Ocean, an incredibly deep part of the ocean that interrupts the Bahamas Banks. It was 1500-1800 meters deep! The seas started to build with winds in the 18-20 knot range. The winds also clocked around to the SW and then momentarily to the W and finally to the North. It got a little lumpy, but Star of the Sea has never sailed so well. We were just flying. OZ was flying even faster, all of us with big foolish grins on our faces. Big heavy boats going fast. What could be better than that?

We were moving fast when Peaches was first to spot New Providence Island where Nassau is located. We moved up, hoping the last couple of hours would go fast. The long night was catching up with us a bit. Bob was up most of the night so he wouldn't miss anything. He did a pretty good imitation of awake while balancing his head and sleeping the sleep of the needful as we hobby-horsed our way to the marina. The first buildings we saw were those of the Atlantis Casino and Hotel complex on Paradise Island just outside the Nassau harbor. It was a lot like Atlantic City rising out of the ocean in NJ, this was entirely too big to be true.

The seas were heavy when we entered the harbor to make our way past all the big cruise ships, under the bridge by the blue Mail Boat and into the Nassau Harbor Club Marina, where we had reservations for a few days. We learned two very important things while getting into and secured to the dock. First, keep up a little bit of mainsail while pitching and rolling into the harbor from the Tongue of the Ocean for stability. Also, do not have your fenders down over the sides when they bring you into your slip. They catch on the dock and make the work of the really nice guys who tie you up a lot harder. Other than that, no harm was done. It was so good to be stopped and standing on the dock in the sunshine, blue skies and our work almost done. How nice to get in just as it is happy hour.

I had all the passports and customs papers filled out, and after about an hour, I was able to go up to the patio of the marina and get the papers stamped, share stories of the crossing to others waiting in line. It finally was my turn to get our cruising permit that lasts until the end of May. $300 later and many signatures done, I had my fishing license, permit, and receipts in hand and could move about the islands at will.

Before customs and getting settled, Bob was up in the cockpit in his bathing suit, goggles and a safety rope provided by Peaches as he went over the swim deck to check the prop. He soon emerged with a wad of very fibrous seaweed (Sargasso weed) in his hand and the news that the cutter had done its job well. No damage. We dodged another bullet and came out fine. I would like the testing to stop now so we can have fun. Everyone who crossed Tuesday to Wednesday said it was one of the nicest crossings they could remember. We are so lucky to get this weather window and to have people to lead us through for our first time.

Bob took us all out for dinner down the street from the marina at the Poop Deck. As we walked, we all looked drunk from being on the boat for so long. The land seemed to be pitching and rolling under our feet. To make things a little more complicated, the people were driving on the wrong side of the road. The food and drinks were great. Ken, Connie and Bob seemed like they had been friends for years. Many stories later, and after no sleep in the past 30 hours, we all trundled back to our boats and passed out cold. All the hatches were open and the breezes were warm, dry and comforting. We have arrived.

Bananaquit taking sugar from Peaches' hands, Exuma Park, Bahamas

Chapter 43

Nassau to Exuma Park

02/12/2010 Exuma Park, Warderick Wells, Bahamas

Monday morning, dawned clear and sunny so we slipped our lines at the Nassau Harbor Club and started south with OZ. Katmandu stayed behind, waiting for a replacement bilge pump. But they will catch up with us later this month in Georgetown.

We missed Bob a lot as we started out to Porgee Rocks, then to Yellow Banks, Norman Stake and then onto a mooring ball at Shroud Cay. Navigation isn't like in the British Virgin Islands, all visual. It is more like point to point travel as you plan a route before you go to guide you through the shallow water, the coral heads, around shoals and sand bars. This longer day trip was beautiful, warm and sunny with enough wind to sail easily along our route.

In the skinny section (10-11 feet) we saw Connie go out onto the bow to spot coral heads, and so I did the same. It will take me more than just this year of sailing these Bahamas Banks waters to get used to the amazing color of the water over the white sands. Everyone I know with a pool at home tries to imitate this color. So, forgive all the water references I make, I can't help myself.

You are probably so yawning now because, nothing happened except we got where we were going without mishap. No broken anything, no frightening noises, not even a spill to wipe up during lunch. We did have a good time and told each other several times how very lucky we were to be here and sailing our own boat.

Yawn! There was a beautiful sunset but without a green flash after getting onto the mooring in Shroud Cay. We had a bit of conversation about the upcoming cold front going through on Tuesday night so decided not to go ashore and explore all the high tide rivers through the Mangroves at this time. We voted to move on to a more secure mooring at Exumas Park in the morning. Exuma Park is a 176 square mile area set aside by the Bahamian government as the Exuma Cays Land and Sea Park, a marine protected area where you bring nothing in, take nothing, pick up nothing, and just enjoy the area in its natural state. Warderick Wells is the home of the Park Headquarters. This is our destination on Tuesday.

So, Tuesday morning we got ready to leave before the winds got too heavy, but late enough to arrive on a rising tide. The way into the park is shallow for our 6 foot draft vessels. It is always a balance between beating the weather and having enough water to do it safely.

It was (I know stop it), sunny and warm, the water sparking and bright. We left with the winds rising and going into the wind, so motored all the way. It got steeper and steeper, with the last of the five hours the worst with the wind and the waves coming at us broadsides. We were heading for Emerald Rock mooring field. Ken and Connie had some anxiety because they hadn't been to this mooring field. We did well despite the high waves, the winds and not being able to read the numbers on the mooring balls. We got the mooring first try, pure luck.

I'm going to talk a little about mooring balls. You usually pay for their use. You hope that they have been well maintained so that they don't fail you while you sleep peacefully rocking in your bunk. You love them just for that reason; you can sleep at night and not get up constantly to check your anchor. And lastly, you have to have a system to pick them up. Ours is to have Peaches on the foredeck with a boat hook and a couple of strong lines. She has an intercom strung around her neck and I have the other one by me at the wheel. Now, you need to go slow, you need to get it close to the bow; you need to stop the boat when she tells you to. All of this is blind as I can't see through her, or see the mooring ball when I get up to it. So far, so good. This mooring ball was the hardest yet, because of the waves and the wind, but Peaches hasn't let one go yet.

Exuma Park is a wonderful place and we had been regaled with stories about it since meeting Ken and Connie. They both work as volunteers while there and get their mooring fees waived. There are several mooring areas; the most preferred is the northern one near the office that is protected from winds on all four sides. We called in our request for a place there Tuesday morning before going down and found out that so did half the fifty or more boats on the banks. We each got a mooring in the Emerald Rock mooring field and are on the list for the northern mooring field in the morning.

The woman who handles this whole "who gets what and when" dance at the park is very good at what she does. Darcy is polite on the VHF at 0900 when the assignments are made, but there are always the pushy people who cannot believe that they won't get the one they want. She juggles everyone like it is a waltz or the guy on Ed Sullivan who used to juggle all those plates on sticks and not drop a one! Cruising is a big leveler of the playing field. Who you are isn't the key any more, it's just 1) where you are, 2) how long is your vessel and 3) how deep is your draft. So, we want to stay here for a week or so, and will remain on the waiting list for the better "balls."

Ken has done everything from clean beaches to fill diving tanks, from rebuilding boats to cleaning up trails in years past. He thinks he will propose that he clean the mooring balls and repaint the numbers so they can be seen more easily. He will broach the "ball" subject at the office tomorrow. The cruisers do a lot of wonderful things down in the Bahamas, and this is one of the examples. Over the VHF this morning the cruisers are doing a big benefit for the medical clinic in Staniel Cay, inviting people to come eat, volunteer, and donate.

My first dinghy trip into the park office today was with Ken and Connie. We were drenched within one dinghy length of leaving the back of our boat. I looked back quickly at Peaches who stayed behind to watch the boat (dry and smiling). As we got going, we got wet and then it didn't matter anymore. The waves were still pretty big from last night's rocking and rolling 20-25 knot winds. We all slept poorly, trying to keep from rolling out of bed all night long. It took a while for our stomachs to catch up with us this morning, so a slow start to the morning with coffee and cold cereal.

As Ken, Connie and I got into the office dock; lots of people were old friends of OZ stopped to talk. I got most of the names straight, I think. We registered and then went out to walk around in the sun to dry out from the dinghy ride. There is an endangered species of rodent who looks like a small woodchuck or a very large rat with no tail. The Hutia are nocturnal and apparently have no predators here, as their population is soaring to over 5000 on the island at last count. A lot of the natural ground cover is gone, eaten by the numerous Hutia. I suggested that they take a boat full of them to some of the other islands. That fell on deaf ears I think

We walked through tidal flats, over volcanic rocks and up through baby mangrove trees and sand to Boo Boo Hill. This is where the cruisers place the name of their boat on a piece of wood or stone (something natural) so people will know they've been here. The view from the hill is super. We walked over to the blow holes on the Exuma Sound side, but the surf wasn't high enough to shoot the water up. When the waves are large, it sounds like thunder. Did I tell you how blue the water is and how warm and sunny it is every day? Oh, another big yawn from you-all. Well, you will just have to come join us and stop shivering up there in snow country. We miss you all.

PS: Starship 12, February, 2010

We spent a happy hour yesterday and hours today getting ready to abandon ship. There is a very large low front system coming through tonight that will have a constant 35-40 knot winds. There will be some 50 knot winds during the squalls as it passes through our location in the south-central Bahamas Banks. We don't have any qualms about the boat surviving this big blow as we are on a strong and well maintained mooring ball. The time on the boats during this blow will be terrible, hard not to get sick and for sure there will be bruises. We are not in the northern protected field of mooring balls, so will be very vulnerable to the winds as they increase over today from the S-SE to SSW and then quickly W and then NW and north. We are particularly vulnerable to the westerly winds. We took a vote, led by Peaches telling me yesterday morning that she was not under any circumstances staying on the boat during the blow and I was not either (there goes the democracy). We talked to Ken and Connie and after considerable gin, rum and beers, we set up a plan (they're in on it).

I am sitting on the porch of the park office finishing the blog so you will be up to date. Peaches and I set longer and stronger lines to the mooring ball, took all the fenders and fuel tanks (8) off the decks, tied down the boom and the bit of mainsail that sticks out. We also wrapped the furling jib a few more wraps for safety's sake. We packed our half of the abandon ship rations (booze, snacks, computer and movies for later), blankets and warmer clothes, lights VHF radios, toothbrushes and the important ships papers and our passports. Connie cooked a delightful cold supper for us to have on the beach. We are spending the night on the beach and up on the porch while the tropical storm blows through. Now be quiet about this as the staff think we are just having dinner on the beach.

We are having a little night out. Peaches likens it to going to sleep with the street people for a night. I think she will be very surprised when all the Hutias on the island crash our party and crowd in front of us to see the movie better. A story will surely come out of this experience. I will let Peaches write that one. This was totally her idea.

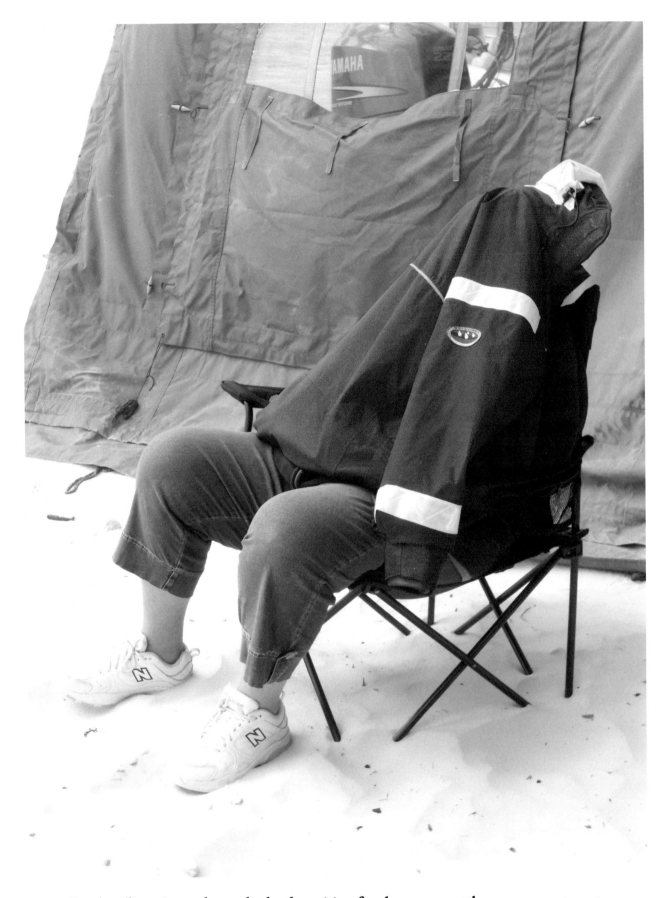

Peaches (listening to her audio book, waiting for the seas to settle so we can return to our boat) the afternoon after The Longest Happy Hour, Exuma Park, Bahamas

Chapter 44

The Longest Happy Hour or How We Survived the Storm

02/14/2010 Exuma Park, Bahamas

Now that I have you on the edge of your seats, be they couch, boat or snowmobile, we are alive and well. The picture above shows Peaches 24 hours after we came ashore on Friday afternoon. This will be explained a little further on.

Now, weather prediction is a very tricky thing. The guys from Channel 4 in Buffalo are heroes when they are right but never to be trusted for the real story. Around here we have our own brand of weather guru-type people. The best of the best for the Bahamas is a guy named Chris Parker. We hope to go to a lecture by him in Georgetown later this month. We have heard that his is the most complete report and he will answer questions from vessels on his 6 days a week program on the single-side band (SSB) radio at 0630 (boaters go to bed very early so 0630 is the second pot of coffee for us).

When we checked into the Exuma Park last Tuesday, Darcy said Chris Parker was Mr. Doom and Gloom. I think that Connie of OZ said it best when she said he has to give as much info as he can so everyone can make their own plans for their next voyage to say Georgetown or to Cambridge Cay. Well, all the predictors from NOAA and Chris Parker said that the low pressure front coming through on Friday between midnight and 0600 on Saturday was going to be a strong one, with gale force winds and possible gusts in the 50 knot range (that would be about 58 mph). He also said it was one of the strongest fronts he has seen in the last 10 years for this time of year.

So, you got the message we were abandoning ship(s) on Friday. When we awoke Friday morning it was another beautiful day in paradise, warm, sunny with just a 10 knot breeze blowing from the south. We were in a mooring field that would give us good wind and wave protection from the East, SE and NE winds, somewhat from the North. Westerly winds like those predicted after midnight was what we thought about as we made our decision.

Peaches gets up and immediately starts running through the list of 100 things she wants to do before we leave to make the vessel safe from the storm because we won't be here. In fact, she said she wanted to leave by 1100. I thought maybe we could have coffee and breakfast, listen to the weather on the VHF from Highbourne Cay, listen to the announcements from Exuma Park and then call Connie and Ken and see what Chris P. predicted. Nope, she had an agenda, most of it was right on the money. I didn't think it needed to be done so fast. Connie said she would like me to come over in the dinghy to consult on the menu (for the abandon the ship night). We were talking code over the VHF so nobody would pick up on our possibly slightly outside the park rules plan. I helped switch out the mooring ball lines for a really strong black nylon three strand 2 inch line, moved all eight of the fuel tanks off the deck along with the fenders and holders. I went over for a few minutes by dinghy to OZ and Connie had already done most of the prep for dinner on the beach, so I came back and got the happy hour supplies done, and packed blankets, small pillows, and foul weather gear. We packed the VHF and short wave radio and tons of batteries (you know how Peaches is, there were actually tons of them) and the ship's papers, especially the insurance policy just in case.

We left Star of the Sea around noon and by then the waves were up over 2 feet and there were white caps in the bay. The wind was starting to whine through the rigging of the ship. This is, for those of you who might want to know, a 4 of 12 on the Beaufort Wind Scale (11-15 knots, waves 3-6 feet, small waves, breaking crests with fairly frequent white horses). Enough meteorology to the story.

We had trouble getting all of our terribly necessary stuff into the dinghy and surfed the waves all the way into the beach on the other side of the Park Office. Ken, who'd been working for the Park, went out to get Connie and the rest of the supplies as I didn't have enough hp in my Honda 5 hp outboard engine to get back out through the waves for her.

When we finally all gathered on the beach, sitting at the table under the thatched roof, Connie spread the cloth and we started the happy hour, way before the "5 o'clock somewhere" rule. We talked and laughed, drank some very good rum, gin and white wine and generally thought how very smart we were being on the land rather than being on the hobby-horsing vessels out in the mooring field.

The festivities lasted until after dinner was served and consumed. The sun was still out, although there were occasional cloudy periods. The temperature was getting a little cooler, but we were like good doobies, very prepared for anything. We noticed that there weren't too many others around and decided to move our party to the porch of the Park Office. We settled into the chairs up there, supplemented by Connie's two camp chairs.

After dark, a long unmarked and unlit cigarette boat arrived at the small dock. There were 4 men dressed in all black. It turned out to be a supply boat for the Bahamian Defense Team (sort of like our Coast Guard in the US). We watched them unload and a big party for them with our Defense people was happening just around the corner from where we were "hiding in plain sight," so to speak. Actually as their night went on, they got louder and louder and sounded like they were arguing, but maybe it was a story telling with a lot of F bombs liberally shot through it. They were still going strong after 1 AM.

We were still pretty happy and after I worked on the last blog and cleared my email, we decided to watch a movie on the computer. We huddled around the screen and found that with all the wind blowing (it was definitely increasing and starting to come from the S to SW) we couldn't hear the dialog. The guys in the back of the office didn't help either. The movie was *Hunt for Red October,* Ken and Peaches' favorite one, so dialog was provided by the two of them. We started changing into long pants, jackets and ultimately foul weather jackets as the temperature cooled and the wind kept clocking around.

Ken and I were surprised that there still a sky full of stars, no clouds to speak of except at the horizon. Chris Parker's predictions for wind shifts were coming true. We moved from the south side of the porch to the west side where we finally decided to try and catch some sleep. Ken and Connie used their camp chairs. I tried somewhat successfully to use the yoga mats on top of the bench used to hold bones and fossils (now on the porch floor). Peaches took the other chair. This didn't last long, with Connie saying she thought we should watch another movie, because she always could sleep better during a movie. I know the feeling.

The wind got stronger still so we moved all our paraphernalia again to the north side porch (the last side available) and lined the chairs up along the office wall. Finally the wind gusts were more what we thought they would be (50 or more knots) because we couldn't stand up easily if we went around to the west side to check our boats. There was lightening and then a downpour, over in just a few minutes. Peaches must have said a hundred times since landing on the beach how glad she was to not be on the boat.

Ken thought earlier that it might be a good idea to move into the "kitchen" for the rest of the night so we would be dry, warmer and safe. He made a reconnaissance hike to see if it seemed okay, and off we went, hauling coolers, bags of stuff and finally ourselves. The kitchen, by the way, is a building with shelves, cupboards, a sink, and the reason it is called a kitchen, it has a refrigerator tied shut with a bungee cord. You could see light through most of the walls of the building, but we were safe. One foray out and down the path to another building with a composting toilet in it found us face to face with the dreaded Hutia. They are brown, chubby, rat-like things without the long tail. They are totally unafraid of anything, especially people. If you see three in the light of your flashlight, think of how many are outside the beam of light. UGGGGGGGGGGGGH!

We settled into our new accommodations and learned the art of rotating your posterior cheeks from one side to the other on a rather frequent schedule to avoid the pain of sitting so long. We had been sitting mostly for hours and hours by that time (around 3 AM). We all, surprisingly, slept some, the Hutia did not invade the building or our space, at least we don't think they did, and morning came. We all thought, very erroneously that we would have some breakfast, catered by Connie, of course (fresh muffins, coffee, and scotch eggs, wow), and then pack it up and go back to our boats to recover.

OH, HOW WRONG WE WERE. Actually, we were wrong on a couple of points. The winds were still very strong, in the protected anchorage the boats were rocking and rolling still, and out around the corner we could see our boats. They were bobbing like toys in a washing machine. The other point came through our door shortly after the first park employee found us in the kitchen. As it turns out we weren't as invisible as we thought. The Park Ranger/Warden, Henry, showed up. What a nice guy. He is a Bahamian with relatives in Rochester and Pittsburgh, who had been in law enforcement (stopping the drug trade from the Dominican Republic and more, I am sure) and had been working for the Bahamian government and the Park for several years. He asked a lot of questions, laughed at our predicament and acted like he believed our story of coming in to have dinner on the beach and then not being able to get back to our boats because of the severe weather that "suddenly" happened (sure, and I am the current Queen of England). We became the talk of the park.

Ken decided to volunteer to work during the day for the Park as long as he was there so we made him up a lunch of all sorts of leftovers from the night before. Peaches, Connie and I finally found a place out of the wind and in the sun. It was just plain cold when the clouds blocked out the sun. Other people came in from the boats in the safe mooring fields in the afternoon, all coming to see if we were still alive. They offered help, peanut butter sandwiches and hopes that we could get out to the boats soon. We said we were fine.

Henry found us again, asking if we were still okay. We were horribly tired of sitting around and not being able to get "home", but said we were fine, great, actually. After he left, Peaches said again how glad she was we came into the island. Now her picture at the top isn't as bad as it looks. We were still on a windy beach, with sand flying into out mouths and noses all afternoon. She was sitting in the chair, listening to a really good book on her iPod, staying warm and relaxing. Connie and I were getting as much sun as we could, reading and killing time (ducking the sand). My mother said that by the time you die, you will have eaten a whole peck of dirt. I looked it up and a peck is 32 cups of dirt! Ugh! Add to that the half peck of sand we ate since the landing on the beach yesterday and I should be a beanbag, not a person.

We are alive and well, got back to the boats in the very late afternoon, after taking the overloaded dinghy back through some rough seas. The boat and the dinghy were both pitching and rolling, but not to the beat of the same drummer. Peaches finally took the leap and got onboard, and with great difficulty we got the boat unloaded, attached to the davits and hauled out of the sea. We left all the sandy stuff in the cockpit, came below, looked at each other and said, "we're home at last". We had some cheese and crackers, a cut up apple, and at 6 PM we called it a night and went to bed. We braced against the 20 knot pitching and rolling gladly (it must have been horrible during the night) and slept deeply.

We moved into the secure North anchorage today, happily, although somehow the mooring rope got pulled under the boat along with the mooring ball. This never happened before to us, but it was an odd combination of strong current pulling the boats in the opposite direction as the wind was blowing. Between Peaches in the water with her mask and fins, and Ken in his dinghy, the ropes got exchanged and all was well. So, got to go. Happy Hour is starting on the beach. Actually, it seems like it's our beach. Will write again soon, although internet sites are pretty scarce where we are.

PS: From Peaches: After 30 years of racing with the Buffalo Harbor and Sailing Club, we have all been out in very nasty seas and strong winds. The nice thing about racing all those years, you could get off the boat, go into the Yacht Club bar and talk about the ripped sails, the broaches, the stupid thing someone else did, or you could go home to your own bed. Cruising is a different animal. The thought of being in 7 ½ feet of water with a 6 foot keel with 50 knot winds or perhaps greater hit my threshold for abandoning ship! I wanted my own two feet on solid ground.

Last night when we returned to the boat, the winds were in the 22-23 knot range. The seas were still about

3 feet. In my V-berth, I got tossed from one side to the other side. I called to Chris from my rolling berth "Can you imagine what this must have been like last night?" My heart and soul felt right when my feet hit the sand on Friday afternoon. I talked to a gentleman yesterday afternoon who rode it out on the mooring ball near ours and said it was the worst thing he has ever gone through. My special black three-strand-line from Charlie Obersheimer held the boat firmly throughout the night. Thanks, Charlie.

Honey wheat bread and reverse osmosis water, all in the same day!

Chapter 45

Bread and Water

I am the king of the world! No, I didn't produce the movie *Titanic* or even *Avatar* like James Cameron (who does think he is the King of the World). Yesterday, I produced clear drinking from sea water and made two loaves of bread in a bitty oven in a boat in the Bahamas. It was outrageous.

We bought the Spectra watermaker for the boat at the same time as we bought the reverse heat and air system, Annapolis Boat Show, 2008. Now, you all know we used the heating system for months on the way down the coast, but there sat that expensive watermaker, with bags of spare chemicals and spare filters, all protected from the ill effects of moisture, doing nothing for us at all.

Oh, I made (with the help of Andy Lopez of RCR), water from the Black Rock Canal in Buffalo, off the docks of the Buffalo Yacht Club. You all can surmise what a feat that was. What must lie under that stretch of water is unimaginable (dead mobsters with cement shoes, hundreds of cell phones, winches, spare parts from all the hundreds of years of boats resting on the surface, oil jugs, old batteries, sunken boats and dinghies, maybe even a Christmas tree or two). Andy and I could see through the glass of water we made. I needed to check out the watermaker before we left the next day. We even touched our lips to the glass and pretended to drink. We saved it for Peaches to drink!

So, we've been gone about six months and water has been free at the marinas wherever we went. No incentive there to pull everything out of the 5 foot deep storage locker where the watermaker resides, untouched by human hands since I pickled it before Christmas at Amelia Island. I had to hire an electrician to find out why it wasn't getting electricity. Answer: Andy had thoughtfully put a shut-off valve on the back water tank so the watermaker wouldn't keep filling it when it was full. Water was still free, the tank was full and $75 later we knew why (the tank was full so it wouldn't trigger the electricity).

Now it is mid-February, we've been away from Nassau for about 10 days and our water is starting to get low in the tanks. At Exuma Park on shore, there are no water facilities, actually no rest rooms for non-staff and no place to dispose or recycle garbage. Since it had been a while, I read the how-to manual and thought "Piece of cake, Mama!" I can do that.

With Peaches help and encouragement, we took everything out of that storage place in the cockpit. This filled all the available seating in the cockpit. Then, to make the boat a little more disorganized, we took all the objects stored where I sleep in the back berth (Whuppa whuppa, portable spin dryer, all our liquor, bags of food that won't fit anywhere else, cushions and spare table leaf to make the couch into a bed for company, bag-o-bedding and towels, packages of TP, you can never have enough of this in the islands, and more) and placed them on every flat surface in the salon except the galley.

You get the picture. In my berth, Peaches opened the thru-hull lever and turned on the electricity. I set up the generator on the bow and had it covering the batteries and now the watermaker because I didn't know how many amps it would draw. I placed a cushion carefully on the floor in front of the Spectra and start pushing levers and toggle switches and wonder of wonders, into a large glass comes sparkling clear water. I get out the electronic tester to test for particulate matter and it reads 310ppm. Anything under 790 is potable (that means you can drink and not DIE!). I did, and I didn't, if you catch my reasoning. We started filling 5 gallon blue jugs while the pump kept pumping 80 gallons of sea water through a membrane and getting one gallon of drinking water. I checked the Link 2000 and it said the Spectra was only pulling about 12 amps/hour. I thought it was a bigger amp user than that.

As the day went on, all was well. I did 4 loads of wash in the whuppa whuppa (turn the handle) washer and spun the clothes dry in the centrifuge dryer (the generator was on, only coasting, so we might as well see how much it can handle at once). All I need now is a cup of fresh coffee and a piece of toast, the Honda would self-destruct (a joke). It was 80 and sunny so all the clothes dried sweet smelling in the light breeze. Now, the whuppa whuppa takes about 100 revolutions with the left arm and another 100 with the right before you drain and then the same for the rinse cycle. By the end of the 4th load and after lifting full jugs of water out of the deep lazaret, I couldn't lift my arms over my ears. Peaches and I were so pleased, it was a perfect day. It was so perfect that we just turned off the Spectra switch and will turn it on again tomorrow and fill the other tank. We even have a couple of jugs of water for OZ.

The next day dawned and we were at it again. Remember, we have nowhere to sit or essentially stand so what else could we do but continue. Then we could put the boat back together and sit down. Did I tell you I had to sleep in my berth with half the mattress out in the salon and a big hole down into the engine gaping beside me? All night I felt like I might roll into the hole and become impaled on the various pieces and parts sticking up. I didn't though.

We made more water and I found a couple of bread mixes so I kneaded enough dough for two loaves of wheat berry bread. I had a fire the last time I tried to make dinner rolls back up in the Erie Canal, so this was taking things to a whole new level of risk. The dough rose, then into the pans and rose again, just like it should. I heated up the oven and the first loaf (one at a time in the miniature oven please) came out beautifully. The second was just as good. The boat smelled wonderful, the water tanks were full and our heads were too big with pride to pass through our doorways.

So, that's my story and I am sticking to it. Today we went in the dinghy to the beach where Peaches replaced a defective valve in the Zodiac dinghy. We had to pump up one of the sides every time we went anywhere this past week, not doing much for our confidence in the dinghy. We went for the long hike up to Boo Boo Hill where we laid the wreath….no the piece of wood with Star of the Sea 2010 on the pile where others have done the same for their boat. Peaches did her first engraving with one of her Dremel and it came out sharp. The view from the top of the hill was spectacular.

We're having the time of our lives. It would be great if some of you might like to come and join us. E-mail us and we can give a tentative schedule of where we will be. Fly into Nassau and take one of the puddle jumpers to the island closest to us. Have a little adventure in your lives!

Footprints in the sand, evidence of the mighty Hutia on Wardwick Wells, Exuma Park, Bahamas

Chapter 46

Exuma Park, What Lies Beneath?

02/22/2010 Exuma Park, North Mooring Field, Bahamas

Hi, back again with more adventures. I've come down off last week's high of making water and bread in the same day. Old geeky stuff to be sure. I'm making water again, just for our tanks this time. All systems are go. It's an overcast day with scattered warm showers, so a good day to stay on the boat and monitor the watermaker. The bread making has gone from pre-made mixes to an Italian favorite. I found out how easy Ciabatta bread is to make and have decided that it is all we need, a simple daily bread just like the loaves we bought at Dash's in Buffalo.

We've thrived in these mill-pond mornings in the north mooring field. It's better than being tied to a dock. OZ is on the next mooring ball and through them we have had contact with the wild side of the park. Ask Peaches what is new and she shouts "SHARKS"! There is a nurse shark under our boat. We are in about 10 feet of water most of the time and it is crystal clear. The shark seems to like the wreck under the aft end of OZ in the afternoons. Some others in the park have seen a nurse shark with a baby shark swimming right beside it.

Peaches was all set to do a lot of maintenance work on our boat, clean the waterline around the boat of small baby barnacles, the green slime, and work on the knot-meter wheel under the boat that hasn't worked since Georgia, but, there are sharks. You might remember she went in the water to fix the mooring ball when we came in here last week on Valentine's Day. That was pre-knowledge of the shark. She finally went in yesterday after a thorough look-see for the shark and got the rest of the waterline done with me holding her line to keep her close to the boat and I'm on shark patrol from up on the deck.

Peaches had a lot of concerns about sharks before she left Buffalo. We were planning (and did) spend about a month in the Chesapeake where you wouldn't expect sharks. She read an article that stated there were 75+ different species of shark in the shallow waters from Maryland to Virginia. This is despite the water being just brackish, not salty like the ocean. Now we are here, in salt waters and there are more sharks! Do-do-Do-do-Do-do-Do-do...

Despite the shark population, we went snorkeling in the southern end of the mooring field, me as boat tender and Peaches, Connie and Ken as the snorkelers. They saw lots of coral, a ray, some Nassau grouper (who are protected from fishing right now because they are breeding), sea cucumbers, barracuda and lots of other reef things. They didn't stay long as the water isn't very warm; after all it is winter down here too. We were snorkeling with another Canadian couple from the sailing vessel Mad Cap, Beth and Jim. The three dinghies all put-putted to a beach at the edge of the north mooring field. It turned out to be warmest sitting on the big rocks rather than sitting in the shallow waters. I found there were the unmistakable footprints of the not-so-elusive Hutia. More about that later.

It's a tradition for there to be a communal happy hour on the beach near the office at Exuma Park every Saturday night. The staff lights a bonfire for us and provides ice for drinks. The weather has not been particularly conducive to this until the last couple of days, so everyone moored at the park came out. They were dressed in their best low-key beach wear, carrying something to pass and drinks for them to consume as the sun set on the beach. I'll bet there weren't more than three or four pair of underwear being sported on the entire beach Saturday night. It is the first part of civilization to hit the sand, so to speak. It also cuts down considerably on the laundry load. Bathing suits are the norm. I brought about six and Peaches even more bathing suits. This is the one time where more is better packed into the boat.

Oh, the happy hour, it was not as elongated as ours was during the storm by any means. We had a great time trading stories and passing boat cards out. Most of us have boat cards with our blog sites, single side band call numbers, emails and cell phone numbers as well as a picture of our boat. You tend to be known by your boat name, like OZ. This is the true leveler as I mentioned earlier. It doesn't matter who you were before cruising. What matters is where you have been, your sailing experiences good and bad, and what you bring to happy hour. How wonderfully simple this life is.

We were reunited this week with the Famille ChamBou, Natalie, Stephen and the kids from Katmandu all looked happy. Looking around the beach, it seems perfect, all the dinghies pulled up onto the beach, their anchors dug into the beach so they won't float away with the tide. Kids were playing and adults were talking, starved for adult company. The sun set and then moon rose in the sky. The stars were low and there were millions of them.

I went hunting, just as dark descended for a photo-op of the Hutia. Francis, Stephen's son helped me greatly in the hunt, chumming for them in the bushes next to the beach with popcorn. For the longest time, there was nothing, but there are 5000 of them at last count, so we were going to get the photo. Little did we know, we didn't need to chum for them. They were everywhere when dark fell, coming right up to the picnic table where all the appetizers were being consumed! According to our friends, Gail and Don, they were thought to be extinct until the mid-1990s when some were found on an isolated island in the Exumas. They are now flourishing. No need for worries. They exhibit some strange behaviors according to the article I read. They urinate on everything, not as a territory marker, but just as a nice community blending of scents. They also groom each other and wrestle just for fun, not for sex or aggression (there is obviously sex going on, the population is through the roof!).

Speaking of animal life, Peaches and I went to the dock to get our dinghy and go back to the boat after the happy hour. The partial moon was out and you could see so much without the need of a flashlight. I climbed down off of the dock (about 10 feet above the water) and started pulling the dinghy back around to where Peaches could get in. I saw a shape in the water, as long as the dinghy ....Do-do, Do-do another shark. This one was definitely not a safe nurse shark; it looked like a big reef shark. I called for Peaches to watch it go under the dinghy and out to the reef. It made a big impression. We both took a little extra time getting into the dinghy so we wouldn't be sharing swimming space with that bad-boy! Stephen and his family came over with us, escorting the old ladies back to their boat. He's sort of become our older brother, protecting two ladies loose in the Bahamas. So, another escape from the sharks. It is kind of like Captain Hook and the crocodile; they are always lurking in the waters below you! Poor Peaches.

We are hoping to leave here tomorrow to go to Staniel Cay to get diesel and gas to refill the jerry cans on the deck. We have used up all our gas in the generators because we are unplugged. Our battery banks are full and healthy. There is still a full gas tank in the dinghy if we are delayed. Our plan, OZ and Star of the Sea, is to try and get to Georgetown by the weekend, attend the weather guru, Chris Parker's seminar, and take part in the festivities around the sailing regatta. It will be fun to go to a store, see new territory, and maybe even get a haircut. I am on week 8 of a 3-4 week hair cut schedule, as is Peaches. Other than internet, some ice and our small mooring fees in the park, we've not spent any money (at last living off all the stuff we packed into the boat months ago). We have really loved it here, such an easy time with lots of reading done, naps, walks on the trails and a large amount of rum imbibed.

Another use of our gentle time here is listening to the VHF radio. It's like having a scanner on top of your refrigerator at home. You can snoop and know what is going on. It is definitely like a telephone. You hail someone on Channel 16, the emergency high frequency channel and then say go up one or go to 18 or 68, wherever you want that's empty for your conversation. There are weather forecasts from Highpoint Cay on a prearranged channel. A lady named June lives on a nearby island and every morning she does a commentary on the weather. Along with the weather she makes comments on how bad other forecasts are and what you should do today, like fish today only as the winds are down on the sound. Her dry humor breaks through. All the marinas, the stores and the restaurants monitor the VHF for reservations, to answer questions or to order parts.

So, about the snooping part, Peaches calls it lurking. It is the Cruisers' National Sport. You listen and if interested follow the person to the alternate channel. You are then lurking. It is a free state of mind down here, not much to fill your time, and what the hell, you might learn something really interesting. Well, like the guy who lost his dinghy from the back of his boat on mooring ball #2. Because everyone listens, it was picked up and returned from around mooring ball #9 or #10 right away. Interesting stuff happens, like hearing about a fire on a freighter out in the Sound from others' conversations on the VHF, and did I tell you about the torrid affair between.........naw, I won't go there.

Peaches has some timely tips for those of you who might be in shark infested waters. Listen up: Never jump into the water because it attracts sharks who think you might be food. When in the water, don't splash or kick your fins wildly as you will appear to be injured food. Don't go in if there is more than one shark, or if there is a shark with a baby. Many of the Bahamas sharks inhabit water from 1 foot in depth to 60 feet. She says you are obviously much safer in deeper ocean waters than in the 7-10 feet we usually have here on the banks. When in doubt, Peaches says, "have a drink and stay on the boat". I concur.

Ken and Connie, from OZ, in their dinghy Toto, Black Point, Bahamas

Chapter 47

Black Point and Georgetown, On the Move Again

03/02/2010 Georgetown, Monument Anchorage, Bahamas

We left Exuma Park on Thursday 2/26 with no shark incidents. We were famous by the time we left the Park, mostly because of our night out on the island. It was new all over for us to be traveling; we were so excited that we could hardly sleep, all in anticipation of our trip to Black Point. We headed south on the banks after making all the waypoints to Warderick Bore. WE WERE IN THE LEAD THIS TIME!!

Did I tell you we were in front on this part of the trip? It felt a little strange not to see the graphics on the stern of OZ, but we managed. The seas were flat after the blow the day before in Exuma Park, not even in the protected mooring it was a little lumpy from the winds. We drank the rest of the morning coffee, took turns checking that Stella, the autohelm, was minding her Ps and Qs. I finished a book in my free time and Peaches was listening to one of her books on tape. What a nice journey. We left early so we could get into Black Point in time to have our cheeseburger in Paradise and look around to see what real civilization had to offer.

We decided on the way down that we had pretty much stopped wearing shoes and underwear and opted for the bathing suit du jour and maybe a shirt when it got cool at night. We weren't even combing our hair consistently when we didn't get off the boat. Exuma Park was a joy and a true vacation from have-to-do things. So, we needed a real wake up call. I had one a couple of days before we left, a picture of me in the dinghy with enough hair blowing around to be considered Robinson Caruso material, although my swimsuit wasn't tattered enough. We need civilization before it is too late!

About 12:30 I noticed Ken of OZ coming up on our port side and passing us, taking the lead. He lured us along into the shallow bay of Black Point. We followed closely, but not quite close enough as our depth gauge said 5 feet 9 inches and we draw 6 feet. We plowed along through the sandy bottom and after about 300 feet of this we were back in 9-10 feet of water and found a good anchorage. Connie said I must have cut the corner over the shallow sandbar a little close. All sandbars shift with the tides and the winds. Lesson learned.

We got the dinghies down and loaded them up with 18 days of garbage in our case, and some garbage and a bunch of water jugs in Ken's case. We dropped off Connie and Peaches at a dinghy dock and went to the large government dock to fill jugs and mostly to get rid of the garbage. My two heavy black bags almost killed me, but I manned up and carried my own. Ken is always so kind, but makes me feel guilty, a little wimpy when he carries things for me. Garbage gone, he pointed me to the main (and only) road into town.

I walked by small houses, some with signs out front, some gorgeous views out toward the water, lots of shore birds (sandpipers and Bahamian Mockingbirds). There was a polite hello from everyone (all three of them) who walked by me the other way. I was getting jittery; it was starting to feel like a crowd to me. A pick-up truck went by and then a golf cart. I knew I was back in a town. I walked until I could hear Peaches talking to someone near the grocery store (a green building, doors open, and lots of green shelves with food prices on a paper at the end of each 10 foot aisle). The straw items and handmade jewelry were placed at eye level so you would want it. Peaches was talking to the owner who regaled us with stories. She remembered Connie from two years ago, OZ's last visit to Black Point. We continued down the road a bit to the Laundromat, where Connie's clothes were finishing up. The Laundromat was up high on a rocky shoreline with a dinghy dock (where we left Connie and Peaches off) below. It was clean, modern, had a great rest room, a store for cleaning products and some boat supplies, and behind the counter, a deep fryer for fresh conch fritters. But wait……..

The owner and operator was out back of the shop, cutting another boater's hair as the lady sat on a small folding chair. Both Peaches and I stood dumbstruck. It had been over two months since a haircut, way back in Amelia Island, Florida. I would have paid the owner anything for a haircut but Connie stepped in before I made a pure fool of myself, Ida said sure, she'd do our haircuts for $15 each. She owns the Laundromat, the store and cuts hair, makes fritters to order and she owns a couple of rental cottages over on the ridge. I said something to her about the strong women on the island and she smiled knowingly. She said "We are. We have to be." She had children in school and a husband who worked off the island. Bet you never had a haircut with the fresh air all around you and view to die for. Oh, and warm conch fritters on the way back out to the main street.

Connie and I bought the last carton of eggs. We'd been dying for some after the long stay in Exuma Park. Since there was only one carton, we split it, got some romaine, a pepper and a cucumber and were so excited. No fresh vegetables or salads at the Park, we were there for 18 days. We wandered down the lane a little further to Lorraine's Restaurant, a town cornerstone. All the kids were getting out of school and all said "good afternoon" made eye contact and smiled at us as they walked by in their uniforms.

We'd heard about Lorraine's Restaurant from a lot of people, who always managed to mention Lorraine's elderly mother who baked bread for sale, daily. We met Ken there, after his trips to the faucet to fill some of his water jerry cans and then back to his boat. We had cheeseburgers all around, with fries, onion rings and Kalik beer; brewed in Nassau (it was cold and crisp!). Lorraine stopped by to talk to Ken and Connie for a while and Peaches asked about some bread. In 5 minutes it was hot in our hands, coconut bread for us and raisin bread for OZ. Not many people were in the restaurant, but there was free internet, and their computer was free to use, so we checked our mail quickly.

Then, because there was time in our busy social schedule, it was on to a bar down the street for happy hour; two for one rum punch with free popcorn. As we walked, all the men who work on the other islands were coming up the street from the pier. It was Friday night and they just got paid. The little bar we were heading for was going to be jumping.

It was quiet when we came in except for ESPN on the big screen TV. They took care of us at the bar and we listened to their conversations as the bar filled up. Peaches likes rum punch and managed to stay on the bar stool but was having a little trouble stringing sentences together after drinking the second one. Have you watched them put 5 shots, all different rums, in the glass before they put in the splash of fruit juice? We were lucky to be breathing let alone talking! We were fine to take the dinghies back to the boats after the long walk back out of town. We leave in the morning, running in front of a weather front all the way to Georgetown, on the outside, in the Exuma Sound (ocean).

We were just having our first coffee of the morning when Connie called on the VHF to say Ken was going out on the deck to pull the anchor. We quickly did the same and followed them out of the bay, this time on a high tide. Hey! How did we get in the follow-me position again? Oh, well. They took us up the island a short distance to Dotham Cut, a deep passage between the islands into the very deep Exuma Sound.

The current was strong and we were essentially flushed out into the Sound by the current. We hit 10.2 knots over ground at one point. What a thrill. The rough water calmed as soon as we got a few boat lengths out of the cut and we headed south again, 52 nautical miles to Georgetown.

The winds were supposed to build during the day and were pretty consistent from the S-SW. Yep, we were taking it on the nose, but for most of the day it was only about 10-14 knots. We had a little mainsail out for stability. We left at 0645 and arrived in Elizabeth Harbor about 4 PM. We followed Ken through the waypoints to get to the anchoring field near Monument Rock. The water went from 10 feet in Black Point to over a thousand feet out in the sound. It went to 90 feet at Conch Cay Cut. We were back to 10-12 feet or less as we went from waypoint to waypoint to avoid the coral and then the shoals and sandbars. As we turned in we could see the sandy bottom again, beautiful clear blue water. There were lots of sailboats anchored in groups. There were dinghies running everywhere. We'd arrived in Georgetown during Regatta Week. Hooray!

We nosed about the anchoring field to find just the right place. We each anchored and then we both settled in for the night. The winds had built as predicted and it was getting a little bouncy but no problem, both of the anchors were buried in the sand (checked by looking into the water over the anchor from the dinghy to make sure) and we could sleep. It got a little more bouncy, making us get up every couple of hours to check our position, that we weren't dragging, and because it was crowded, nobody was dragging into us. The moon was full and we could see like it was daylight. Peaches finally got up for good around 0300 and watched from the cockpit. We didn't drag, and although the waves were still flecked with some white foam, we weren't uncomfortable. We couldn't wait to get off the boat and explore.

We were in the Monument anchorage field with Volleyball Beach the next one down. Georgetown itself is across the Elizabeth Harbor, about a mile. There were lights on the shore of Georgetown all night long. Monument Rock anchorage has a beach, with a small beach restaurant and a place with picnic tables for shore picnics. The Monument is a white pillar at the top of a hill covered in green plants and low trees. I can't wait to see the view from there!

Part of the atmosphere of Georgetown was from the Cruiser's Net. The Cruiser's Net is on the VHF channel 72 at 0800 and lasts for an hour or more. There are so many activities going on during the regatta weeks that the net is a busy place. You are nobody if you skip listening for a day. There are weather, announcements, welcomes to the new arrivals and safe journeys to the departing vessels. There is a quote for the day, and the cruisers like the open mike to speak. Some reminded us of the speed zones in town near the dinghy docks, or not to anchor in the shipping zone as the all-important food and fuel shipments come several days during the week. Some people put in reminders about VHF etiquette, and others asked for help fixing motors or generators. They asked for missing parts for their engines or, finally to offer some item off of their boat to a "new home" (sell something but you can't say that over the radio or you will have to pay Bahamas taxes).

So, I listened a bit and got more and more awed at the extent of the infrastructure that the cruising community had. There are events going every minute and I thought either you would love a place like this, or if not quite so social, might want to move on before it captures and morphs you into one of them. This place has been dubbed day care for retired adults, and I can see it already. But, I digress.

It was calmer on Sunday, so we got dressed and left to go to Volleyball Beach to have a look about, a drink, another cheeseburger and some cold Kalik beers in the Chat and Chill (absolutely perfect). We took another short dinghy ride and just before dark we were landing at St. Francis, a resort/restaurant complex. We were there to watch the Olympic hockey game between USA and CANADA, a rivalry between the two boats to say the least. The other reason we went there was to join in the every Sunday night trivia contest, four players on a team. Peaches was our ex-nun ace in the hole because there were usually a lot of religious questions. We got our drinks and watched the game (boy, the Americans couldn't even make eye contact with the official handing out the silver medals when it was all over, they were so sad). Oh, those Canadians were happy people at the bar here in the Bahamas. This is a little like civilization. I could hardly take my eyes off the big TV screen. Deprivation I guess.

Well, you probably know how we did. There were 40 questions. You write your agreed upon answer down, leave those blank you just can't come up with an answer for and fill them in later. Peaches handled the six religion questions as best she could (you know, it was a long time since her nun days). We all bobbled around with the rest of the questions. Interesting what you can find out about another couple by playing trivia. You can tell the book readers and the movie goers for sure. You pass your paper to the next table and you correct theirs. We were soooo bad! (16 missed out of 40). The winners only missed 4. We may have missed a lot of the religion questions. We will have a ways to go to make any favorable impression at this venue, but it was fun. I think we will stay below the social radar here if that is the best trivia we can manage.

We had a wet and sloppy ride home in the dark, going into some waves. We were safe enough, but I am not a fan of getting soaking wet, salt water in your eyes and try to guess in the dark when the next big wave is going to come. We'll have to get better at it here in Georgetown, where the dinghy is your key to all wonderful and some very necessary activities.

Today, Ken and I each took our dinghies and went across Elizabeth Harbor to Georgetown for gas (3 cans for me) and a water and 2 cans of gas for Ken. He was so kind, his 15 hp outboard would have gotten him there in no time at all, but my 5 hp was pretty wimpy and he slowed down for me (I kept mumbling I think I can, I think I can....all the way). We went into Victoria Lake, through a narrow fast current underpass from the harbor and pulled up to the dinghy dock at the ESSO sign. There were lines of cars for the fuel pumps, more cars than I've seen since rush hour in Nassau. We walked our little bags of trash through the park to the government dock and returned to get the fuel. I can't wait to go through the town.

Touring Georgetown is going to have to wait a couple of days as another low front is coming tomorrow afternoon and through Wednesday. We re-anchored this morning a little closer to shore as some other boats moved out. We wanted to be as protected and well anchored for all the westerly winds coming. This is Chris Parker, the weather guru's, Hum Dinger of a low front, so we have taken note. No real land protection this time. Not bad enough to abandon ship again. Peaches dove on our new anchor and it was not as we would have liked, so we re-anchored again with much success. We are making water and getting ready for a lumpy couple of days. Sounds like a good time to hunker down with a new book. More adventures later. We will be here through the month. Come visit.

Waiting outside the internet store in Georgetown, Bahamas

Chapter 48

Georgetown

03/08/2010 St Francis Restaurant and Resort, Bahamas

Our first real dingy trip into Georgetown was a good one. The crossing was smooth, but might be a different story when we go back to the anchorage and directly into the wind. Peaches has started wearing her foul weather red coat whenever we go in the dinghy so she doesn't get so wet. I go completely the other way and wear my swimsuit and just get wet. The Honda isn't a big enough engine to get our boat up out of the water and plane along. We just plow thorough. I'm thinking another bigger motor for next year, maybe like Ken's a 15 hp Yamaha (so sorry to my sons at Honda, the 15 hp Honda is too heavy for Peach and I to lift up onto the rail).

We entered through the narrow entrance to Lake Victoria, watching for boats coming out even though we have right of way. The gas dock to the right is short and usually has 3-4 dinghies tied there with gas and diesel cans tied into them. The regular dock, provided by the Exuma market, is full of dinghies from one end to the other, often there are two to three layers of dinghies, making it hard to push your nose into them and get to the dock to disembark. With some books to drop off at the library, groceries to get, we had folded grocery bags and my computer in tow in the red box on wheels. We had lots of time to go slowly.

Peaches has to stop occasionally to rest her back, so we got to do a lot of people watching. At the library, I found out that it is run by the cruisers on a volunteer basis. There are hundreds of books, all shelved by author and mostly paperbacks. You join for $3 and can take as many books as you donate. There are some hard bound books for sale too. I took as many as I gave, although I knew that made Peaches a little anxious about boat space. I read so fast, it will be a momentary pain for her.

We stopped at the Market, a long one story wooden building near the park. Like a lot of other buildings, it is painted turquoise. Inside, looking out at us are many women, selling straw hats, baskets, shells, jewelry and T-shirts. We didn't get anything there, although the vegetables looked nice. Any of you that know Peaches well, know she has an incredible collection of T-shirts from all the places she's traveled, all the races she has participated in, and from all the gifts people bring to her from their trips. I'll bet there were over 1000 shirts when we started cleaning out her basement before we left, all hanging on hangers. She hasn't bought one T-shirt since we started our trip! I got her one in Amelia Island because she has trashed a couple of hers by leaning over the batteries while working on the engine........holes everywhere. We didn't get straw because other cruisers have told us not to bring it on the boat unless it is sprayed with insecticide first and kept in a plastic bag for 6 weeks.

The next stop was the internet place. You could get internet for free close to the Exuma market, but it is sketchy at best. The other part is there is a lot of car traffic, with trucks pulling in to unload and people talking all around the one picnic table there, so on we went, all the way to the other side of town (on the same main road, not really a street except for the heavy traffic) I'd been to the internet place before with Connie and Ken and told Peaches about it, but you really have to go there to understand it. We finally came to it on the left, a long, low green building with a door not much taller than I am. You step down into the building and it is a little dark. There is a slanted board attached to the front wall, full of cruisers and their laptops, all frantic to get their internet business done or contact their families, or like us, trace our financial wellbeing. A couple of freezers are on the right when you walk in, with people standing and using them for desk room for their laptops. We waited our turn to sit on the white plastic chairs. While we waited, Peaches said this reminded her of her Fullbright Experience in India. "We called this a mud hut, painted." She might have used the word undeveloped in her description, but we did get on the internet and we got our business done for only $5.

Everyone's power cords snaked to one central outlet. The young owner and his wife scurried around helping people get on the internet, selling frozen Kool Aid cups, some cans and boxes of food items and for a small fee, the use of their cell phone to call home. The guy's main responsibility was to reboot the internet when it went down, every 30 minutes or so. He had a bunch of equipment piled in the center of the long room and on top of that was a huge wrench. When everyone was getting down on him for the lack of connection he would grab the wrench and go out back, supposedly to beat the server back into submission. He had a good sense of humor.

Our business done in the cramped room, we shuffled back to the center of town and got ready to do our grocery shopping. It looks like a grocery store, smells like one, and has carts like one. The produce section is your key to how recently they have gotten their supplies from Miami (not much local vegetables or fruits because there isn't much soil on these coral islands to grow them, almost all food is imported). If there is plenty, you can get just about anything. There are always onions, potatoes, limes, and unidentified tubers. The apples, peppers, melons and citrus fruit is expensive but when you want it, you get it. I have never carried apples home from the store so carefully or chose the time to eat it with so much thought! Everything is more expensive, the meat is all frozen, the beef cuts were hard to identify, so we used our frozen supply. Chicken was okay though. Butter was the best, either from Ireland or New Zealand and so sweet. The cookies were all from England, how nice. Potato chips were $8 for a bag as were snack crackers. It helped that we worked so hard to provision. I ran out of a couple of things that I just got, no matter what. I remember paying about $8 for a small bag of Panko bread crumbs, but I had scallops and just had to. Cheese was available, Swiss cheese and cheddar were both sold in big chunks for less than a dollar a pound. The problem, it was there sometimes and not others. You could always get eggs and bacon. It's not sounding too healthy so I'll stop with my gastronomic tour.

We got back to Star of the Sea, but the ride was long and wet because we went so slowly, hoping it would make it less waterfall-like. We had to hurry up and put stuff away and get dry and presentable because we were all invited to the motor yacht Utopia for drinks. An Austrian named Herb lives there and has loads of room for happy hours. All bearing food and drink, we arrived to join John, Jack and Linda from "New Attitude" who are from Cobb Island, MD. Reto and Sally were there from LaDanza, both from Switzerland (and Oregon). OZ was with us, from Toronto. We had a great time. The boat was so tall (high in the air) on the upper decks that we all felt like we were on a small plane. The talk ran from introductions to boats, to weather, to trials and tribulations of cruising to fishing stories. I was at that end of the group, so got to hear Herb's stories about shark fishing in an 8 foot dinghy.

Yep, you heard me right, lots of teeth, sharks usually longer than the 8 foot boat and it was a rubber boat! He apparently hooked what he thought might be a 12 foot hammerhead shark. It bit through the bait, pulled him around some then bit off most of the fish, eyeballing the little boat with the big man and all that bait in it. Herb said some lobster fishermen came along in a larger boat and one of them looked down over the side, shouting that it was indeed a hammerhead shark, but it was more like 22 feet long. The lobstermen pulled him out of there. There were more and more stories, each more unbelievable, but true. What a great time. I could hear the conversation at the other end of the boat, Peaches talking about not having any lights or electricity on the boat going down the coast of Florida. I was glad to be here listening about sharks instead (she wouldn't).

Herb showed Peaches and me around the boat before we left and we were very impressed with his art work in oil, wood, and some metal sculptures. He had an amazing hammered copper piece over his bed. He has reinvented himself several times during his life, but come back each time as an artist. We have met some truly intriguing people on our trip.

Saturday night was a great lasagna dinner on OZ with Reto and Sally from LaDanza. Connie didn't have all the regular ingredients for the meal, but cruisers are great at substitutions. Connie has done some awesome catering in her time and I've never eaten anything she'd made that wasn't top drawer. It was rich and flavorful and totally gone by the end of the meal (along with several bottles of red wine). We taught Reto and Sally how to play Nufie Poker, a card game we play with Connie and Ken a lot. It is easy, fun, and the most you can drop in a long evening of laughing is 75 cents. My brother caught on while he was with us and has spread it across Texas by now. Reto had a long run of beginners' luck ending with him taking home the pot of Sacajawea gold dollars Peaches and I play with, mixed with some Loonies from Canada (we didn't use quarters; fancy company, fancy coins).

Have I mentioned ARG (the Alcohol Research) meetings? This is an approved gathering of cruisers on Hamburger Beach for the express purpose of drinking, eating and talking (in that order I think). Everyone brings their own alcohol of choice and a finger food dish to pass. The time is well spent and our devotion to pure research like this is strong! Once a week in Georgetown during regatta week, ARG takes place. Rumor has it that this tradition carries on up the chain of islands as we head back to Nassau. I sure hope so!

Our plans are to stay here some more and relax. We entered the trivia contest with OZ for Wednesday and hope to do better than we did last week. We thought we were going to ace the last one with Peaches, the ex-nun, taking care of the religious questions. She didn't relate to the questions very well. We'll do better next (and the last) time. We'll go up to the top of Monument Hill for the Around the Island race to help the race commentators know who is in the front. I hope to get to the computer store and do my taxes on line. Always civilization is poking into our adventure.

Oh, Georgetown is called Chicken Harbor (as opposed to Velcro Harbor like Vero Beach) because people get this far and decide that it is too comfortable and safe to go any farther. The other thing that happens in Georgetown is that people come this far, stay and then start back toward home. There are people who leave their boats here in one of the hurricane holes (from June through November) and just fly down every winter. On the cruiser's net I've heard them say that they are going to pull up the chains at both ends of the harbor to keep everyone here (an old military trick). Georgetown turns out to have a little something for everybody. We look forward to a visit by our friend, Jeanne Wiebenga in a couple of weeks. Think about coming down yourselves. Despite the frequent low fronts coming through during this El Nino year, it is usually beautiful here. I'll keep on blogging.

Surf on the Exuma Sound side of Stocking Island, Bahamas (Photo: Jeanne Wiebenga)

Chapter 49

Georgetown Rediscovered

03/28/2010 Monument Anchorage, Georgetown, Bahamas

It is always a gift to see a place that has become yours, because of your length of time there, through someone else's eyes. Jeanne Wiebenga came from the hustle and bustle of Washington DC this week to spend time with us on our home anchored in Monument. She had her normal everyday stress to dump overboard and a strong desire to get some healthy tan (not as much an oxymoron as you might clinically think). She has done both as well and taken long walks on the beach and treks through the bush. Big smiles on her face and her shoulders are tan and relaxed. We've done our job well!

So, through her eyes, we've seen the beauty of the land and the beaches again. Also, through her eyes, we've seen our new Canadian friends. A new member added brings out stories you haven't heard before from your companion boats. Her good humor and sharp wit along with her Dutch accent, won her immediate inclusion in all we have done this week. We'll be sorry to see her fly out of Georgetown tomorrow.

It's been an interesting learning curve for her being on Star of the Sea. Jeanne didn't mind the motion of the boat at anchor, didn't have any problems clambering around the boat above and below decks, getting in and out of the dinghy or onto the docks. Her appetite was good, her ability to follow the strong research protocol of ARG (Alcohol Research Group) was perfect. She only had one small problem with life on the yacht. She doesn't like the head (bathroom) protocol. To us it seems common sense, something to be done to save the plumbing and the environment. Placing used TP into a small plastic bag and tossing it into the garbage does not come easily at first. There is always some fishing around in the bowl when you automatically drop it in. Pumping the handle to flush the bowl out with sea water and pumping it all out is also not pleasant. Your head is bent over the bowl so you can reach the handle and all you have deposited while you pump and pump and pump is swirling around right in your face, so to speak! ENOUGH SAID (even for a medical person). We didn't tell her about dumping in vinegar to clean everything out and salad oil to lubricate the rubber valves (a veritable salad dressing). Oh, sorry, again, enough said.

We took a great hike across Stocking Island (where the Monument is) to the ocean side. We walked and walked the beach looking for shells, taking pictures of the surf hitting the rocks and finally going around an outcropping of jagged rocks to the beach hidden on the other side. Tucked into the rocks in the tidal pools were black long-spine sea urchins. First a very large one and then as our eyes became better attuned to the pools, we saw hundreds of baby urchins between every crack in the rocks.

It was so different walking the rocks and tidal pools of the coast of Maine as a child and walking these rocks this week. The water here is absolutely clear, making it impossible to sense what the depth of the water you are going into with your next step. Do any of you remember the Scientific American magazine picture of an experiment done with kittens on a black and white tile floor, but with some of the tiles replaced with clear glass? I felt just like those kittens, unsure and so tentative to step out into nothing. In Maine, the sea water has more sediment in it and it is very clear what is rock and what is deep water. Today I only made one misstep and only lost a sliver of knee skin. A successful day.

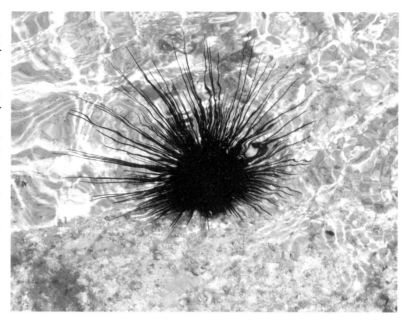

Jeanne is an OB/GYN doc but also a photographer. She saw the rocks and the edge of the sea differently than I had during many walks over the same beach. She found little families of snails, small multicolored shell dwellers in little "villages." There were some tenacious lichens, one cell plants who survive by breaking down the rocks. They were in deep pinks and reds and were everywhere.

Looking down into the water, not much is seen. There are very large starfish on the bottom that stand out on the pale sandy bottom, 10-12 feet down. We have seen small silver fish that come around the boat in the morning. There are some larger fish, needle nose and others, but not many and only in certain locations. There is a very rare dolphin in Elizabeth Harbor. There are numerous stingrays of all sizes that really stand out against the light sandy bottom, flying away under the water.

In the air, there were not as many birds as I thought there would be. Yesterday was the first day, in downtown Georgetown, that we saw gulls. I think they were black headed gulls, a large flock. When we climbed Monument trail up the steep hill, there was a large osprey nest sitting on top of the monument, made up of twigs, some over 2 inches in diameter. There were lots of man-made touches to the nest; blue and red braided marine line

and some plastic pieces. When we first crested the hill, the osprey took flight and soared above us for a while, hoping we would go away. When we didn't go, she did. I wish Peaches could have come up to see this with us, but the climb was too steep. Then, we heard the long, complex call from the small trees around the monument. A single Bahamas mockingbird was trying to draw us away from the monument and maybe from her nest. We followed her while she pretended to have a broken wing, taking short flights and dropping down again to chastise us roundly for still being there.

We went down the other side of the island and walked the beach along the Sound for an hour, totally alone on this huge stretch of perfect beach with only a couple of small sandpipers running in and out of the surf for company. Jeanne said that it could be a beach in any number of countries she's been to, from Australia's northeast coast, the Tasmania south east coast or the islands of Maui and Kauai on Hawaii.

On our return visit to the monument, the mockingbird was in the osprey nest, still with her cacophony of noises and her short broken wing leaps from the nest. There must be quite an arrangement between the female osprey and the mockingbird for her to be such a zealous guard of the big nest. We loved it, standing for 10 minutes at a time, arms outstretched with cameras at the ready, trying to catch her in her flights from the top of the monument, 50 feet above our heads.

Jeanne's time with us was short, but because it is island time, seemed slower, and gentler. It has been filled with good food, drink, and good company. Jeanne even graced our dinner last night with her rendition of the Dutch National Anthem, stirring!

We all took off Friday, the three of us from Star of the Sea in our dinghy, meeting up with Connie and Ruth, her company from Toronto, representing OZ. We went to volleyball beach to pick up Stephen and Natalie from Katmandu, who anchored there so their kids could join the crowd of teens and pre-teens on the beach every day. Our goal was to get further west on Stocking Island, to cut through a creek at high tide and go to Sand Dollar Beach on the Sound side to hunt shells. Unfortunately the waves were high and the winds were strong. The sun was warm and we were determined to get to our goal. In the short ride to Katmandu's boat, we were all soaked to the skin, salt in our eyes and on our lips, bailing the dinghy as we went. But, as I said, we were determined. Unfortunately, or fortunately as it turned out, we did not go as fast as the others in our dinghy with the 5 hp Honda, and soon the others came back to us, and we were headed to the Elizabeth Harbor side of Sand Dollar. Whew. Once you are wet, you cannot get any wetter, but we were all done with bashing into the waves.

We found a trail that went up one side of the mountain and down the other. The ocean beach was a huge pile of tumbled boulders of every shape and size. The cliff down to the beach looked impossible. Stephen and Jeanne gave it a try, with Jeanne persevering and making it down to the beach. Stephen, Stephanie (his youngest daughter) and I found a long convoluted way along the cliffs that eventually lead us to the beach. Our goal was to rescue Jeanne, who really didn't need rescuing. We couldn't stand watching her poke through the boulders for sea life and be content standing up on the cliff. The others eventually drifted off back down the trail to the safe beach. We had great fun climbing over the rocks, getting splashed by the surf and finding so much life in the cracks of the rocks. Oh, we got great pictures of it all. We finally returned up the convoluted path and reluctantly joined the others. They were all huddled around Natalie and Peaches on a wooden bench. Back on the beach, Natalie was patiently teaching her how to make a woven sailor's bracelet out of string.

Something to note; if your passage to the beach or wherever you go by dinghy was hard, wet and generally miserable and most importantly the winds don't change direction, your ride home will be smooth, dry, and fast. Ours was!

During Jeanne's stay, we still had some chores to do yesterday. We dropped her on the beach to walk and we took the dinghy to Georgetown for groceries, more rum and some new ($5) DVDs. No wind, smooth dinghy rides both ways, it was a real treat. We also started making water again yesterday and today for our trip to Staniel Cay on Monday after Jeanne flies back to Nassau, then to Baltimore. OZ with their company from Toronto will not leave until their company departs on Thursday. Weather is everything when you plan so we might all end up going together Friday if there are weather delays. We are ready whenever the weather gods are.

We're starting our 4th week here and my feet are itching to move on. Oz is ready to move north too. After their company departed I could see a big change in them. They were planning the near future, their lives in Canada poking into their nice time in the islands. Connie has a deadline to get back to Toronto by the end of April. Ken will stay with the boat in Titusville, Florida until it is ready to be put away for the summer.

So, sometime on the trip north through the islands, we will part company and make our way a little slower home. I can't even think about cruising without them. We will miss their company, their sense of humor and most of all their willingness to bring along a couple of smart but inexperienced Americans on their maiden cruising voyage to the islands. No amount of R/O water given to them during our stay will compensate them for what they've done for us! Our boat will be stored up the Cooper River in Charleston at Detyen's Boatyard for the summer. We have no real time schedule except we need to be out of the hurricane paths by June 1st (above Cumberland Island, GA).

First we will stop at Nassau again as Peaches' niece Kristen and her constant companion Mark will be there in a resort for a few days at the end of April. It will be so good to see them. I hope they can get tanned and de-stressed as effectively as Jeanne has done in a few days here with us. We look forward to seeing everyone this summer while we stay in my home near Chautauqua Lake, NY.I can't imagine being on dry land that doesn't move, walking from the living room to the kitchen without climbing up and down a ladder and lastly, being able to flush the toilet without watching it swirl away or bagging the TP!

Junkanoo, Easter Eve in Black Point, Bahamas

Chapter 50

Black Point Revisited

04/03/2010 Black Point, Bahamas

We pulled up our chain after more than a month in Georgetown, and the anchor actually pulled up out of the sand. It was buried by time and the frequent cold front winds passing through the Monument anchorage. It felt like weightlessness to be moving again, out the crooked path between the shoals in Elizabeth Harbor and out to the Exuma Sound, thousands of meters deep. The sea looked the color of the darkest blue ink, with white crests. The wind clocked around to the east, where we were the most protected in Monument. In the Sound, away from the protection of the island, the waves came from miles and miles of empty sea, where the fetch (or the distance that waves have to build up) was long. Today, Friday, was the third day of easterlies, so we're sloshing through 4-6 foot waves. The air is fresh, the salt spray from the bow was crisp white, and we are on our way back to Black Point. Perfect.

Both Oz and Star of the Sea have been left somewhat empty by our parting company, so we took Thursday, before we left to clean up the vessels, gather the dirty sheets, try to find places to pack away breakables and batten down the hatches again. The water tanks were full of our reverse osmosis water; we did tons of laundry (mostly salt encrusted clothes made wet on the long dinghy rides in strong currents and waves on the bay). Once clothes are wet with salt water, they stay wet until washed in fresh water (they actually attract water from the air until cleaned). We learned early in the game to strip up in the cockpit and never bring anything wet with salt water below (Connie from OZ is particularly insistent about this as she has real upholstery on her couches). We also learned to try to keep as much sand out of the boat as possible (an impossible task) .

We got familiar with moving at the slow pace of retirement in the islands. We read insatiably and even Peaches found she loved the Kindle. Connie became the newest and most enthusiastic Texas Hold-Um poker player, and we all became credible Nufie Poker players. We made all decisions based on the winds and the tides, nature being the controlling factor everywhere (yes, even where you are right now), but blatantly relevant in this boating community, where all transportation is by dinghy.

Our starting time today was fixed by the time we needed to cross through Dotham Cut back onto the banks and to Black Point. We needed to get there at slack tide or on an incoming tide; otherwise we would experience something called THE RAGE. This happens when the winds and the currents oppose each other and the huge waves are square topped and almost impossible to cut through for smaller or underpowered larger yachts. I checked our bucket list, and THE RAGE wasn't included. We set our arrival time at 5:30 to 6 PM, right after the tide turned. We set out in the easterly waves I mentioned above, so there was some wallowing. Stella, our autohelm, handled herself like a perfect lady, strong and dependable. Only an occasional big 7th wave threw us about. I decided early in the day that there would be no cooking going on in the cabin, and, peevishly felt sad we probably couldn't read en route.

Well, I was proven wrong. We set our sails (the main was a little recalcitrant and could only come out three quarters of the way) and off we went, OZ in their place at the lead. We each have GPS programs that tell you from minute to minute when you will arrive at your destination. It varied from 5:05 to 6:02 depending on our speed. The wind varied from 9-15 knots and the seas never changed, coming at us from the starboard side, white caps frothing. We settled into a good routine and I found I could read like a champ. This comes from someone who occasionally got quite car sick in the back seat of my parent's car. I started out carefully though, looking at the chart book, and gradually getting to the trio of Barbara Kingsolver books I started a couple of days ago. Peaches even reclined for a rest on the cockpit seats. Her vigilance when she awoke probably saved us from another clogged prop. There were batches of Sargasso weed floating, and one particular patch looked just like a large piece of particle board. We turned Stella off and swooped around it before it could foul the prop.

Just about 5:00 we neared Dotham Cut and went through it like greased pigs, no resistance, no square waves, an anticlimax due to good planning. We anchored in Black Point with many other boats filling the bay. We were with four others on our trip south. After anchoring, we took hot showers, dropped the dinghy and went to OZ for conversations and drinks. Home in the quiet darkness we dropped into bed, the sleep of contentment.

We've been taking thousands of pictures, thanks to living in the digital world. We get immediate gratification by downloading them to my computer. Jeanne allowed me to download all the pictures from her camera onto the computer before she left. The pictures are all in the raw state, needing sharpening, deleting, cropping or occasionally nothing done to them. I came across some pictures we took just before we left Georgetown. The subject, dolphins, finally! We were coming back in the dinghy from St. Francis and some internet time when we spotted a mature female with a baby going along the surface in front of us. Pictures at last. They seemed so big up close and from the one foot elevation of the dinghy. We followed along slowly behind them until we realized there were three other dinghies moving in on us. At that point it felt more like we were chasing the dolphins, not just enjoying their company. We broke off and went home.

We plan to stay at Black Point until Staniel Cay empties out after Easter. Then we'll stay there a while and work our way up to High Point when Ken and Connie will depart. Katmandu has arrived and the party has begun. It is just so much more fun with the three kids around, asking to visit the boat, hoping we'll let them play Nufie Poker with the adults. Stephen and Natalie are great friends, the ages of my boys but the age difference has disappeared down here. Another Canadian boat, Breathless with Doreen and Rick, was anchored near us in Georgetown. We met them on OZ for a happy hour a month ago. They are also moving slowly up the Exumas on the way back to Florida. We spoke with them and they are very willing to plan their crossing of the Gulf Stream to coincide with ours, giving us the buddy boat we want for safety going back across to Florida (we later found out that Ken and Connie set this up). How amazing that people come into your lives just when you need them. We are so lucky. Their boat is a Beneteau, about our size and their speed will be just about the same as ours.

It was Easter eve and we all got ready to go into "town" to watch the festivities. It was a night for Junkanoo! A Junkanoo band from Nassau arrived earlier in the day and the town was preparing for an all night long party. There were booths set up to paint the kids' faces, food stands lining the main (only) street and basketball contests going on. It was almost dark when we arrived after a hurried dinner on the boat. There was no room left at the big Government dock for the dinghies.

As we walked into town, the number of people on the street increased, kids were running around, teenagers were bumping into everyone, golf carts darting among the pedestrians. You had to watch your toes in your sandals so they weren't run over! The food smelled good, rum was flowing and we found Katmandu right away. The Junkanoo band was dressed except for their huge headdresses and they were tuning their instruments, shaking their tambourines, and talking the high quick talk of the islands. The whole town was vibrating.

Eventually, sometime after 9 PM they formed rows and started the music. I have never heard anything like this, trumpets, trombones and lots of drums. The beat was infectious, the noise way above the decibels of a fire siren, but it needed to be just like that. We moved to the music standing at the side of the street,

you couldn't help yourself. The musicians went by dancing and laughing as they played. It was totally dark but I was holding my camera at the ends of my arms, over my head and shooting blind. The shots were incredible. I didn't know who I got or what I got in the shots until we were back on the boat and I could download them. People's faces were transformed, elderly people were dancing along behind the band and children were on their father's shoulders. Young women, worn down by work and family, were free to shake their booty. It was perfect. I won't forget this night. As we walked back to the dinghies, the music kept on. The Junkanoo Band marched half a mile down the street then turned and marched back, all night long. Back in our boats, the music came across the water, just the beat of the drums.

Easter Sunday we all (Katmandu, OZ and Star of the Sea) went to OZ for a pot-luck Easter dinner. There was plenty of rum, wine, good food and extended Nufie Poker to keep us entertained. While we played in the salon, the kids watched a movie on the computer up in the cockpit. Speaking of entertainment, before dinner Ken and Stephen, two engineer-types, were trying to make fresh coconuts from the beach into rum cups for their Easter drinks. Two men with knives, plastic Kool Aid cups and a lot of ambition to drink their drinks finally

succeeded. The cups leaked but like two 4 year olds, they were happy because they did it themselves!

We left Monday afternoon late to come the hour or so to Staniel Cay. The winds were in the 14-18 knot range, big waves, and the water was about 12 feet deep. We managed to anchor in the middle of a pod of super yachts at a place called Piggy Beach. More on that later. Peaches and I went into town with Ken and Connie, stopping at the Staniel Cay Yacht Club for lunch. I say this like we go out for meals all the time, but we just don't. There aren't many places and Connie, Natalie and I are such awesome cooks, we prefer eating together on the boats. The Yacht Club is going to be the source of internet for us while we are here. On our way back, Peaches and I will take the dinghy into the beach near our boat and feed our leftover lunch to the swimming pigs. More stories later.

The picture at the top of this chapter is me, working extra hard to get the last blog out to you before going to Black Point. You can see the strain and fatigue running off of my face.................really. It's hard to write this stuff, really it is.

Piggy Beach, Staniel Cay, Bahamas

Chapter 51

What is the Name of this Beach?

04/09/2010 Staniel Cay, Bahamas

I am not able to confirm that pigs can fly, but, boy oh boy, can they swim! We anchored right in front of Piggy Beach at Staniel Cay. The anchoring over near town in the next bay is not as sheltered and is very shallow with some rocky areas.

There are 4 wild pigs that live on this island and they are not the kind that needs to forage for their food. It is hand delivered to them by the hordes of tourists who visit Staniel Cay, either cruisers or the paying guests on the mega yachts anchored all around us. Our lunch at Staniel Cay Yacht Club (definitely not a stuffy wear your tie to dinner place!) yielded a lot of leftovers so Peaches and I couldn't wait to feed the pigs.

When we got to the beach, another boat was being assaulted by the swimming pigs. They float like corks, for sure. Well, it seems that they're not really vegetarians but are "carbitarians" as they only wanted the bread. They let all the good lettuce and other vegetables bob out on the waves, fighting for the bread. Pigs at a distance are interesting, but up close with us sitting in a rubber boat, they are like vicious sea creatures with wide open mouths and lots of teeth. Their sharp hooves as they tried to climb into the dinghy with us to get more food looked like sharp knives! My tactic was to wait until they closed their mouth and then pushed on the convenient pink snout (nose) to get them away from the boat. During the day, every day, more than 30 boats feed these floating eating machines!

We've been in Staniel Cay for 4 days and our family has finally been completed when Katmandu arrived on Wednesday afternoon. We have so much fun with Stephen, Natalie and the kids. Wednesday night we had another big card game, this time on Star of the Sea. We six adults went at it with all the concentration that people have who are not worried about going home to sleep because they need to get up the next day for work. We laughed, told stories, drank rum and generally battled our way to midnight. It was Connie and I at the end, everyone else had their quarters to the kitty. Connie, the Queen of Poker, had luck as well as skill working for her and won. Despite my command of most things, I am so not the Queen of cards.

On Thursday, we calculated low tide so all three dinghies could go to Thunderball Grotto to snorkel into the grotto and around the island to see the fish, the coral and all the stalagmites and stalactites. It was great fun, but because of my claustrophobia, I declined to swim as I thought you had to dive under the rocks to get in and then under the rocks on the other side to get out again. That was not my idea of a good time. As it turned out, there was an opening about the height of your head at low tide, so I would try it another time. I was official dinghy watcher and picture taker. All the others came out so excited, Stephen saying I should jump in right now and he would pull me though. What a guy.

Everyone in the dinghies and the diving stuff stowed away, our three dinghies turned around to the back of the island, past a rocky beach that had a wrecked sailboat, not much smaller than ours, up against the rocks. We landed the dinghies a little down the beach where the rocks were less treacherous. Francis immediately saw some wild goats. Even by getting a big stick for a staff and pretending to be a shepherd, he couldn't lure them out of the bushes. We all explored the wreck, but everyone felt like we were trespassing on somebody's grave. Our hairs were standing straight up. We managed to launch the dinghies without putting holes in them. The waters and the shoreline (called the Majors) deserved one picture after another, they were so colorful. After about an hour we got back to Piggy Beach, yep they were being fed again.

Late Thursday night, Ken from OZ came to our boat and had our water cans, some tools we lent to him and his apologies that they were leaving in the morning. I knew this was coming, but I don't think even Ken thought it was going to come so fast. They must have worked very hard to get everything tied down, but Chris Parker's weather forecast made it clear to them that they had a two day window to get back to Florida. There wouldn't be another window for weeks, so off they went. Remember, true sailors and especially cruisers don't make firm plans until the weather sources are consulted. Sometimes precipitous leave taking happens, sometimes longer than wanted stays happen. We all talked in the morning in the VHF before they sailed out of the harbor, but with big lumps in our throats. We felt a little like orphans. They'd become such good friends and such mentors (even if we never did win at cards!). Connie is a weather guru, a consummate chef, and has a heart as big as the boat. Ken is tall, with a dry sense of humor and a laugh as big as he is. They will be missed. We have planned to get together at home this summer, maybe half way between our homes in Niagara on the Lake. We hope Katmandu can come too.

So, this morning, I don't feel so much like an orphan as I do empowered. We really have learned a lot, gained courage, and magically, we can see our way home by ourselves. OZ, as I mentioned, already set it up with Breathless to go back across the Gulf Stream with us.

Today we are in Staniel after our snorkeling trip to Thunderball Grotto, where I went into the water with all the others. Stephen and Peaches stayed close to me just in case I freaked out or cramped up. I got a couple of free rides from Stephen when the current got strong. Good friends. We are doing internet at the Yacht Cub and we filled our diesel and gas jerry cans. Peaches has made arrangements for a 4 person golf cart to tour the island and get groceries from the pink store, the blue store, the bread lady, and anything else we see on the way. She couldn't have walked all the hills and valleys of the island, so this was cool for her, decadence for the rest of us. (As it turned out, we ordered the golf cart but it was on island time, so wasn't going to come today). Stephen and I took off across the island on our own two feet (each) to the stores. We hit the blue store, the bread lady store, and ended up at the pink store to get onions, tomatoes and butter. Who needs a golf cart? Stephen's arms got pretty long carrying the majority of the bags........nice to have a young, strong friend along. We will be relaxing on the boat a few days and then start working our way up the island chain toward Nassau and more adventures.

Oh, the pigs. I just downgraded them from pure sea monsters back to pigs. Francis, from Katmandu, rode with us this morning in the dinghy to go snorkeling and he said he'd seen 10 baby pigs on the beach when he woke up this morning. Katmandu is a catamaran and can anchor in very shallow water, so they are close to the beach. BABIES, I'd better get some more old bread out of the galley. She is eating for eleven.

**Sharks in 3 feet of water at the dinghy docks, we were careful
climbing down to our dinghy! Staniel Cay, Bahamas**

Chapter 52

Anchoring, the Long and Short of It

4/10/2010 Piggy Beach, Staniel Cay, Bahamas

We are sitting in Staniel Cay, newly anchored closer to Piggy Beach so we will be more protected from the northeast winds that are coming in. With OZ gone, our immediate access to Chris Parker is cut off, although Katmandu does get it and it is posted in the Staniel Cay Yacht Club. I guess what we really don't have is Connie's interpretation of Chris' weather report. We are staying here through next Thursday so the day to day predictions are not as life changing as they might be if we had a definite schedule to keep. I might not set the alarm to get up for the local weather lady at 0800 from Blue Yonder. I talked a bit about her earlier, but here's some more now that we are in her backyard. She is very technical, telling those at Staniel what days are best for snorkeling and especially calm enough in the Sound to fish. She takes her reports from Chris and also from NOAA/Nassau weather predictions throwing in her own comments if she feels the others are wrong or hedging their bets. She's been on the air since 1995, lives on one of the small islands and is an institution all unto herself. The thank yous coming from all the listening boaters after she is done via the VHF radio are only small compensation for such a big service for the cruising community.

Our new anchorage closer to Katmandu is just off the beach in 8 feet of clear blue water. An improved view (of all the pigs) is part of our new position in the harbor. We haven't talked much about anchoring in the blog as we were in Georgetown on the same anchor for the whole month. Now, we have re-anchored three times, not because we dragged, but for better and better positioning with the winds and the other boats in the bay.

Peaches and I have been anchoring all the way down the east coast and in the islands, but you can never learn enough about getting it right. Conversation, everywhere there are cruisers, will always have an anchoring component. So, here is what we know at this point in our cruising lives. You need an anchor that is heavy enough for your boat. You also need an anchor that does the job. Some are better in sand, some in rocky bottoms, some, but few in grassy areas. You also should have a spare anchor.

We have a CQR, 35 pound anchor with a plow on a swivel arm (see picture from Beaufort about the Anchor Buddy). We have 250 feet of chain attached to the anchor with a swivel connector. There is another 50 feet of rope rode attached to the chain with a splice (thanks to Charlie Obersheimer of Buffalo). Last, but most important for everything to work out perfectly, this rope rode is tied firmly to the boat!

It takes two to tango and it also takes two to anchor. The famous comment of those who are anchoring goes like this: some days you are the audience and some days you are the entertainment, we have been both. A sure source of entertainment and a little anxiety for those already anchored in the area (and who have staked out their area of comfort around their vessels) is watching a newcomer come at them.

The large mega motor yachts come in and use their bow thrusters to position, drop their massive anchors and because of their size, they go where they want. The rules feel a little different for them than for us. The entertainment connected to the mega yachts is in watching the crew making the boat ready for the passengers. Cooks are running in the power boats to get the supplies, the other crew are launching the ski boats, getting the sun protection up, and in the most recent case, the treadmill onto the top deck (sweating with a view rather than to the oldies). The real show with these mega yachts starts when it gets dark. The underwater lights come on under the back deck and it looks like there are blue lights shooting 20 feet out of their back ends. Peaches felt my jealousy and hung her diving light over the edge of the swim platform but it just wasn't the same.

The anchoring entertainment comes when another sailing yacht arrives, weaving itself into a position where there will be good holding, protection from the winds and currents, and in a lot of cases, near their buddy boats. This is when those sitting with their cool drinks under the bimini of the cockpit, their books abandoned for the moment, get protective of their space. In the anchoring boat, one person is at the helm, one on the bow of the boat with the remote control for the windless in their hand, the walkie-talkie hanging around their neck (or in more electronically advanced crews, the headset with microphone). This is so that the married couple or in our case crewmates don't yell at each other (high entertainment for the crowd).

In our case Peaches is on the bow and I am at the wheel. We use hand signals a lot; go left, go right, slow down, back up, go forward. Perfect conditions are no wind, no waves, no currents. The anchoring this morning was like that. Peaches lowers the anchor after I have stopped the forward movement of the vessel, letting out 30-40 feet of chain. Then, I slowly back at her direction, as straight as possible, to see if the plow part of the anchor catches in the sand (mud). If it has, I back down on it at 1000-1500 rpm. This sets the anchor. Then we back slowly and straight (ly) until the right amount of chain is out.

Beginners usually put out too much chain (paranoia), and we are still considered beginners. Normal anchoring situations use a scope of 5 feet for every foot of depth. Storm conditions require 7-9 feet for every foot of depth. We are in 9 feet of water, expecting extended days of 28-30 knot winds so put down 120 feet of chain (this is a very common length of chain to place for a boat our size)......we have had as much as 200 feet out for the big blow we went through in Georgetown. Ken says we will get a better feel for it after a while.

The only drawback of more chain than needed is the boat swings around the anchor almost the whole length of the chain down, so with 120 feet, you might move as the wind clocks around the compass as much as a 200 foot diameter circle. So, the good news, we have lots of room around us right now. The winds are expected from the northeast. The island is to our east and it curves around so we are well protected.

If you are yawning or skipping ahead to find some humor in this tiresome dialogue, here it is. More cruising adventures have ended abruptly because of the anger and frustration generated between couples trying to anchor under difficult conditions. Things are said in fear and frustration that would never come up in any other land-based arguments. I have heard a perfectly lovely couple call each other idiots, threaten bodily harm if the person on the bow doesn't stop shouting and, in the worst case scenario, advise the person on the bow that as soon as the anchor is down they are taking the dinghy to the shore and a cab to the airport.

Most of the conversation is done at full voice, using all of the colorful swear words attributable to sailors (no shit!). With a particularly botched anchor job in a heavily populated anchorage, at the point where the swear words are flowing, the other boat owners are out on their bows or their swim platforms. They are getting ready to fend off the newcomers before they put a hole in the side of their homes, boat hooks pointing at the offending newcomers. Often the audience also has their VHF radio mike in their hand, doing some shouting of their own.

So, to let you know, the cruising fraternity is normally a helpful and willing teacher to newcomers, but you need to ask for help before it will happen. Barging into a harbor full of anchored boats without using the VHF radio for assistance makes you all on your own. Boat hooks with be pointed at you. But, if you try and fail or if you are hesitant or unsure of the local waters, make a call on the radio and they will give you more information than you could possibly use and a lot of people who will help.

What classifications do Peaches and I fall into? How about beginners with about 7 months of anchoring experience? We no longer shout at each other much, we try not to take offense for anything said during the anchoring procedure and we are usually successful. We have anchored in totally pristine creeks in the estuaries of the Carolinas and in swift and deep harbors, notably Beaufort NC. We've anchored in soft conditions like this morning; with crystal clear waters, no winds and no appreciable currents. We have also done it in crowded conditions in 26 knot winds (last Monday afternoon here in Staniel Cay). We will still be perfecting this when our eyesight is not as good and when it is harder to hear over the noise of the chain, but by then we will be not just old, but old salts.

One more thing about anchoring. Our friends aboard Katmandu have teased us unmercifully about our unwillingness to move our big boat to see new places (in Georgetown) or make shorter dinghy rides to get to town. Stephen indicated (with a straight face, mind you) that we must have bought the anchor that expires after 10 uses (it goes up in a puff of smoke like the tape player of instructions on Mission Impossible). He, on the other hand bought the one that you can use as much as you like. Up and down as many times as necessary. Their 28 foot catamaran goes to town and anchors to shop and take on water, returns to the anchorage with their buddy boats, then to volleyball beach for the kids. In Georgetown, they must have moved 10-12 times while we sat in one secure spot. So, we have moved three times here already and the anchor is still there, stuck into the sand. A point well taken, Stephen.

One more thing, there is a thing called a lookey bucket, a bucket with a clear bottom. With this bulky tool, you can go in your dinghy, follow your chain to the anchor and look to see if it is truly buried in the sand. We did that today, using Katmandu's bucket. It was buried deeply in the sand. PERFECT.

So, this is one of the chores on the boat that never comes up in our land-lives. We are going to have quite a shock coming back to a house where you don't have to think about where the electricity is coming from or whether your water supply is sufficient. We won't have to protect every single item of clothing, books or electrical equipment in plastic zip-lock bags.

But, we won't get to see the stars every night, feel the wind in our hair, sense the motion of the waves and currents under our bare feet on the deck. We won't be rocked gently with the waves to sleep or hear the gurgling of the water against the hull. We won't have nearly the excitement looking into the water when a shark or a large ray swims by or dolphins play near the boat. We won't see birds normally in our woods and fields at home sitting on a rocky shore or running on the beaches of the islands. We won't feel the freedom of setting our course and sailing with all sails set, all flags flying and smiles on our faces. Driving to the store will be very anticlimactic. We shall have it both ways.

Star of the Sea, Out.

**A trip to the Blue Store, all meat is frozen includingthe tube of conch!
Staniel Cay, Bahamas**

Chapter 53

Hitchhiker in Paradise

04/16/2010 Staniel Cay, Bahamas

So, what do you do if you are trapped in paradise by some bothersome winds out on the Sound and small craft warnings? You just have a good time. Other times when the weather has been stormy, bad weather has been a big brick wall to get over to make passage to where we wanted to go. This time, it has been a pleasure. Despite the strong winds, we are totally protected here at Staniel Cay near Piggy Beach. Our anchor is dug in, we are close to shore so we have a full view of the tourists feeding the pig families and our friends on Katmandu and Mad Cap a couple of boat-lengths away.

June from Blue Yonder has kept us entertained with the weather forecast every day at 0800. Every morning we tune in and, almost with relief, we decide to stay another day because it is so nice here. Our only concession to the winds is that we haven't gone into town for three days. Today, we venture forth. The winds have slowed us down and made us realize we don't have to rush to Nassau for our company until the weekend. So, what have we been doing?

First of all I want to report that our buddy boat OZ made it to Lake Worth, Florida (above Miami) last weekend. They crossed the Gulf Stream in a very narrow weather window and all on their own. OZ is a heavy, beautifully intrepid vessel and she carried Ken and Connie safely to the US, despite some big waves and rain just before Florida (and their radar was out). We were so relieved to hear they made it safely, and thought you would want to know too.

Peaches has become a voracious reader. Tom Clancy seems to be the most likely author but I think she is reading Bill Clinton's autobiography today. I've just finished the three novels by the late Swedish author Stieg Larsson (*The Girl with the Dragon Tattoo*, *The Girl Who Played with Fire*, and *The Girl who Kicked the Hornet's Nest*). They were convoluted and great reading. We also trade DVDs with the other boats, so movies at night are a treat and an excuse to pop popcorn the old fashioned way, on the stove. There is no TV reception, so we are still very news ignorant. It actually feels pretty good. Watching the news is very stress producing. I don't miss it right now.

Peaches has been in the water as much as possible. The bay is shallow (isn't everything on the Bahamas Banks?) and safe to jump off the back of the boat. The kids from Katmandu come daily, sometimes twice daily to see if she "can come out and play with us." She usually does, snorkeling with them into the beach, finding treasures all the way. Someone has the zip-lock bag full of scraps to feed the pigs and then carry back their treasures from the deep. On both of the vessels, there is a bag filling up after meals and snacks just for the pigs (being "carbitarians" they even like popcorn, but so do we so they don't often get that in their bags).

Snorkeling is a sport that is low in cost (no tanks to fill with air, no regulators to get certified), is good for every age (there is a 50+ years difference in age between Stephanie and Peaches, for instance), and you never know what you are going to see. The Hermit crab is one example of a surprise for the kids. They have seen barracuda, rays, sharks, yellow jack and lots of unidentified fish. Francis has a great fish ID book on Katmandu so he could tell that it was a Remora under their boat. Yesterday they were surrounded by miniature jellyfish, thousands of them. We found out this morning that they are called thimble jellyfish and they will sting you if you caught them between your shirt or shorts and your skin. It is recommended that you not wear a

T-shirt that is loose, as they will get under it and you will be an itchy brother for a few days! This swimming is perfect exercise, better that a Stairmaster or an elliptical.

So, I hitchhiked a ride aboard Katmandu today. As I said in the anchoring chapter, they move their home to where they need to be rather than transport the five member family in a small boat with their water jugs, garbage, computers, and fuel jugs. I rode over along with two other hitchhikers from Mad Cap. Beth and Jim hooked their dinghy on the back of Katmandu so they could go home (with the wind, surfing the waves rather than crashing into them like they would have to go to town). In a boat absolutely full of Canadians, I rode with a fresh cup of coffee in my hand, my camera at the ready and not a drop of sea water touched my freshly washed shirt and shorts. It was a miracle!

We plan to move back up to Exuma Park to anchor overnight. We'll go with Katmandu and it should be a nice short day, only 15 nautical miles. Then we might then go to Norman's Cay, a place where there is a plane wreck in the bay from a drug runner who was shot down. Every little island and cay has a story for sure. We are heading to Nassau so that we can meet our company on Tuesday. I expect a fresh wave of homesickness to hit us when they leave after a few days with us, especially Peaches. As we come back up through the islands we are seeing old friends who are also going north. Everyone is tan, relaxed, and trying to use up all the extra supplies and provisions on their boats before hitting Florida. At that point, anything still in your boat needs to be transported home or donated to a soup kitchen. Our meals are starting to be strange combinations of non-related food items.

In my mind, I'm already making piles of items that probably won't be needed next fall when we head back to the islands. We don't need so many clothes, so many hats or quite so many books (I can't imagine I just said that, but the Kindles have overtaken our need for new books every other day). A lot of the packing we did "by the book" was pretty much on the mark. We had plenty of paper towels, garbage bags, zip lock bags and TP (all expensive in the islands). Thanks to OZ we were well supplied before leaving the US with crackers, chips and stuff to make happy hour munchies (pistachios were the big hit!) These are triple or more the cost in the US. Peaches slept in the V-berth with these delicate items on the shelves surrounding her bed. Any tossing and turning on her part at night was a potentially crunchy event. We ran short of pretzels and pistachios. Sam's Club here we come before we leave in the fall.

We'll need more shrink wrapped coffee beans from Premiere. Most of the coffee I tried down here has been little more than dark colored sawdust. All my "useless" spices and seasonings" and the salt and pepper grinders survived the damp and sometimes bumpy conditions on the boat, and they were all liberally used to make chicken taste different every night of the week. Peaches thought we could just get away with the salt grinder. Also, for anyone who has to pack away for a trip like ours, Knorr Leak soup can be incorporated in anything and make it taste better.

The long shelf-life milk is not really palatable to Peaches at least, but it works well in cooking. We should make our own bread for the most part, unless there is a bread lady on shore. We needed to pack more of the single serving ice tea mixes to put in our reusable water bottles. We needed a great deal of fluids to stay feeling well.

Another last thought on our packing job, you can never have enough rum, gin, bourbon or wine on board. In our case, we originally packed it all on the starboard side of the boat and only now that we are ready to return to the US, is the boat leveling off due to our consumption from our liquor cupboard and wine cellar (all those happy hours). I am waiting for my ride back to Star of the Sea. Being on the internet for the better part of today has really been a treat, but I am ready to get back to the quiet of the boat, my home.

Passage from Shroud Cay through the Mangroves (by dinghy) to Exuma Sound, Bahamas

Chapter 54

Shroud Cay, A Day in the Mangroves

04/20/2010 Nassau, New Providence Island, Bahamas

We broke free of our anchorage in Staniel Cay, leaving Katmandu and Mad Cap behind us at Piggy Beach. Peaches broadcast the Canadian Nation Anthem, played by the Orlando Philharmonic, over the VHF as a tribute to our dear Canadian friends. I don't know about them, but we had huge lumps in our throats. It's hard to leave such good people. But, we are Star of the Sea and we are spreading our wings, solo this time. It feels just super!

We hit the first waypoint on the navigation program (and on Peaches handheld Garmin), turned north and tried valiantly to set our mainsail (an in-mast furling mainsail). It would come out past the first batten, then it wrinkled up terribly at the top. We reeled it in and out, in and out carefully with no success. Finally, Peaches remembered how we fixed this in the Chesapeake, two circles of the boat fast through the eye of the wind and the sail was free. Out it came, and with the wind on our starboard quarter, off we went, with Stella our trusty autohelm keeping the course.

It was a beautiful day to sail, the wind at our backs, surfing the small waves comfortably. There were big white clouds with streaks of mare's tails up higher. The winds were in the 10-15 knot range and, for a change, I could have asked for a bit more wind. We were moving at about 6.2 knots over ground. All was right with the world.

Our trip was exciting in a calm way, all alone on the Bahamas Banks for the first time. I kept thinking I would see the back of OZ somewhere, the yellow brick road winding up their stern, but no such luck. They are safely in Florida, working their way to Titusville where Connie will fly home and Ken will stay to slowly work on the boat. Our first solo voyage went very well. I read a lot, made lunch for us, monitored Stella a bit while Peaches monitored the Garmin, watched Stella and relaxed (key word). Before we knew it, we had covered the 30 nautical miles and were pulling up to a mooring ball right next to Breathless.

We watched a movie during dinner and before bed and slept the sleep of solo sailors. This morning, we heard from Katmandu and found they were underway, as was Mad Cap, with all their electrical problems behind them. Jim had some disturbing electrical failures on the boat and Stephen spent a couple of days trying to get him functional again. They were en route to Shroud! How great is that!

Rick from Breathless suggested a dinghy trip through the Mangrove trees. It is a creek that is only able to be used when the tide is high, and goes through the island to Exuma Sound. We readied our cameras, pumped up the dinghy (still a valve problem), checked the gas tank and off we went. Another couple, Elaine and Bill on Triumph from Toronto, came in their dinghy. They were anchored near Breathless.

We followed Rick and Doreen around the end of the island and into a cut in the shore. The Mangroves swallowed us up as we carefully watched the shallow waters. In this case, it didn't hurt to have experienced guides to lead us through all the twists and turns (all the turns looked the same). This is part of Exuma Park and the moorings and the property is all managed by them. Some of the channels are off limits to motorized dinghies but sea kayaks are perfect to protect the mangroves. All the dinghy drivers, myself included, stood to drive with the extension handles on the outboard so we could better see the shallow waters. We are in a no wake zone this morning. We planned the trip for high tide so we could go, walk the beach on the Sound, and (a big and) have enough water to get the dinghies back. Rick and Doreen said they once pulled their dinghy close to 2 miles to get out to where the water deep enough for them to put the outboard down into the water. I said we had experienced guides, very experienced.

There weren't as many birds or fish as I expected. Doreen told us that the white birds flying over us near the shore were White-tailed Tropicbirds and a small number of Rose-billed Tropicbirds. They are white with tern-like wings and a long narrow tail feather. They are about 30 inches long, the rose-tailed are a bit smaller. They do an amazing mating dance in the sky, but seem to be all in pairs now (we missed it). My Sibley's Guide say that this is one of the only places that they are seen in the east as they are normally seen in lower California and Mexico. They are beautiful, but fly too high to get a picture.

Our day in the mangroves and later going up to Driftwood Point for the view and the lizards was perfect. The piles of debris on the Sound beach were unbelievable. We found bits of line and some interesting boat pieces and parts. Bill even found a motorcycle helmet. Cruisers walking this beach (actually most beaches) pick up man-made debris, especially plastic, and pile it in one place for pick up. All you drop overboard eventually finds a home on the beach. It makes you think hard about what you do. We walked and walked on the beach, head down, looking for shells. Peaches didn't walk far, but she went in the other direction than we did and found a sea bean.

Doreen, Rick and Peaches all found sea beans that wash up from the shores of Africa. There was a hamburger bean, a heart bean and a Mary bean (has an indented cross in the surface). Doreen said people polish them and make them into really stunning jewelry. Along the way we saw a lot of shell-less crabs buried in the sand to stay safe. You could see right through them!

Later, our happy hour on Star of the Sea was so much fun, with Natalie and Stephen, Jim and Beth from Mad Cap and Doreen and Jim. Triumph left for Norman's Cay shortly after we got back from the Mangroves. The stories went on and on, and we added ours on top.

We intend to leave early in the morning to make our next solo flight to Nassau. The weather looks good, the winds will be behind us and then to the west, no rain predicted. The other boats will move on to Norman's Cay to see the sunken drug-runner plane. Katmandu and their kids will stay to do the Mangroves first. We'll see everyone later in Nassau.

We left at 0715 and had coffee and pancakes along the way. It got windier and it went from westerly to winds from the north as we entered the eastern end of the Nassau Harbor. About two thirds of the way to Nassau, we crossed the Yellow Banks, an area of dense coral heads. We timed it perfectly, to go over them at high tide, about noon. Even though it was 10-18 feet of water, the coral heads (they look like dark round formations) make you want to steer around them as it was impossible to guess how far under the surface they were. The winds were 18-20 knots through this section so, with Peaches on the bow pointing where I should go, and me calling the depth meter readings, we got through. It was hard, but we weren't experienced enough to feel safe just going through with our 6 foot keel hanging down.

We reserved a slip at the Nassau Harbor Club a week ago, but couldn't confirm this until we were almost there. Lady Hawk, people we met in Georgetown (and who grew up in Kenmore near Peaches) heard us calling the marina and said they would stand by if we needed anything.

The dock handlers and the manager himself were at the slip to catch the lines. As we made a last tight circle to come into the west side of the dock, I realized that I hadn't been this close to other boats and particularly a big heavy dock for over 2 months (since we left Nassau). It all came back in a rush, with Peaches' guidance from the deck and we slipped into the spot just like we'd been doing it daily, all or our lives. Slick as...............well, slick stuff.

We got the lines secured, hooked up to shore power (a shock for the batteries, pun fully intended, although they were fully charged from the alternator). We hooked to the water with our hose and gleefully washed all the accumulated salt off of the decks, the anchor locker, the canvas, the cockpit and cushions and the dinghy. Then we tumbled down the stairs into a puddle of tired, fortified ourselves with some popcorn, a G&T for Peaches and a Dark and Stormy for me. A hot shower for each of us was next. Wonderful. Kristen and Mark fly in tomorrow, so first thing tomorrow, a civilized breakfast and a cup of real coffee (and free internet). I hope to get all the bedding washed in the marina laundry (too big for the whuppa whuppa).

It is morning, Tuesday April 20th and we are in Starbucks, higher than kites on the caffeine and putting our internet lives back together. Someone warned us to be sitting down when we took our first sip of coffee, it will hit us like a brick bat (it did).

We can't believe the noise around us now that we are back in civilization. There are people talking, horns blaring, and music everywhere but discordant, and lights that shine into your cabin when you're trying to sleep............hey what is this? We'll get used to this, but we will be back on the boat again this fall, looking for the quiet and the darkness at night with stars above us again.

The "prisoners" from the Cruise boats, packing in every
minutes of their 5 hours of fun the Nassau, Bahamas

Chapter 55

Nassau and Eventually the Berry Islands

04/29/2010 Frazer's Hog Cay, Bahamas

Going to Starbucks every morning never got old. Internet and coffee, a little Skype phone conversation thrown in, how could that be bad? With Kristen and Mark in town from Tuesday (4/20), we saw a totally different side of Nassau than we did in early February. With OZ and my brother Bob, we went through customs, had some dinner and shopped for supplies. We've become tourists this time around.

We went to Harbourside Marina just down the street from our marina to look at Yamaha outboard motors. We were very underpowered (read this totally wet dinghy occupants) with our 4-stroke 5 hp Honda. We loved the reliable engine, but we were WET. I think every blog I wrote made mention of at least one horrible journey to get groceries, get diesel and gas or all three at once. We were soaked with salt water and had to dump all the wet clothing in the cockpit. NO MORE!

We bought a 2-stroke 15 hp outboard that is bigger than the Honda, weighs only 17 pounds more and we'll be able to go in the high seas with the best of the cruisers (I know this is not particularly an eco-friendly move on our part but it is all about the weight and ease of repair down here, everyone has a Yamaha). We also found out that it is the #1 stolen outboard in the Bahamas. So, anyone who is interested in an intrepid Honda, only driven by 2 elderly 62 year old ladies for one season, please call or email us today (end of advertisement).

After purchasing the motor, to be delivered tomorrow morning to the boat, we took a taxi to the Wyndem to meet Kristen and Mark. Well, it was kind of an island time taxi as we went to pick up the driver's son from school first, heard all about his family and the older son who was going to start college in IT-computer training. During the detour, we saw parts of Nassau we never would have seen on our own. We were shown where the doctors and lawyers lived, where the best local food is served, where the fort is located. There is a big

pile of sand dredged from the harbor for the luxury liners to enter and dock in the harbor. Finally we were where all the hotels are. He said he heard the Chinese have bought the Wyndem Hotel, where Kristen and Mark got such a cheap deal on the flight/hotel package. The Chinese want to go head to head with the huge Atlantis complex on Paradise Island. It may have taken an hour to go 5 miles, but it was worth it. We walked into the Wyndham and Peaches got to see her family for the first time since September, down on the Hudson River.

Mark made sure we didn't want for liquid libation and we talked and laughed, talked some more and couldn't get enough gossip about Buffalo. Then we did a little gambling in the casino.............not particularly lucrative for us, but fun even though Peaches and I were only playing penny machines. Kristen and Mark seem to know their way around a casino for sure. Remember, we are still trying to get used to civilization. We were taken to dinner at the Angus Steak House, red meat......yummmmmm!

We lured Kristen and Mark to the boat the next day for dinner, so Kristen got a good start to her 4-day tan during the day and Mark read a great Steve Martin book (and passed it on to me, I've finished it too). We did shopping in the grocery store, bought DVDs in the DVD store to take along on our trip home (they come out of a mysterious drawer behind the counter and are all the latest films to hit the theaters at $5 each (no copy write laws in the Bahamas). We also picked up the old James Bond *Thunderball* because we all snorkeled in the grotto where he was being chased in the film. It was very good, showing an upscale Nassau that is no longer here (no matter what unofficial tour we take). They had a lookey bucket in the movie too.

Thursday we met them after noon to shop the duty free shops near where the cruise ships dock, everything from Gucci to T-shirt stores. Lots of jewelry stores and perfume stores are on the street too. Then there was the straw market, where you can bet everything was manufactured in Taiwan or China except for the occasional vendor making straw baskets. It was huge, but we bought nothing (imagine that). Peaches made quite a few attempts to see if anyone was selling jewelry made from sea beans, but they didn't even know what she was talking about. It must be just an Exuma Islands thing.

We had drink and snacks at Senor Frog's. We saw a lot of the cruise ship "prisoners", let off the boat for 5 hours only, eating and drinking at warp speed in order to do it all before curfew. How can that be relaxing? It seems wrong that what they are doing can be called cruising. Where's the quiet oneness with nature, the occasional shot of adrenaline when something goes wrong, the loose schedule and the go only when the weather is good principle?

Breathless with Rick and Doreen has arrived and anchored across the harbor from our marina. They are coming to dinner Friday to get better acquainted and set up plans to go back to Florida. We compared weather reports, printouts from www.windfinder,com and www.passages.com, www.weatherunderground.com and others (Chris Parker included).

We decided to leave Nassau and head for the Berry Islands, specifically Frazer's Hog Cay, to the north on Saturday morning. If the weather pattern holds, we'll just continue on to North Rock, north of the island of Bimini, and aim for Lake Worth, Florida (about 186 nautical miles)

When we were getting ready to go and making dinner for that night, Kristen and Mark stopped by the boat on a motor scooter they rented, no helmets required. We talked a bit and then they were off to enjoy their last day on the island. We are ready for our last day too, dinghy up, new motor on the back rail, the Honda on the dinghy, thru-hulls closed, fluids topped off in the engine, provisions on board, charts and waypoints gathered and entered. If we could only learn how to sleep soundly the night before these journeys, we would be golden.

Before Kristen and Mark even got to the airport at Nassau to clear back out through customs Saturday morning, we were underway through the Nassau Harbor and out past the lighthouse to set our course for Frazer's Hog Cay. Breathless went first and set the pace. They unfurled their jib as the wind was soft and the main would have just flopped. We did the same and settled in for a nice 30 nautical mile trip, and only 30 miles as the weather window closed to cross the Gulf Stream. On the way out of the harbor, we heard from Katmandu who came into the harbor last night, anchored inside Paradise Island near Atlantis. Stephen, as our official big brother, said that we shouldn't go beyond the Berry Islands as the weather wouldn't be good to cross until Thursday. He turned out to be right. His other advice; "Don't take drinks from strangers and don't drive while drinking." What a nice guy he is.

We'll wait for the window to open back up while at anchor in the Berry Islands. Our trip north was a short hop in building seas of 2-4 feet and winds building to 18-20 knots. The trip was a little lumpy with the waves sometimes up under our stern and sometimes slapping us on the beam, but only 30 miles of it. The sun was out and we took a lot of pictures. We spotted a whale and some dolphins about half way there and were so excited that, you guessed it, we didn't get the picture, only one lone dolphin fin to show for our excitement.

When we came to the islands, we followed Breathless in, it was so shallow. There were some red and green markers near the shore that Rick didn't remember from their last trip here. We followed them off the lane and anchored beyond them. On the bottom, there were lots of grassy spots with light places that looked like sand traps on a golf course. Rick said make sure we hit the sandy spots with the anchor as few anchors do well in grass. They drag and don't set. Peaches did a great job while the bow pitched up and down and the boat rolled. The wind and the waves were not from the same direction, making the water chaotic. After the anchor was set we stayed up in the cockpit and watched to make sure the anchor held in the 20 knot winds. This was not going to be a comfortable anchorage. We added boiling water to a dehydrated meal of sweet and sour chicken, given to us by Peaches friend Linda Britbach for just such a time, and ate sparingly due to the motion of the boat. We quickly became horizontal in our beds (the best place to be on a rolling boat). Surprisingly, we slept well, although you had to use one leg against the hull to keep yourself from rolling like a hot dog on a commercial cooker.

It's better today, and best at low tide where the waves decrease, but we are boat bound and from our weather reports on the Sirius weather program, it will be several days before we are able to leave. Not the greatest news, but it is better today and we are catching up on our sleep, our reading and oh yes, blogging. Doreen on Breathless is a great cook and she has been presented with 2 fish Rick caught on the trip up from Nassau, a barracuda and a Mahi-Mahi (a 3 footer got away). She saved me some fish fillets and a dish of chowder from her freezer. Yum.

So, we wait and wait, but as Peaches says, "I would rather wait for the right time, a three day window so that I can enjoy the trip. I want to have fun!" I agree because, if Peaches isn't happy..........

It is Monday morning and we were awakened during the night by some rain, so up to close the hatches. Peaches stayed up to try and get Chris Parker on the small radio/ single side band radio. No luck at 0630, probably because of the bad weather in Florida (we later found out it is a radio and a short wave radio, we were never going to get Chris Parker on that). Florida is getting 40 knot winds and possible tornadoes, more than an inch of rain an hour. Rick on Breathless couldn't get all the report either, so we stay put here. Peaches was yanked out of her idea of going back to bed by a small tanker ship that plowed right between Breathless and Star of the Sea and then turned hard right and kissed our stern(so close). All Peaches could see was the huge prop at the tanker's stern as he went through. We were going to try and move to a mooring near the Berry Islands Club around the next bay later today, but now that we find we are sticking out into the channel, we are going right now.

We pulled anchor, but not quickly enough, as the tanker unloaded his gas and diesel and was charging out between us again. One of the other boats near the Club said to us that "at least the tanker had some excitement in a rather boring day of going in and out of many little marinas." Like we've said before I don't like being the entertainment. I like being the audience.

We picked up a nice new mooring ball in front of the dock with the Club sign on it. There are a couple of fuel tanks on shore and a small shack......um, the clubhouse, I think. We are hoping against hope that there is some internet so we can drop this blog and pick up our email. At one time, this club used to be bigger, with a restaurant and bar, but I don't think that would fit into the shack I see from the boat.

We are comfortable at last, although it is raining, but not as hard as in Florida. Most of the truly bad weather should pass north of us, the Sirus program shows all the lightning strikes and heavy rain going over Florida and east out to sea. Our own Doppler weather animation is pretty telling. There is no rolling here, a huge plus for comfort. I was getting dizzy at times from working down below while rolling 30 degrees each way every 5-7 seconds. We watched a movie at anchor last night (*Men Who Stare at Goats*) and I was queasy by the end from sitting sideways in the boat. All better now.

We'll probably try to cross the Gulf Stream either Wednesday or Thursday, so time to get out my book again. The VHF radio is full of people discussing the weather and when to cross, so we will most likely go with the pack. This is one time when being inventive or trying to go solo is a very bad idea.

One more short story. The Honda outboard motor was sold in less than 12 hours. A couple we met at Point Abino, Canada wants it when we return home, and agreed to the price. I should advertise more, huh? Star of the Sea, Out.

Star of the Sea on the Bahamas Banks, heading For the Tongue of the Ocean, the Gulf Stream and, eventually, Lake Worth, Florida (Photo: Doreen Itenson)

Chapter 56

Crossing the Gulf Stream II

04/29/2010 Berry Island Club to Lake Worth, Florida

Hi, this is short but we want to tell you we made it to Lake Worth from the Berry Island Club. We departed yesterday at noon and arrived at Lake Worth about 10 AM, all in one piece. We took what we could glean from the weather from Chris Parker, Rick's interpretation of his forecast and what we got from listening to the boat people waiting to go across and talking on the VHF (like polling the audience). For us, our Sirius weather program corroborated Chris Parker's thoughts. Yesterday was a perfect day to do the 12 hours from the Berry Islands to North Rock, just north of Bimini. In reality (not the forecast), there was some wind, flat beautiful seas with sunny skies. The outlook for the Gulf Stream across to Lake Worth (Palm Beach) was also good, no northerly component of the winds to ruffle up the north flowing Gulf. There is hardly any wind and only some northeast swells to ruffle our feathers.

We went through the Tongue of the Ocean, a really deep portion for the first 12 hours, and then, back onto the Bahamas Banks, shallow waters of 10-18 feet. Piece of cake, we'd been doing that since February. We even took the time to take pictures of each other under sail (Breathless and Star of the Sea) before we took a tack that only allowed us to have the main to be used (not a good picture opportunity). The sun set and we were doing fine.

We saw several other vessels, motor yachts, other sailboats, some trawlers and at one point a huge luxury liner bearing down on us, collision course (or at least it seemed so). When it passed in front of us, going 20 knots, it had every light lit on all the decks. It looked like a city moving by us at the speed of a freight train.

In the morning, after the sun came up, we saw more vessels, but only one big container ship. The large 10 foot northeast swells were like climbing one mountain after another, but they were smooth, without waves to interfere with our progress. They were most impressive to see coming in front of you. We spotted the Florida coast from a long way out and Peaches got her first cell phone coverage in months...............excuse me, iPhone coverage. Her apps were all intact and she looked whole again. She called her sister Susanne from about 11 miles out to say we were back.

The entrance to the shipping channel into Lake Worth is wide, like a major highway. We went left around into the ICW and found a great anchorage a 10 AM. We thought we felt fine after being up 22 hours but found we weren't efficient at anything we tried to do. We made breakfast, showered. I got my phone activated and then Peaches crashed. So tired, so glad to be back in the USA. I called my Dad for a long talk, answered some emails, found I was all thumbs when I tried to text my friend Brenda , the words were all backwards and it sent before I got done, so very out of practice. I gave it up and slept. Oh, before we slept, we reported into customs by phone, with 24 hours to show up at the customs office. Tomorrow, not now! Star of the Sea, safe, home, and out.

Passing Katmandu in the ICW, going north to Vero Beach, Florida

Chapter 57

Welcome Back to Vero Beach

05/07/2010 Vero Beach, Florida

We slept long and hard after the crossing and then got ready to go into customs on Friday. We called in about noon Thursday after we arrived and answered 20 questions (mostly with numbers) and were given a clearance number to use when we showed up the following day. We took the dinghy and landed at the Tiki Bar where we promised to come back and have lunch (free docking, $10 at the other dock). We walked a short distance to the customs building and Peaches was pulled off course part way by an 80 foot Farr design boat being launched later today to join in the big Bermuda race. It was spectacular.

On Saturday, we left Lake Worth and started up the Intracoastal Waterway toward Fort Pierce and ultimately to Vero Beach. We spent a week in Vero on the way down and loved the free bus service into town, the number of cruisers in the mooring field, and the Saturday night happy hour at the marina.

Breathless pulled anchor at about 0700 and we left Lake Worth and made our way around Peanut Island and into the ICW. We needed to pass through 7 bridges in the first 10 miles. Some bridges opened on the quarter hour, some on the half hour and some on demand. It went surprisingly well. Going up the ICW, we passed by some incredible houses with large complex piers and very big boats. A lot of the homes had For Sale signs up and one poor rich guy in a particularly huge house had a MAKE ME AN OFFER sign out front. All is not well among the very rich in Florida. We took a lot of pictures (lots of time, not very complicated navigation work).

As the day progressed, Katmandu came into view. Stephen and his family crossed the Gulf when we did, but got into the harbor later in the day. We were glad we could stop worrying about them crossing the Gulf Stream. They did so well. We finally came up to them in the ICW. Katmandu left earlier in the morning that we all did. We all waved and waved. The kids looked happy considering they were in school (every morning until 1PM even when underway).

We came to an area where there were no more bridges except a 62 foot clearance one, so set our large Genoa (jib) and used the wind to push us north. The wind was building from behind us and we were moving along at a great rate of speed. This is the first time we raised a sail in the ICW. Breathless was being a good example for us. The winds built to 26 knots just before we were going to anchor near Fort Pierce. It took a lot of strength to furl the jib. The ICW between the markers canal is very narrow, and we couldn't easily turn into the wind. We anchored and spent a very peaceful night. Peaches has really relaxed in the ICW and seemed to enjoy the trip (coming down the coast we were really hung up on the shallow water and swore that we wouldn't go back into it, but here we are, happy and content).

The next morning we left Fort Pierce and the view became more familiar. We'd been here before with OZ. The weather was nice, there were people camping on the spoils islands and there were lots of birds swooping around the islands and following the small fishing boats. We arrived in Vero Beach at 10 AM on Sunday, pulled up to the diesel dock and got fuel, water and got rid of our garbage, some of it from the Bahamas (getting rid of garbage makes me happier than a lot of other chores, even well bagged garbage stinks sitting in the dinghy in 90 degree sun). Breathless went to mooring #16 and we joined them when we were done. It is humid in Florida and 90 degrees or higher, so the inside of the boat is damp and there is nothing as bad as being hot and then lying down on damp sheets. Ugh! We went to a Super Wal-Mart on the free bus

(I know, we have gone right back to the dark side) and got groceries, some desiccant to soak up the damp in the boat, and generally had a ball wandering in the air conditioning. We were with Katmandu and it took an entire Taxi-Van to get us back to the boat, and all but Stephen, Peaches and I went back on the bus! Stephen bought real food for his family while we bought mostly things for happy hours (no comments from the peanut gallery, please).

Peaches got the oil changed in the boat, a messy job no matter what we do to prevent spills. I got the watermaker cleaned with chemicals to take off the minerals and bacteria from the membrane, and then I pickled it. Sounds terrible, but it all went smoothly (except I was in a deep locker in 95+ degree temperatures most of the day). Stephen taught us how to tap, drill out and then extract two sheared off bolts in the engine. I never thought we'd need to know this, but we have the tools and the T-shirt to prove it now.

I can't imagine what fixing the bracket for the fuel pump would have cost us to have it done by a marine technician. We were so glad it worked, but we were all shaped like pretzels when we were done. The place where the bolts sheared off was in a horrible place on the big diesel engine under the stairs. We don't know if it was vibration that did this, if the bracket didn't fit right or if the ½ inch bolts were not strong enough. Stephen is such a valuable resource for us and he is so kind to help. He teaches while he does things to the point where we can do it and be a lot more independent. The beautiful French accent doesn't make the experience boring at all. He's now trying his hardest to get us to stop paying top dollar for boat parts and get them from E-Bay. He has a real point. You don't usually need anything shipped the next day. Wait and save.........a foreign concept (get it?).

Happy hour on Breathless with some of their old cruising friends, Linda and Ron was fun. There are more beginner stories to tell, and Linda's to hear. These two belong to the exalted group of cruisers who have sold their boat and decided to live in Vero Beach full time. The group is called CLODS, Cruisers Living on Dirt. Natalie and Stephen were there too and we finished off the night with fresh coffee (from our newly fixed coffee maker, just saved by Stephen and Natalie who fixed the loose wires) and rum cake from Natalie and a no-bake cheesecake from Doreen. We were killing ourselves with kindness.

After five days in Vero Beach we managed to tear ourselves away and left for Melbourne, Florida. It was a 30 mile trip, but with sunny skies and light winds, it was easy. Just before we left, we had two nights in Vero with heavy, heavy rain storms. The rain on Wednesday night almost filled our dinghy to the top, the first time, ever. The sad part of the rains was that Ken drove down from Titusville to see us and go out to dinner, but the rain made it so we couldn't get over to the dock safely in the dinghy. We'll find him when we get to Titusville for sure. We are happy and moving north.

Peaches' first Manatee, belly side up, enjoying the fresh water shower, Titusville, Florida

Chapter 58

The Bucket List

05/09/2010 Titusville, Florida

Well, as you can tell from the recent chapters, we are coming to the end of this first adventure with Star of the Sea. Rick and Doreen on Breathless and Peaches and I on Star of the Sea are slowly moving up the coast of Florida. The days are hot and humid with occasional amazingly strong rain storms lasting only hours, but dropping inches and inches of rain into our dinghy.

Breathless has always gone about their passages by getting up early in the morning and leaving at or before 0700. It sounded barbaric to us at first but then we saw their wisdom. They stop after 7 hours or less and drop the anchor. They have the afternoon, often the most hot and windless time, to rest, read, and eventually make a lovely dinner and sleep. I have a completely flat forehead from bashing it with the palm of my hand in ignorance! Start a couple of hours earlier and be done when all others are still slogging up the ICW or from island to island in the Bahamas. KISS (keep it simple, stupid). They have left a huge cadre of cruisers copying their methods of cruising without fatigue or stress. Thank you, thank you.

We are sitting at anchor outside of Titusville, Florida, where our friends from OZ (Ken only, Connie is back in Mississauga) as well as LaDanza and Ten Years After are up on the hard. That means their boat is out of the water, on stilts or in a cradle. We went into the marina for a happy hour with all of them. This marina wins the Happy Hour award, as there is one here every night (I know, I say happy hour too much). We took the dinghy in about 5 PM, going very slowly through the entrance to the two side by side marinas, behind the breakwater. Ken said there were at least 4 manatees inside and we wouldn't want to hit one. We saw none of these "sea cows" on the way down from Buffalo because it was too cold for them. Now is our chance.

We were wandering about in the dinghy at idle speed and asking folks if they'd seen the manatee. I guess they are so common here, and such a bother to the boaters, that they could hardly bother to answer us. One guy looked at us, two 62 year old women in a dinghy and asked us "Are you guys lost or something?" He didn't answer the manatee question. We puttered on and finally ended up at the dinghy dock with Rick and Doreen. We got out, found the nice place with tables, a grill and a roof to keep the sun off of our heads and we settled in waiting for Ken.

Some of the people at the next table, drinking their beers and looking like they were the unofficial greeting committee, asked us how we were. Peaches piped up "Where are all the manatees?"

A balding guy made some mumbled derogatory comments about them, then said "Why would you want to see them? They are a pain in the ass, they make the water dirty, they get in the way of the boaters when they take their naps just at the surface with their snouts sticking out to breathe (remember they are about 1200 pounds of sleeping blubber)."

Peaches didn't miss a beat "I still want to see one!"

I thought that was the end of the conversation, but the guy smiled and got up out of his chair, left his beer on the table and wandered over to the dock at the end of the shelter and turned the water spigot on to a dribble and resumed his place at the table, leaning his chair way back on its back legs. The conversation went on among the people there comparing boats, where we've been, any problems we've had, where we were going, etc. The guy sat up a little straighter and said "There's your manatee now" pointing over to where the water was dripping off the dock into the water.

A snout, kind of grey in color with whiskers, was under the dripping water, with his lips pursed into a funnel. This huge, immense, white underbelly stretched out for about 5-6 feet with a finned tail at the end and two flat paddle like "arms" at the sides. He was rolling around and around, belly up, back up, belly up. All the time the funnel-face was in the fresh water. There were plenty of minor scars on the animal, but nothing gross. I've heard they often get nicked by boat propellers.

I guess from what people were saying the manatee loves fresh water and are very attracted to it. In the marina, they show up when people are hosing off their boats or filling their water tanks. I think they know the sound of the fresh water from the spigot hitting the water. Peaches took several video clips of the manatee, and I got a couple of still shots, our proof of seeing one up close. The coolest thing was watching Peaches follow it from one side of the dock to the other, camera in hand, so excited about finally seeing a manatee.

About the manatee: They are huge, often 1200 pounds or about the weight of my horses when I was in that business. Manatees are often referred to as "sea cows" as they are very large, appear very "simple" and are vegetarians. Peaches looked them up on her iPhone and they are thought to be descendants of the elephant. After seeing one closely yesterday, they look a lot like the dancing chorus line of hippo in Walt Disney's *Fantasia*. They also remind me of the mechanical "realistic" hippo who come up out of the water in the old river ride at Disney World.

Peaches' source on the iPhone (and it is true because it was on the internet, don't you know?) said that manatee are much more intelligent than first thought. More like a dolphin, they show in experiments that they have the ability to learn, to have long term memory and to show problem solving. I piped up and said this to the guy who turned on the water, and he said "You got to be kidding me, they are about as smart as a tree stump. Did it say in your fancy computer that they fart?" No it didn't, but yes, they certainly do, lots of little bubbles coming to the surface from their tail region. Makes me think this one was a male. Enough said.

So, our bucket list is pretty full now that we have seen the manatee. We are waiting for the winds to calm down a bit so we can go in and see them again. Our bucket list is being filled as you go through this long winded story, from leaving Buffalo September 4th 2009 until last night. Bucket lists can be long and unwieldy, so we are going to dump our bucket list and start fresh for next fall. I'll keep writing though, because there is always something new to see or say.

Towboat US hauling us out of 4 feet of water in the Ponce de Leon Cut in the ICW, Daytona, Florida

Chapter 59

OOPS!

05/10/2010 Daytona Beach, Florida

The picture tells it all. We are now officially in shallow water, just turning into the Ponce de Leon Inlet. We followed Breathless who bumped the bottom and got off the sand shoal and yelled to us to "Go right, go right!" Well, we were immediately in 4 feet of water. Not his fault though. A barge was aground there a week ago and filled in the 18 feet of water that should have been in the middle of the channel with lots and lot of sand (about 14 feet if I have it right). The fact that the barge was there for 4 changes of the tides made it easy for that amount of sand to be moved.

The guys from Boat US were great (we've said that twice before I think).We got off in 15 minutes and the bill was over $1000. We paid nothing. Our membership for towing wasn't used up until the end of June and we have been well served. We are anchored safely with Breathless in Daytona Beach just in time for a happy hour libation. Lots of birds, manatee, dolphins, jumping fish and turtles swimming went by us today. Great day too as we had our sails up for almost 20 miles of the trip. More later.

Our view of OZ; our friends, out buddy-boat and our "giver of courage"

Chapter 60

OZ, How Two American Ladies Found Their Courage

5/12/2010 St. Augustine, Florida

Once upon a time in the faraway place called Florida, two American women navigated their sailing vessel named Star of the Sea into the pier at Fernandina. They were hard working women who were at the end of a long and arduous journey to find warm weather. Their travels had taken them into canals, rivers, creeks, bays, swamps and even watery cuts through tall forests. They also stopped in many small villages where the fine folks and shopkeepers were kind to the weary travelers.

Great surprise was often noted by the inhabitants of these villages at there being no men-folk to steer this handsome ship. No men-folk onboard to carry the heavy water jugs and to gather the food. After a few words with these women the town women were interested and maybe even had the green-eyed envy of them. Such a brave undertaking for two women who appeared old enough to be home at the hearth, telling stories to their grandchildren.

Little did the people know that these women, Peaches and Chris, were not as brave or as confident as they appeared. Surely they appeared skilled and were sure of their docking and fixing the ship to the pier. Their ease filling the tanks with fuel and the water containers with fresh water was obvious. But, these women had bitten off more than they could comfortably chew. Their trip had become drudgery, every morning preparing the ship to slog on through the swamps and navigate through the raging rivers and every evening preparing a meager pot of soup or stew for the evening meal before falling, fully clothed into their cold beds. There were few smiles and even fewer words spoken between them.

What reason could anyone imagine for their long journey? Were they fugitives from the dirty streets of New York City, for their vessel was registered to this place? Were they running away from abusive husbands? Were they running toward somebody with whom one of them wanted to share her life? Why would they go to such extremes to go a thousand nautical miles from home? They told the friendly folk along the way that they were just looking for a place to live where there was no snow, no blowing and blustery winds, no governors to make them slave in the hospitals any longer. They were looking for their freedom and their comfort, as simple as that.

So, our tale progresses to the time they tied to the pier in the fair town of Fernandina. The town was aglow with decorations for Christmas. The winds were cold for this far south, so it seemed that they had come a very long way only to have a cold and blustery holiday without the comforts of their families. The town was very welcoming and the other ships at the pier all seemed to be pleased to be here for the holiday. One ship, OZ, was tied closely to the Star of the Sea at the large pier. The Canadian man and woman seemed very friendly and willing to share their information about possibly going further south. They would go out of the only country that these women had known, and to the islands of sun, sand and the landing place of the great Christopher Columbus. The women were very interested but among themselves, they talked of fear. Fear of the unknown is one part of it, but for them it was more a fear that their new vessel was not seaworthy enough to go to this wondrous place.

Many chance and not-so-by-chance meetings were had with Connie and Ken of OZ. The family from Katmandu also seemed to need OZ to give them direction for their first journey. OZ seemed to have all the information needed to make this trip as well as many years of experience in this journey. They had charts and books as well as pictures of these islands. The women were entranced and decided to make every effort to find a journeyman or some other representative of the ship builder to repair Star of the Sea. Weeks passed, Connie traveled back to her home to visit her sister while Ken kept talking and counseling the women. The American women paid homage to him with many tasty meals and much conversation. Star of the Sea was repaired at last. When Connie returned, preparations were made for the start of the journey to the islands along with OZ. The women felt confident that they would see the islands at last, after all, OZ had returned eight times, safely back to their home. The women were overjoyed, daring to smile.

With their hearts in their throats and their pulses beating fast, they left behind the coast and set offshore for the distant Port of Canaveral. This was to take a day, a night and part of another day, but OZ would lead and be there for any problems. Problems a plenty came up in the night when all the lights and instruments on Star of the Sea stopped working. They followed OZ's light until the sun came up on the horizon. The night was long and frightening and the women were grateful for the light of dawn. They read and reread the pages of words about the electronics, they prayed to their God. Peaches found all the religious medals given to her before the start of the journey. They thought of turning back many times, or of asking to be rescued by the towboat people, but Ken said they must soldier on, and they did.

OZ became the beacon for the rest of the journey. They made long day trips, short stays in friendly villages, fishing villages, and finally another long jump to the fortified city of Miami, surrounded by large walls with many windows. Some of the walls were very high and the ships in the harbors were as large as a whole town in far off New York. The women's ship remained dry and the women became more used to the traveling. The days did not seem so bleak or so long when you travel with another vessel beside you. The women thought that they were much less afraid, but hated to admit it was because there was a man there to bolster their spirits when things got rough.

Finally the day came to leave the shores of America and head across the wild Gulf Stream to go to far away Nassau. Chris sent a messenger to her well to do brother in Houston in the far away state of Texas. He sent word back that he would travel with them to this home of Christopher Columbus. In their hearts, the journey became less ominous with family involved. Both women had read many books about this journey and had all the information they needed to be successful in their quest for warmth and sun. They just needed the courage to make it happen. Their pulses hammering in their heads and their hearts in their throats, they followed OZ out of the harbor and into the ocean. The seas were light, the sails full and the sun glinting off of the waves. This was breathtaking, this was beautiful. This was perfect.

The rest of the winter journey was full of adventures, windy days, but warmer weather. The clear blue waters of the Bahamas were mesmerizing. The islands were so different, one from another. The sky was big and bright with stars. They made friends with other peoples of the country of Canada. When OZ had to leave early to return to America, the women experienced their first stirrings of fear again. We will be like orphans, left on the beach to wither and die. The yellow brick road on the stern of OZ was no longer in sight.

Shortly, it was time for them to head north and they awoke that morning with an awesome feeling of certainty in their skills of navigation, weather forecasting, and how to sail their ship. Their hearts were beating slow and strong in their chests, their pulses were steady and smiles were on their faces. The women knew all along how to accomplish this journey, wherever it might take them, they only needed the courage from OZ to find it. They will never forget this precious gift and will pass the courage along to anyone, man, woman or child, who needs it in the future.

They all (Ken and Connie, Natalie, Stephen, Sabrina, Francis and Stephanie) lived happily ever after.

Star of the Sea following Breathless through the ICW, Palm Coast, Florida

Chapter 61

Anchoring in a Mud Puddle

05/12/2010 Palm Coast to St. Augustine, Florida

We've had one nice day after another coming north through Florida. The weather is warm but not too humid, sunny with huge cumulous clouds and enough wind to feel comfortable. We went to Palm Coast to visit friends of Doreen and Rick. Jill and David Royall are retired air traffic controllers from Atlanta. They live in an old canal housing development (a canal village) off of the ICW near Palm Coast. After our towboat experience the other day, we were a little hesitant to go in the reportedly shallow entrance, but Rick said to just do it, so we did. It was not 5 feet deep as he thought, but mostly 7 feet. It felt odd to be gliding our big sailing vessel down a narrow canal with houses and docks sticking out everywhere. No room to pass unless you are a kayak! We went into a larger basin where the canals went off in every direction like spokes of a wheel.

So, it felt like we anchored in a water filled pot-hole or a mud puddle. I definitely felt like we were trespassing in all these expensive backyards. It was beautiful, quiet and fun once we got used to it. Normally, we anchor in a much more open place, at the edge of the ICW, or a river or creek.

We rested, having arrived at 11:30 after only 4 hours of travel. There's lots of time for naps, showers and to prepare our part of the dinner. Doreen is bringing chicken and beef shish kabobs and a couscous salad. I brought the cheese, chutney, pistachios, apple slices, dried cranberries, almonds and crackers. We got in the dinghies and went about two blocks and arrived at the Royall's dock. Their large yacht, Shibumi was tied right in front of their home. What a treat. Jill is a master of canvas work and has done all the canvas work on the boat which looked in pristine condition. They love cruising and hope to make it again next fall. I hope so too, they were great fun to be with. The house was beautiful, Peaches headed for one of the stress chairs, "Oh, finally a real chair to sit in." Dinner and conversation was all over the place and fun. Time passed way to fast. Tiramisu and fresh fruit was served by the hosts and we reluctantly called it a night. We returned to our boats to sleep and then off again in the morning.

The rumor that the canal was going to be shallow was just that, rumors. The morning trip was fun because the sides of the Matanzas River were close to us and there was a lot to see. One stretch of this river had shoaled in badly and was the subject of a lot of Coast Guard warnings. They put in some drop markers to help people from going aground, and they worked, we didn't. Whew!

One thing that stands out to me every day as we moved north is the number of abandoned sailboats anchored along the ICW. Some of them appear to have been there for years, others for less time. Long green algae cling to the waterlines and below. Some are nose down because of water in the boat. The fiberglass has no shine and often the boats are stripped bare. Some we saw have broken loose and are tipped over on the shore. It is a terrible financial problem for Florida's economy. It costs them so much to salvage or to junk these boats, and a sad sight for us.

We finally heard from IMIS, our boat insurance company, about whether we could store the boat in Amelia Island rather than go all the way to Charleston, SC. What a joke. They said we could stay in Florida, one mile south of their arbitrary line that you must be above before June 1st (hurricane season), for a mere additional $1600. Are they kidding me? We are, obviously, going on to Charleston SC after resting in Fernandina for a few days. We hope that Katmandu is still there. It would be fun to see them one more time. They are scooting as fast as possible all the way back to Quebec. Stephen got a possible consulting job in India for three weeks and would like to take advantage of that before he takes another permanent job in the mining engineering field. They are really driving themselves, and we hope they do okay.

Peaches is talking with her good friend Frank, from Myrtle Beach. She hopes he can come with us on the overnight trip from Fernandina to Charleston, out in the shipping lanes. Going from port to port along the Georgia coast is a lot longer distance to go as well as a logistical nightmare. If you aren't in the ICW you need to go out quite a distance to run offshore and then make the long trek back to the shore at the end of the day. No, I don't think so.

Both Peaches and I were quite burned out today for a while because we thought we were almost to our goal, Amelia Island, and now we aren't. Now we are perking up, thinking about going into Charleston Harbor and the neat things we'll see. It was so foggy and rainy when we went through the harbor the last time, so getting a picture of Fort Sumter would be cool. More adventures to come.

Return to Fernandina, Florida Pelicans napping after their feast when the fishing boat came in

Chapter 62

Welcome Home to Fernandina

05/14/2010 Amelia Island, Florida

We made it back to Amelia Island this morning. We rounded the last marker of the ICW and there was Fernandina Harbor Marina, right between the shrimp boats and the paper factory. It was like coming home for us. We spent a month here in late December and early January. Remember when we had ice on the deck and had to go out to buy long pants and sweatshirts to survive the winter holidays in Florida? Well, the sky is blue, the weather is perfect, and it is a non-humid 85 degree day (sorry all you western New York people. I know your spring weather hasn't settled down yet).

We anchored last night in the Fort George River and had a nice quiet night. I was unsure it would be a comfortable one as we'd been inundated by huge horse flies and tons of no-see-ums. Peaches convinced me to unearth the electric fly swatter from the storage under her bed. It makes a terrible crack when the fly hit's the wires. The horse flies were so big that when I stood up at the helm to steer and ease my sitting muscles, they hit my face like I was on a motorcycle (I was not smiling or showing my teeth).

This morning, the flies were mostly gone, but the laughing gulls were everywhere. Peaches even recorded their voices with her iPhone. I was watching the birds go by while drinking the first cup of coffee and a Wood Stork flew low down the river, right by the boat. I had never seen one before. My jaw was hanging open and I couldn't scrabble for the camera in time. Still, very cool to see it. Peaches got a great book this evening as we walked through Fernandina and into our favorite book store. It's called *Florida's Living Beaches*. It has everything from birds to sea beans. The sea beans sold it to Peaches. I would have loved to have it this morning to identify some of the insects and the birds.

We have a long list of things we want to accomplish over the next few days: redo the varnish on the teak (lots of sanding first), wash and wax the sides of the boat (will drop the dinghy down to do this), clean the stains off the deck and wax it, go through the lockers and make lists of what is never going to see the inside or the outside of this boat again, list what is going to stay, clean the interior woodwork and Pledge it, wash the non-wood parts of the walls with anti-mildew cleaner and then the same with all the insides of the storage places, on and on (sorry, but by now you know that books about cruising contain lots of lists). It sounds daunting and unobtainable at this point (Sorry, most boat related books end up with long lists that need to be done for part of the prose).

We've been talking with Frank. We spent a couple of weeks staying at Osprey Marina and visiting him in Myrtle Beach. Now we are collaborating with his wife, Valerie, to get him on the Star of the Sea for the overnight to Charleston. He will love it, and so will we. He is a storyteller! Peaches tells a story of how he got her to buy her first boat from him. He taught Peaches to sail when she bought the Bluenose, her first boat. She said he would have a picture of this boat in his pocket and when they were at Mass, he would shake her hand during the Sign of Peace and flash the picture, saying she should buy it. It worked and she did. Frank is wonderful and I am so glad he and Valerie are my new friends.

It is a real luxury to be tied to a marina dock again after so long. We have covered the 300+ miles up the Florida coast, inside, from Lake Worth by anchoring here and there. We are sorry we said all those bad things about the ICW, especially in Florida. We had a great time. Lots of pictures and comfortable anchorages.

We have power plugged into the boat, garbage bins for the garbage, water anytime we want, and a beautiful old city to walk in anytime. We are going to try to work hard the first part of the day and rest and play in the afternoon (sounds like the Breathless protocol for no stress). I can't wait to walk and walk. It has been a long time on the boat with only the climbing up and down, sitting, standing, walking 2-3 steps at a time and sleeping as exercise. Connie from OZ said in an email that she returned to her land-lubber status very quickly as she drove her car home to Toronto. Ours will be a slow transition, but we look forward to it.

Doreen and Peaches showing off their Sea Beans

Chapter 63

Sea Beans and Other Beach Stuff

05/18/2010 Fernandina, Florida

A couple of days ago we put up a Photo Gallery of sea shells and sea beans. There were a lot of emails liking them so I thought I'd better write a story to go along with them. We did a good deal of beach walking in the Exumas, with the best shells found on the deeper Exuma Sound side of the islands. There the surf is strong and often the larger shells are broken into beautiful but unidentifiable bits. The smaller shells, most of what we saved, are hidden in the tide line under the dried out seaweed clumps. Most of the beaches were almost barren of other people, not like Florida's beaches that are sometimes shoulder to shoulder with people, especially during spring break.

I digress. The first time Peaches and I heard about sea beans was on our first night in Vero Beach when we went to a happy hour on Orient Express. Bruce and his wife, Gail, make sea glass jewelry and some spectacular pieces out of sea beans. We filed this info away until last month when Peaches found a sea bean at Shroud Cay at the end of the Mangroves on the Sound side. Sea beans come in with the tides from other tropical lands. They travel from Central to South America and to the Caribbean islands, the Bahamas and sometimes due to the Gulf Stream to European shores. Beans in their pods also come from Africa. Peaches' heart bean came from a long, twisting pod of the monkey ladder vine. These grow in the rainforests of Central and South America (the book *Florida's Living Beaches* says that the ladder vine has the longest bean pods in the world). Now you know enough about these beans to render a fellow happy hour friend comatose!

Sea beans also come as a hamburger bean (in red and brown). They look like miniature wooden hamburgers. They develop in spiny pods hanging on long stems from tropical rainforests in the Americas. Brown hamburger beans come all the way from Africa. Wow! So, when you find them, what do you do? You carefully sand them and then rub beeswax into them. They glow like beautiful wood. People make great jewelry with them, especially pendants, some very dramatic statement pendants.

The rest of the shells and beach stuff are pretty well described by their names, Most of ours are in the tiny, but amazingly beautiful, kind. The only exceptions are the fan corals that are large and delicate and impossible to figure out how to get home on an airplane. Most cruising boats end up with a large conch shell or two aboard. These are beautiful, especially the insides that are every color of pink from pearly to Pepto Bismol pink. The use of them as horns blown at sunset at the anchorages comes from a long lineage of cruisers. I'm sure the Caribbean pirates used them too. Every person has their special combination of one or two notes, either held as long as they can with one big breath or thousands of two note songs. We had one but never made it into a musical horn. Lots of beaches near small towns are covered several feet deep with the conch shells because of the amount of conch eaten. Their gardens are bordered with them; they even make walls of them. Ours went back to the bottom of the sea.

Peaches favorite shell is the checkered Nerite snail (see picture). They are all less than an inch and we saw them in every nook and cranny of the rocks on the beaches. They cluster together at night to graze on the algae covering the intertidal rocks. The little critter inside has a calcified plate that it uses to close the door to the shell when it is out of the water and in the direct sun. Evolution working just as it should.

We've settled on a day and time to do our trip to Charleston, SC on the "outside." Frank couldn't make it as his grandson is graduating this weekend, so he misses out on some fun, but for a good reason. We are leaving Amelia Island Thursday, just before noon to go the 149 nautical miles to Charleston Harbor. We want to enter the harbor on an incoming tide so we don't have to fight the current and the nasty waves that sometimes develop. We should get in about 2 PM at the latest on Friday. We have a slip waiting for us in the Charleston City Marina so we can relax and rest for the night.

We saw Walt Thayer, a young fellow who lives on his boat across the harbor from Fernandina Harbor Marina when we went ashore today. Peaches met him in the Captain's Lounge and he offered to help her with her iPhone back in January when it was too cold to be anywhere but in the lounge where it was warm. He does computer consulting jobs as they come along and seems very talented. Cruisers need people like Walt around as we are all increasingly dependent on our computers, cell phones and electrical navigation aids. He hasn't sailed much yet, although he has lived on a sailboat for several years. This might get him started sailing. We've invited him to travel with us and he is excited about going. We are glad to have one more warm body to allow us to all get some real sleep, not just the 20 minute to 2 hour naps we usually get on overnights. We'll get him to a bus or a train station when we get into the marina in Charleston so he can get back to work in Fernandina before Monday.

Peaches and I will then take Star of the Sea to her summer resting spot 20 miles up the Cooper River. While at Fernandina we got 6 coats of varnish on the teak toe rails so that is one chore out of the way. We are working on getting a car to travel north to Western New York and then eventually back to Charleston to finish up the work on the boat while she is out of the water. Peaches spent a lot of this afternoon checking out a lease deal on a Honda Odyssey LX (my sons will be proud). It has lots of space for boat stuff, and will even hold Peaches' scaffolding. What were we thinking, selling both of our cars and going to Trinidad for the summer?

Walt Thayer and Peaches almost to Charleston after a night of smooth sailing among the "big boats" in the shipping channel

Chapter 64

Moonlight on the Sea or How We Got to Charleston

05/23/2010 Charleston, South Carolina

We are alive and very well as of 12:30 this afternoon at the City Marina in Charleston. We left Fernandina yesterday about 0930 and it was hot, sunny, with an easterly wind at 10-12 knots and we were so ready. Waiting for a window was particularly hard this time because our original Thursday departure date looked perfect, warm and sunny etc. Friday looked just as good, but another boat that left couldn't even get out of the harbor because of the heavy easterly seas. So, Commander Weather was right, Saturday was perfect. We saw lots of dolphins, no whales, some flying fish and small fish swarming at the surface in a large ball, probably being chased by the dolphins.

All our newly done teak is gleaming in the sunshine, our deck is clean, and I had a couple of days to go through most of the cupboards and cull out what can be given away (to Walt), what to keep, and what to drag north. We are still eating kind of strange combinations for dinner because I'm using up stuff. Peaches says if she sees another batch of couscous she will scream. I understand. I can't look chicken (in any form) in the face at this point!

We crossed from the Bahamas to Lake Worth in a full moon and it was almost full again last night. We put up the sails and motor sailed the course Peaches set for us, a direct line from the end of the jetty in Fernandina to the S004 buoy outside of Charleston. We went over 6 knots most of the way, often more like 7 knots. There were no waves, just moderate easterly swells that we rode over easily. About 3 AM the wind totally died so we furled in the sails and motored off into the moonlight. It was a sweet, gentle night.

How did our crewmember, Walt, do? Great! He seemed to be really enjoying himself and learned like a sponge. Like all good friendships, we learned a lot from him too. The best part of having Walt with us was that we all got a chance to sleep. Peaches showed him how to go out on deck with a tether, what an EPIRB is and where ours is located, the life raft, on and on. During the long night, he learned a lot about sail trim, the autohelms (Stella was stellar!) and ships in the night (radar). The radar worked well and it kept us safe in the dark. It also kept you awake, totally, watching for new blips and lights. We sure were in a major shipping lane, as many as 12 blips on the radar at once!

Food: we did fine. The sea state was relatively calm, so we ate real meals. Dinner was a little harder than I imagined. I could only get one of the two pots clamped to the stove so the pots wouldn't fall off when the swells went under us. So, I was making chicken, garlic, tomatoes, onions and shallots into a fresh pasta sauce. That needed the clamp. I hand-held the pot of boiling water for the pasta and cooked and stirred things one handed as the boat went up and down the swells. Everything cooked and we ate in bowls. It was warm and good and better than another sandwich. I will never hold a pasta pot for 20 minutes on a rolling ship again, for anyone!

We came into Charleston harbor with lots of photo ops. Last time it was foggy and raining. This time, we got a picture of Fort Sumter, lighthouses and bridges. We pulled into the City Marina on the Ashley River (where the low bridge was that Peaches thought was on the ICW). After we tied up at the marina, in the midst of hundreds of millions of dollars of white fiberglass, we could relax. Rows and rows of private motor yachts, larger than Tiger Wood's yacht, were around us. We looked like the pizza delivery yacht or something.

It seemed like I walked a mile past these yachts, some with matching Vespas on the dock in a line (so the

216

owners didn't have to get tired feet walking to the office I think). I finally got to the office to check in. Now I know why all the dock hands used golf carts to go from one boat to another, helping them to tie up to the dock. All we cared about was that we were done. We worked on the air conditioning, needing it more than any other time in the 10 months we've been gone. Peaches and I bled the water line to the air conditioner and in the cool air, we were able to sleep.

Walt is going back to Fernandina probably by train, another new experience for him, tomorrow. We will go back through the harbor, up the Cooper River and get Star of the Sea a rest too.

My only question is where is OZ? I still look for them. I know that OZ is up on land in Titusville and Connie and Ken are home in Toronto working hard to get their cruising kitty filled up for next fall's trip. You never lose the attachment to those friends who help you through a new challenge, a new adventure, so I will always be looking for them. They would have been proud of us and our trip to Charleston. We "done good."

On the way to the Cooper River, under the Ravenel Bridge, we first noticed the rapidly moving storm, Charleston, South Carolina

Chapter 65

Hey, Who Said it Was Okay to Rain?

05/24/2010 Detyen's Boatyard, Goose Creek, South Carolina

There were two American women sailing a beautiful yacht called Star of the Sea. They had learned so much over the past eight months about sailing, navigation, weather, getting along with others, risk management and conservation of strength and energy. These two women just executed and carried off an overnight passage from Fernandina, Florida to Charleston, South Carolina without a hitch and with a great deal of happiness and satisfaction. So, why, oh why, did these same two women take off from the Charleston City Marina about noon today to go up the Cooper River without even looking up at the sky?

Peaches and I tossed around renting a car to go home from the Detyen's Boatyard and found that it would cost us almost $1000 for a one-way 879 mile trip to Buffalo. So, finally we decided this morning to fly and got a couple of seats on USAIR for 8 PM tomorrow. Cheaper and quicker. Hey, tonight will be our last night on Star of the Sea! What a sudden and weird attitude adjustment. So, again, why didn't we check the weather before we left the dock?

We unplugged the electric lines, called the dock guys to help us off the dock and before we thought, we got going. The winds and currents in the harbor were both against us, the wind at 17+ knots for starters. And, finally, looking up at the sky, the two American women felt the first sharp stab of conscious. We continued on through the somewhat confusing harbor and headed for the bridge. The pictures Peaches took today will show a steady and very dramatic progression of the weather as we went up the Cooper River.

So, sitting in the boat tonight, watching Dancing With the Stars, I thought I'd better fess up and tell you how we became foul weather navigators today. The Cooper River is very forgiving as it is wide, very well marked, and dramatic in the amount of ship building, marine commerce and military installations along it's edges. We would have shown more pictures, but, well you know, the weather deteriorated.

Peaches and I made it up to the first big naval shipyard when we knew our goose was cooked, or drowned. We could see the curtain of rain coming across the river, along with the wall of misty fog. We closed all the canvas, lowered our speed and kept making forward momentum. Well, forward momentum until we couldn't see because it was so dark and raining so hard. We idled back and forth in front of the bows of the big docked ships as they were all we could see in the rain. It let up and we progressed a bit further and repeated this idle speed waiting again, and again, and then again.

The good thing about this lapse in preparation for our trip up the Cooper is that we worked out a good plan for how to handle another not so uncommon weather problem. No fair-weather sailors, we.

We called the boatyard a little after 4 PM to see if someone would please, please stay and help us with our lines. We had some emails and a nice brochure about the boatyard but it's always hard to prepare for a landing sight unseen. We were told to go past the last navigation marker in the river (about 20 miles up) and then go around a left bend in the river (still 34 feet deep) until we see a large square building where America's missiles were built. It was white and looked a little like the federal building in Washington, but it was out in the middle of nowhere.

Then we were supposed to look for a rusty barge with a nice blue and white tugboat tied to it. Right there, we were to make a sharp left into a canal that eventually leads to the hoist that will pull us out tomorrow. This we did only because the owner, who waited for us after the others left work for the day, waved us in. Lots of current but a good landing was made port side to the itty-bitty canal. We would have continued right by him. It didn't look like any other marina we've ever seen. But, once tied up, it was a well-organized working boat yard. Whew. I turned off the instruments and the diesel, for the last time until next fall.

The rain and thunder and dark clouds started to fade away to regular nighttime darkness, with stars in the sky along with close to a full moon. It's in the 70s and a great temperature for sleeping. The two American women made lists of what to do tomorrow when the boat comes out, ate probably the strangest meal ever out of their empty fridge and freezer and we told a story about ourselves again (to you). We felt better about sharing this and will always at least look up in the sky whenever we start Star of the Sea's engine, prepare to drive the car out of the garage or even to cross the street. Out bucket is full of lessons learned, perfectly full. Star of the Sea Out, until we get home.

Star of the Sea pulled out for the last time this trip, Detyen's Boatyard, Goose Creek, South Carolina

Chapter 66

Up On the Hard

05/26/2010 Detyen's Boat Yard, Goose Creek, South Carolina

Here is a picture of Star of the Sea as she was brought up out of the canal and onto the jack stands. It was a great experience. Everyone was good at what they did, particularly Miguel who ran the hoist and power-sprayed the boat like it was his own. The whole crew put her up on the jack stands.

Peaches immediately started scraping off the baby barnacles on the hull, the prop and on the waterline. The barnacles snuck up on us just since we came back in from the ocean into the ICW. The knotmeter hasn't worked in a long time because of all the live critters stuck on all the paddles. Peaches was really intent on doing it right away as the barnacles get hard as stone as soon as they dry out.

I went up the ladder and defrosted the freezer and cleaned out the refrigerator. There was only a small bag of unopened cheese, one pound of butter, some cream cheese and yogurt to give to the girls in the office. All our leftover cans went to Walt before we came up to Charleston. There were traps to clean on all the water lines, battery levels to check, the bilge to clean out, the deck to hose off, windows to clean and cover and thousands of surfaces to clean.

We showered in the boat for the last time for awhile, with an amazing amount of sadness. We hung drying (desiccant) bags all through the boat to stop mildew (Florida's State flower), zipped up all the canvas, left the boat and were speeding to the airport (heads spinning, feeling like we hadn't said a proper farewell). For your information, we looked up at the sky to see what the weather might have in store for us when we took off from the airport (well trained captains at last).

We plan to drive down to Charleston as soon as our Honda is delivered to Buffalo in a few days. We need to bring the cover down to protect Star of the Sea from the hot, humid and unrelenting sun. We are also bringing an electric dehumidifier down to plug in for the summer. Boats are so vulnerable to humidity when out of the water (on the hard). People have told us horror stories about coming back to boats with a thick layer of mildew and mold covering everything inside (EVERYTHING). Makes my hair stand on end to hear this. We are armed with lots of helpful hints from OZ and from Breathless to avoid this. My fingers are crossed.

I am writing this after arriving in Buffalo around midnight last night and going to Peaches' sister's home in Kenmore. We all talked and talked and then collapsed at last into the guest rooms upstairs. The bed was still, the house didn't move under me, I couldn't see the sky and the sounds were all wrong. Peaches and I both feel like strangers in a strange land....land bound without wheels, but with people all around us who love us.

A new adventure on land has started. Thanks for riding along with us. We tried to give you the good, the bad, and the ugly, but particularly, the humorous.

**Margaret, Peaches and Chris at the First Annual Put the Boat to Bed
Festival, Detyen's Boatyard, Goose Creek, South Carolina**

Chapter 67

My Whole Body Aches, but Star of the Sea is Resting Comfortably

06/09/2010 Detyen's Boat Yard, Goose Creek, South Carolina

It's a good thing I don't have to raise my arms over my head to write this blog. After washing and waxing the waterline twice, Peaches, Margaret Lane (our best friend from home until we asked her if she wanted to come to Charleston and help us a little with the boat and do some sightseeing) and I are done in! We drove 15 hours last Saturday from Chautauqua to Charleston, barely able to stand let alone walk when we got out of the car at the Hotel. Being over 60 sometimes makes it hard to jump out of a vehicle and walk away gracefully. A couple of gimpy steps and we were fine.

I digress, actually we worked so hard at the Chautauqua house since we flew home that we were already stiff and sore in all of our non-boat muscles, mowing, trimming, moving boxes and settling in. We ran around to see friends and family with great success, then more work at the house. We managed to get our leased Honda Odyssey last Thursday afternoon and started loading it right away: the scaffolding, all the heavy metal poles for the boat cover, the two large parts of the cover, the dehumidifier and miscellaneous tools and stuff to do the job. Friday, our friend Lee came with a pipe cutter and helped us cut each of the long spine pipes (each 20+ feet long) in two so they would fit into the van. We got pipe coupler pieces from the manufacturer in Buffalo when we picked up the car. The Odyssey held everything and still had room for the three of us and our clothes. We were ready for anything.

Our first look at the boat was Sunday morning and all looked well. The boats around her were different from the ones we saw 10 day ago, but nothing changed in her space. The first problem was encountered after having our free breakfast at the Wingate (Wyndham) on the campus of Charleston Southern University was the HEAT! We got to the boat at 1000 and it was so hot we could hardly take in a breath. First, we unloaded the scaffolding and the poles, and then opened up the boat. Up on stilts, you can run the water, not use the head. You can run the fans and lights, but you cannot run the AIRCONDITIONING. Holy shit is was uncomfortable. There were seven desiccant bags hung in the boat when we left and all were full of water. No mole or mildew.

The first day we got the bamboo poles off the side stays, the teak flooring out of the cockpit, all the canvas curtains down, washed and packed. Peaches got the dirtiest part of the hull cleaning done. She applied acid with a brush around the waterline where the small barnacles were scrubbed off. They left behind a lacework of glue-like stuff that couldn't be sanded. It was messy but a job well done. She still has a peachy complexion and only one hole in her shirt and a small one on her hand from the acid. Not bad for working over her head with drippy acid!

Lunch was a sandwich made at the hotel from our supplies in the bar refrigerator. It's always harder to work after you eat but we slogged on. We crawled back to the air-conditioned van and started to drive to the hotel. Our clothes were soaked and we were drained of strength and gumption. Margaret, who has always been thin, wiry and strong, suggested we stop at the golden arches for a $1 hot fudge sundae. We two chubby folks thought that sounded sinful (we must have burned at least that many calories today). In the extreme heat, we consumed as much water and Gatorade as we could manage and were still light-headed and didn't need the ladies room at all. I really felt grubby when we went through the drive-through. The young girl practically dropped the tray of sundaes into my dirty hand (when I looked at myself, there was dirt in every crease of every finger……) and indicated I could place the money on the counter. I don't blame her, we looked like we'd just crawled out from under a large rock. WOW, the ice cream tasted so good. Our core temperatures were so high, you could feel every bite sliding all the way to your stomach.

We went to dinner at a Mexican restaurant recommended by the guy at Barnes and Noble. It was Peaches birthday so we treated her to dinner and some new summer clothes (without acid holes in them). The waiter treated her to a birthday shot of tequila. She said she couldn't drink it all, could she share it with her friends. He said "Oh, you want a three-way shot? I'll get it for you, especially for your birthday." Back he came, three shot glasses, a third of a shot in each one with a salt-rim and a lime floating. Peaches downed hers, Margaret did hers, and finally I downed mine. We were cheap drunks for sure. All it takes is too much sun, a Mexican beer, dinner, and a tad of tequila.

Monday we washed and waxed half the boat. Peached lowered the extra anchor to the ground, took off the New York registration plates and did a little more acid spotting. We got the jib unfurled and dropped to the deck but couldn't fold it up safely with the Zodiac on the foredeck. We cleaned the leading edge of the sail and lowered it to the ground to fold it on the yellow grass. Again, we were rubber-kneed, hot and tired by noon so we went into the Odyssey, turned on the air conditioning and immediately fell asleep.

The heat index was over 100 degrees. We ate a little, then outside again to pull stuff off the boat to take home. We mostly made piles, like things with like things, but it was a start. We went to the golden arches again and it made us feel better. Wal-Mart had large plastic totes on sale, so we got the largest one to put the library of reference books and guides into for protection from moisture on the boat while we're gone. Most of the large charts fit too. We cleaned up, and poured ourselves into bed again. Peaches was in her nightshirt, Margaret with a mountain of pillows and me with my heating pad, a sad commentary.

The problem with all the work we're doing is the crawling up and down the ladder, up and down off of the scaffolding, up and down the stairs into the boat. Margaret, who started out with a sciatic right leg, got better while we both have shooting pains from our butts to our knees. We are all stiff if we sit down more than 15 minutes, but we slog on like good soldiers. Good old soldiers.

Tuesday we finished the wash and wax, knocked down the scaffolding and took everything out of the van again to get it on the bottom of the van space. Peaches started building the pipe ribs for the cover. We threw more stuff down from inside the boat to go into the van. I've been looking forward to this for months, taking stuff off the boat and not bringing it back. All of a sudden, the van was more than half full! We kept going, taking anything that couldn't stand the heat or moisture of the summer in the boat. The van was getting alarmingly full. We quit for the day and we went to the golden arches and……well, you know. We swam and just barely rolled into our beds again.

Today, we really worked hard. The inside of the boat has been emptied of goods to go home and everything is out from under the front berth except a scuba tank and some shrink-wrapped mashed potatoes. We are taking things out of the van and pressing all the air out of the storage bags, trying hard for more space.

The cover got on the front of the boat, with the able-bodied help of Margaret's cousin, Mark. He came to see her and the boat, and like a good fellow, stayed for the rest of the day (kind of like Tom Sawyer and painting the fence). The cover was a real chore because it was so heavy. In Buffalo, the cover magically got on in the fall and off in the spring (accompanied by a bill in the mail). This is another steep learning curve conquered. We got the wrong one in front at first, but man-handled it to the stern and recovered. Everything is a struggle in this heat and 15 feet in the air to boot!

We took Mark to lunch where the crew at the boat yard goes, a lunch buffet place called the Red Bank Club. Wonderful southern fried chicken and endless ice tea were served. The van is completely full, but we have all this stuff still at the hotel than needs to come home too. After a slow, hot afternoon we went to the golden arches…………no comments needed. We have to keep up our strength after all. It was over 92 today with a heat index of 110!

Tomorrow we're not working, but going for a carriage ride in Charleston and then a harbor tour. We're going to shower in the morning, put on nice clothes and not get dirty or sweaty at all while we play in

Charleston. Friday morning, we'll finish disconnecting the batteries, plugging the thru-hulls with paper so varmints don't crawl up into the boat and finally, hang the bags of formaldehyde inside the boat (and quickly get out and close the hatches and parting boards. It'll kill all living things on the boat, mainly the molds and mildew, but hopefully not me). All should be fine until we return in the fall when we'll do the bottom paint and everything gets re-hooked.

We're tired, happy and satisfied with our time well used. Now we understand why Ken took so long to put OZ away, and he was only one person! There are three of us! Actually, we are amazed at what we could do under these hot conditions. Margaret said, and I quote her directly, "If anyone asks me if I would come down again to help a "little" with the boat, I'd say probably not. If they call and ask you to come help put the boat away, I would tell you to walk away, walk away!"

Sweet basket maker at the Market, Charleston, South Carolina

Chapter 68

A Day to Remember

06/10/2010 Charleston, South Carolina

Today we dumped work without a qualm and turned the car to the right out of the hotel driveway, not left to the boat. We took Route 26 into the downtown portion of Charleston, the "old" town, south of Broad. We were dressed in bright, clean, and well accessorized clothes as opposed to the stiff with sweat, filthy and stinky clothes we've worn all week, working on the boat. We were free! But, as sometimes happens in the south, it was stinking hot, over 95 degrees with at heat index over 110. To us, it meant that no matter how bright and excited we were to see Charleston, we were going to do it complete with sweat and that funny light-headed feeling that comes with hot, unrelenting sun and high humidity.

We took a carriage ride behind two mules named Order and Julie. They were a miss-matched pair, with Order formerly partners with Law (now retired). Julie was a fast, perky walker and Order was not. The driver hoped for a happy, slow pace to show off the homes in Charleston. Order was always a few steps behind. We saw so much, and Mike, the carriage driver, was great. Hot or not, it was like looking into people's lives, so different from ours. Both Peaches and I took a lot of pictures of doorways. Everything was in bloom, even the trees.

We walked in the Open Air Market for a while until it was time to eat. Yep, even in the hot, hot whether you need to stoke up a little. We went to the Crab Shack and had a three-way-bowl of She Crab Soup (one bowl, three spoons). It was sinful and yes, we are older, more mature women, and share entrees......no comments from the kids, please. We had some coconut shrimp and felt wonderful when we were done. Off to the harbor tour.

What are two captains of the ocean doing on a harbor tour you might ask? Well, we'd just gone through the harbor 10 days ago, but only remember where the red and green markers were, not what we were going by. We saw lots of ships, forts and buildings but what were they? It was a lot cooler out on the water. The captain came down and wandered around talking to the passengers, so he came to Peaches and I sitting at the stern and said we looked too calm. Peaches told him that we were both captains, and she went on to ask how many gross tons the ship was, 50,000 tons. We were both licensed to be at the helm, but had no experience to get it from one side of the harbor to the other. He docked it perfectly in big winds, fast swirling currents and also as the tide was rushing in. When we walked off the boat, he asked if we wanted to try docking it someday. We both said sure. He didn't say more. I don't think he thought we would really want to do what he does every day. We would, actually!

We drove through the southern part, south of Broad, where the oldest houses are, looking for hidden back gardens. Margaret and I walked around a couple of long blocks taking pictures. We both turned to each other at the same time and said we would not have been able to go to the boat at all today. We were walking v-e-r-y slowly. Peaches ducked this walk and stayed in the van with the air conditioning. Not an unwise choice.

We got home at dinner time, in rush hour traffic. The hotel feels like home by now, so we gladly got out of the overloaded van and into the room. There sits all of our duffle bags and bags of tools and stuff. Where are they going to go? Margaret has a potted sweet gum tree, a gift from her cousin, Mark. It needs room and some air around it. Our fall-back plan is to put Margaret on a plane tomorrow and use her seat for the overflow (and the tree). We'll manage somehow.

We need to clean surfaces in the boat, tip up all the cushions, empty the water tanks, take off the last of the canvas, disconnect the batteries (all of them) and finish the cover. Hopefully it will fit over everything and zip shut at the aft end of the boat. There are no guarantees. Maybe we can be on the road by noon. I can't possibly move any slower than I am now. Hope we make it at our new slower, southern speed.

It was so hot at Detyen's Boatyard that.....
we never got the back zipped up, but the guys at the yard
finished it for us, Goose Creek, South Carolina

Chapter 69

It Was So Hot That…..

06/13/2010 Charleston, South Carolina

This was how last week seemed to us as we drove home Friday afternoon from the Detyen's Boatyard. We did the "It was so hot that….." in the car to keep from falling asleep while we got five hours of the trip home from Charleston under our wheels before stopping at a motel to shower and sleep. It tells the story in short bursts. The whole week we worked in 95+ degree heat, no wind and 100% humidity. Whew!

It Was So Hot That……..

-Our Chapstick melted in the car

-The baby sweet gum tree Margaret was taking home almost died when left by mistake in the van for an hour.

-We wore the same dirty clothes every day because we couldn't smell or feel any worse by the end of the day even if we started out with clean clothes.

-When you spit, it never hit the ground (I know ladies don't spit, but boat workers do if they get a mouthful of dirt).

-We drank two cases of water and a case of Gatorade and almost never had to pee.

-We absolutely had to have a $1 hot fudge sundae from McDonald's every day on the way to the hotel to lower our core temperature (If you believe that, have I got something else to sell to you!).

-By the end of each day, three 60+ year old ladies, sitting over dinner, couldn't even manage a conversation or a simple high-five after a day in the heat.

-Margaret's chronic sciatica mysteriously went away. We plan to install a tall ladder and a series of heat lamps at her home to keep it away permanently.

-Margaret actually walked sideways, although her eyes were going straight.

-A cold bottle of water was warm by the time we got it to the top of the ladder.

-Peaches' holy water in the boat evaporated (guess we'll just have to read the instructions and pray in an emergency).

-The shipyard workers all thought that we'd give it up and ask them to please do the job for us.

-It took three of us to keep remembering righty-tighty, lefty loosey when screwing (no other comments please).

-It took three of us and a cheap corkscrew to get a bottle of white wine open, then guzzle it down (two holding, one screwing and pulling) A sad commentary.

-Speaking of sad, the whole time we worked on the boat in the horrible heat, 5 vultures circled us, making bets about which one of us will drop first.

-After emptying 150 gallons of fresh water out of the boat, there wasn't even a puddle underneath the boat in the dust.

-You couldn't see though the pools of sweat in our sunglass lenses when you worked bending over something.

-The metal tools left out in the sun for a couple of minutes burned our hands.

-Our hands were so sweaty that we lost three spanners trying to get the batteries disconnected. They just squirted right out of our hands and found hiding places (where they shall stay forever).

-By the end of the afternoon, it took almost a half an hour to climb the 15 feet up to the boat.

-Half the water we drank was poured down the fronts of our shirts (no wonder we didn't pee)

-All conversation was reduced to grunts and sometimes crude hand signals.

-If someone tried to talk, they were told to shut up.

-We never want to do this again. But, it's like childbirth, after you are done and 48 hours have passed, you forget how bad it was. I can't wait to go cruising again already.

-Some of the small batteries in the hand held electronics in the boat exploded.

-We retreated to the van and the air conditioning when we lost our ability to reason and fell asleep immediately, like the switch was turned off.

-The workers up from Texas to complete repairs on a tug in the boatyard were sent home because it was too hot, and the locals were hired to finish the job!

-The mockingbird who always sang all day started taking every afternoon off.

-Margaret, who volunteers to do everything for everyone refuses to ever come with us again to do the put-the-boat-to-bed festival.

-Peaches would announce three times, every 5 minutes, that she was getting up to start working again.........then not get up.

-Going down the ICW through Georgia where it was so shallow, sounds like a party compared with working in this heat.

-We had to drive Peaches the 50 feet to the rest room when she had to go.

-I started mentally adding up all the costs: meals, hotel, gas, and the sweat and tears to see if it was a financially responsible decision to pay someone else to do the put-the-boat-to-bed festival. It wasn't.

-The boat swelled up so much in the heat that the cover couldn't be zipped up (so the guys at the boatyard will pull off the new Yamaha outboard, place it in the cockpit, and lace up the tarp). We did need them after all.

We got the nicest compliment from the workers in the boatyard as we left. They thought we would quit after the first day, and we kept coming back. After the second day and third days, they were amazed. They all came over offering to help, just checking on us to make sure we didn't faint and fall off the boat. We skipped Thursday and did some sightseeing, but came back for the hottest day yet. Their jaws dropped. We got respect and the job got done as we planned.

So, we drove off with the Odyssey sitting low on her shocks, with the heavy floor to ceiling overflow from the boat packed in tight, leaving barely enough space for Margaret to sit. When we return, the only things coming back down are the floor boards for the cockpit, and the bamboo poles for the stays. They will get coats and coats of varnish this summer. All the clothes came home and very few will go back for our next cruising season. The learning curves are paying off already. Star of the Sea is safe while we return home to our families for a while. I can't wait to get back to her. I like the feel of my sea legs under me better than my land legs.

Next year's goal:

THE WATER LINE WILL SHOW ALL THE WAY AROUND THE BOAT

The front porch looking out on so much green, we're home

Chapter 70

Landlocked in Chautauqua

06/25/2010 Chautauqua Lake, New York

My head is full of people and daily tasks. My heart is still on the boat. Over the last week, Peaches and I have been dealing with selling her house, boat insurance, house insurance, lawn mowing, tree removal, balancing the pH of the pool, house cleaning and storing all the boat stuff we pulled off during this first year of cruising. More about that in a minute. We thought Peaches home in Kenmore sold last week, but the deal didn't go through. Her nephew who was living there last year bought a house so we hope it sells this summer. She needed a home and so I raised my hand and said please bring yourself and your things down to Chautauqua (well, we didn't kill each other while on a 44 x 13 foot boat for 10 months, my house is big, so why not?).

Peaches just took off for a week to go to Lake Placid for a conference. She needs more credits for her Nursing Home Administrator's license, just in case she wants to consult again. My NP credits are completed ahead of time for the next 5 years. I'm covered. It's like carrying an umbrella to keep the rain away, we are keeping our licenses current so we could work (not).

Being landlocked in a very nice but rural place, we are dealing with a lot of woodchucks, chipmunks and a very noisy batch of crow babies. I put up a couple of bird feeders right away and have all the cardinals, blue jays (they are pigs!) and lots of goldfinches, hummingbirds and even a Baltimore Oriole. I miss the mockingbirds from the south. Nobody has as long and complicated a song as they do (except when it was so hot that…..). So, Peaches' introduction to birds is continuing even on land.

She took the lead picture this time, a baby woodchuck who is living under the front porch and who loves to sun himself there in the morning. He has some decidedly more spoiled cousins who lie next to the pool on the back deck to get their quota of Vitamin D from the sun. They are still cuter than the Hutias at Exuma Park. Our friend (still) Margaret had a black bear sighting at her home across the lake from us. I was glad it was so far away, until I came out the other day to find my raspberry bushes flattened to the ground, by a bear! The sharks and the rays are starting to seem like close friends.

We are seeing and communicating with our families and friends. We missed them so, but wished they would come to us, rather than us coming home to them. They would have loved the boat (well, I shouldn't have been so honest, I guess, if we wanted company). The 4th of July is coming and so are my sons and their families. I can't wait to see the grandkids. They read the blogs as part of their home schooling. I can't wait for them to get here, I need to hug them. Peaches has come home to all her great nieces and nephews, a big houseful of families up in Kenmore.

We have plans for Connie and Ken from OZ to come to Chautauqua when they take a break in their summer jobs. Mixing our land and sea friends will be a treat (Everyone feels they know OZ and Katmandu from the writings).The new plan is for OZ and ourselves to go up to Quebec for the Canadian Thanksgiving before we take off to get our boats ready this fall. A great plan.

All the stuff taken out of the boat added to all the things we didn't put on the boat originally is a formula for frustration (or, the start of a consignment marine store). All of it is dumped in my double garage, in and around about 20 years of my stuff (oh, and the stuff from my father's garage that he couldn't part with when he sold his home) . So, this week, while Peaches is away at her conference, I will toss the used-up and the not used in 10 year things. I am at the "putting things with like object phase" of the garage. I can't see the end of it yet, but with my strong desire to organize things, I'll succeed.

I think I should send away for the fancy white tent-thing they have to photograph item to sell on E-Bay. We could make a bloody fortune.

I keep sneaking looks at the blogs of our friends who are still cruising. It keeps me sane. Good ones to look at are Melodeon, the steel hulled junk we wrote about in Vero Beach http://www.travelblog.org/Bloggers/ MELODEON . The other is our friends Bob and Connie on Meredith. They have gone from Georgetown where we last saw them to Cuba and all the way back to Canada. He has such a great way with words. You'll love them both. http://www.bennersadrift.blogspot.org

So, our time on the land is fun, lots of hard work, good friends, good food and lots of green grass all around us. Actually, it's just like life on the boat except when you wake up on the boat and it's time to move, your front and backyards are blue, the scenery is beautiful and your neighbors and good friends are shuffled and redistributed. I want it both ways. Less than 4 months until we take off again, and more stories to come!